JOURNAL FOR THE STUDY OF THE OLD TESTAMENT SUPPLEMENT SERIES
296

Sheffield Academic Press

The Evasive Text

Zechariah 1–8 and the Frustrated Reader

Mark Cameron Love

Journal for the Study of the Old Testament
Supplement Series 296

Published by
Sheffield Academic Press Ltd
Mansion House
19 Kingfield Road
Sheffield S11 9AS
England

Typeset by Sheffield Academic Press
and
Printed on acid-free paper in Great Britain
by Biddles
Guildford, Surrey

British Library Cataloguing in Publication Data

A catalogue record for this book is available
from the British Library

ISBN 1-84127-020-2

CONTENTS

(IN)CONCLUSION

LIST OF TABLES

ABBREVIATIONS

AB	Anchor Bible
ABD	David Noel Freedman (ed.), *The Anchor Bible Dictionary* (New York: Doubleday, 1992)
AJSL	*American Journal of Semitic Languages and Literatures*
AOS	American Oriental Series
ATD	Das Alte Testament Deutsch
ATR	*Anglican Theological Review*
AUSS	*Andrews University Seminary Studies*
BA	*Biblical Archaeologist*
BDB	Francis Brown, S.R. Driver and Charles A. Briggs, *A Hebrew and English Lexicon of the Old Testament* (Oxford: Clarendon Press, 1907)
BHS	*Biblia hebraica stuttgartensia*
Bib	*Biblica*
BibInt	*Biblical Interpretation: A Journal of Contemporary Approaches*
BibRes	*Biblical Research*
BSac	*Bibliotheca Sacra*
BT	*The Bible Translator*
BZ	*Biblische Zeitschrift*
BZAW	Beihefte zur *ZAW*
CBQ	*Catholic Biblical Quarterly*
CHD	D.J.A. Clines (ed.), *The Dictionary of Classical Hebrew*. I. *Aleph* (Sheffield: Sheffield Academic Press, 1993)
CRBS	*Currents in Research: Biblical Studies*
ETL	*Ephemerides theologicae lovanienses*
ETR	*Etudes théologiques et religieuses*
EvQ	*Evangelical Quarterly*
EvT	*Evangelische Theologie*
FRLANT	Forschungen zur Religion und Literatur des Alten und Neuen Testaments
GKC	*Gesenius' Hebrew Grammar* (ed. E. Kautzsch, revised and trans. A.E. Cowley; Oxford: Clarendon Press, 1910)
HeyJ	*Heythrop Journal*
HSM	Harvard Semitic Monographs
HUCA	*Hebrew Union College Annual*

ACKNOWLEDGMENTS

As is customary, I'd like to thank all who helped me to produce this work. Thank you, coffee club crowd (Noel Bailey, Anna Piskorowski, Ruth Anne Reese, Yvonne Sherwood, and Froo Signore) who bestowed your wisdom through learned conversations, offered critiques of this work in various stages of its production, and made long days in the library not just bearable, but enjoyable. Ruth Ann Reese deserves special mention for helping me choose the terminology I use to discuss intertextuality and refine my thinking about how intertextuality functions in biblical texts. It's funny how much one can miss coffee. It hardly needs to be said that I'd like to thank the editorial team of Sheffield Academic Press for all their work on the manuscript. I especially appreciated Georgia Litherland's help and encouragement in the process. Thank you, Philip Davies, for your friendship, advice and endless supply of jokes. Thanks are also due to Gachon Medical School which furnished me with both time and facilities in its inaugural year: a time when other demands were more pressing on the college's agenda. I couldn't ask for a finer set of colleagues. Most of all, thank you John and Gwen Love for your emotional and financial support without which this project would never have been undertaken, let alone completed.

IEJ	*Israel Exploration Journal*
JAAR	*Journal of the American Academy of Religion*
JBL	*Journal of Biblical Literature*
JETS	*Journal of the Evangelical Theological Society*
JJS	*Journal of Jewish Studies*
JNES	*Journal of Near Eastern Studies*
JNSL	*Journal of Northwest Semitic Languages*
JSOT	*Journal for the Study of the Old Testament*
JSOTSup	*Journal for the Study of the Old Testament*, Supplement Series
JTS	*Journal of Theological Studies*
KAT	Kommentar zum Alten Testament
LVT	*Lexicon in Veteris Testamenti*
NRSV	New Revised Standard Version
OBO	Orbis biblicus et orientalis
OTL	Old Testament Library
OTS	*Oudtestamentische Studiën*
PEQ	*Palestine Exploration Quarterly*
RHR	*Revue de l'histoire des religions*
SBS	Stuttgarter Bibelstudien
TOTC	Tyndale Old Testament Commentaries
TZ	*Theologische Zeitschrift*
VT	*Vetus Testamentum*
VTSup	*Vetus Testamentum*, Supplements
WBC	Word Biblical Commentary
WO	*Die Welt des Orients*
ZAW	*Zeitschrift für die alttestamentliche Wissenschaft*
ZDPV	*Zeitschrift des deutschen Palästina-Vereins*

(ANTE)THESIS

Chapter 1

SETTING SIGHTS

> Really, what I want to do is impossible, for any listing of an endless
> series is doomed to be infinitesimal. In that single gigantic instant I saw
> millions of acts both delightful and awful; not one of them amazed me
> more than the fact that all of them occupied the same point in space,
> without overlapping or transparency. What my eyes beheld was simul-
> taneous, but what I shall now write down will be successive, because
> language is successive. Nonetheless, I'll try to recollect what I can.
>
> Borges 1971: 26

Michel Foucault said that Western society is compelled to confess and
that the confession is 'one of the West's most highly valued techniques
for producing truth' (1990: 59). One only needs to watch a television
talk show like *Oprah* to verify that this tendency is still pervasive in
Western culture. Following the conscious, and subconscious, dictates
my society has set for and in me, I begin with a confession. I do not
understand Zechariah 1–8.[1] As a university graduate who has spent a
fair amount of time reading literature and theories about literature, I
think myself to be a basically competent reader. As such, arrogant
though it may be, I generally expect to comprehend a text, or at least
understand what it is trying to get across. At the very least, I hope to
understand where my deficiencies lie, that is, I may not understand
quantum mechanics, but I hope to understand that it is my ignorance
concerning quantum theory that inhibits my understanding of a book on
it. Still, as a late-twentieth-century male reader trained in religious and

---

1. Carroll extends this confusion to the prophets as a whole, concerning which
he confesses, 'I really do not know how to read the prophets and so I am trying with
every piece I write to make sense of *all* the data contained in the Bible on prophets'
(1990: 34).

biblical studies, I find Zechariah difficult to understand—almost impossible.

The realization of how little I understand Zechariah has led me to examine the difficulties, rather than to repress those difficulties by offering a coherent reading of the text which declares its unequivocal meaning. This is because after my reading of unequivocal interpretations of the text, many of the problems of Zechariah 1–8 remain unsolved. Its misty incoherence is not dissipated in the 'daylight' of academic discourse. This necessitates confronting the incoherence; to catalogue it, to examine the ways it is manifested, to ask the questions, 'what don't I understand about this text?' and 'why don't I understand this text?' My goal is to examine the function of incoherence in Zechariah, in order to understand what effect the assumption that Zechariah is incoherent has upon the reader. While I work within the epistemological grounds of reader-response criticism, which believes intentions are impossible to discover in texts, I recognize that readers still postulate intentions for authors and texts. On these grounds I examine the effect that a postulated writing strategy of incoherence has on a reader (who is herself, actually, the postulator of this intention).[2] After examining the difficulties this text poses for a reader, I will offer ways to cope with these difficulties and examine their shortcomings and implications.

While it is not revolutionary in the guild of biblical studies to claim that the book under consideration is confusing (one is hard pressed to find a commentary which does not state this somewhere in its pages, especially so for Zechariah), no commentator to my knowledge has yet taken this confusion as her or his object of study. Perhaps that no commentator has studied this confusion to date says volumes about the

---

2.   For the sake of clarity in this study, and to avoid the notoriously awkward 's/he' and 'his/her', the feminine pronoun will denote the reader and the masculine pronoun will denote the author/editor and other characters in the work unless they are feminine characters. My choice of the masculine pronoun to refer to the author of the work is simple—I don't believe a female author would write such a sexist work. (To deflect future criticism, I realise that a person could write a text which portrays their own gender in a sexist way.)

field, but I leave those volumes for the metacommentators[3] in the guild.[4]

Note to the Reader

The Hebrew and English texts of Zechariah have different chapter divisions. This book uses the Hebrew chapter divisions. For the reader who is unfamiliar with Hebrew, the following chart is provided.

Zechariah's Chapter Divisions

English Text	Hebrew Text
1.18	2.1
1.19	2.2
1.20	2.3
1.21	2.4
2.1	2.5
2.2	2.6
2.3	2.7
2.4	2.8
2.5	2.9
2.6	2.10
2.7	2.11
2.8	2.12
2.9	2.13
2.10	2.14
2.11	2.15
2.12	2.16
2.13	2.17

This work will use (E) to refer to English chapter divisions and verses and (H) to refer to Hebrew divisions.

---

3.   Metacommentary is defined by Clines: 'When we write commentary, we read what commentators say. When we write metacommentary, we notice what commentators do' (1993: 142).

Perhaps having noticed that commentators do not take this confusion as their object of study already places me in the camp of metacommentary, at least for this excursus.

4.   For the most recent, comprehensive history of scholarship, see Prokurat (1988: 1-99).

Chapter 2

ZECHARIAH 1–8'S LITERARY CHARACTERISTICS

Historical Criticism and Zechariah 1–8

Are there convincing grounds for denying or doubting the documented events? And if there are not such grounds, how may we interpret the motives of those who seek to cast doubt upon the historical record?

Greenblatt 1989: 4

Ultimately, all redactional approaches to the literary problems in Zechariah 1–8 operate within the methodological paradigm of the historical-critical method. Historical criticism attempts to resolve the problems inherent in the text using literary history to determine the original sources that comprise the text, and the original purpose of each of the sources identified (Rendtorff 1986: 184). The basic presupposition of historical criticism is that the text does not make sense in its present form because it contains opposing editorial views. Consequently the text's original sources must be determined and the intention of each understood before we can understand the final form of the text. Bergdall says similarly:

Underlying most if not all of the theories about Zechariah's composition is another assumption, namely that the way to understand the text is to reconstruct the history of its development so that one can place the original prophetic messages in their proper historical framework and also identify the changes in meaning which those messages underwent as they were committed to writing in a new historical setting (1986: 27).

I do not wish to engage in the debate surrounding the redactional history of Zechariah 1–8. Personally, I do not understand the approach of commentators who date portions of biblical texts to different time periods and then proceed to dissect the text on logically unstable grounds (circular logic—many of their grounds for dissecting the text are often based on themes discussed in the relevant portions of the texts; to be fair to modern redaction critics, this process is more common in the past generation of redaction critics). How does one distinguish one author from another except by a name on the front cover? (Some socio-stylisticians might object to this rhetorical question.) My style is capable of taking many forms, sometimes bad, other times slightly better. One need only look at music videos (for example, Peter Gabriel's 'Sledgehammer'), the new wave of postmodern television advertisements that jump from image to image (for example, the Guinness or T.A.G. advertisements), Dali's surrealist art, books like Italo Calvino's *If on a winter's night a traveller...* or Jeanette Winterson's *Sexing the Cherry* to realize the only item needed to unify disparate material is a frame (whether it be cloth, canvas or celluloid).

More directly concerning Zechariah, P. House argues for the unity of the book of the Twelve based on comparisons with *The Canterbury Tales*, *Gulliver's Travels* and *Don Quixote*.[1] On the issue of awkward transitions in biblical texts as evidence of redactional activity, Tollington's assertion regarding the awkward transition between Zech. 1.7 and 1.8 summarizes the issue concisely: 'There is no more reason to accuse an editor of being unable to create a smooth text than to blame the prophet for this literary slip' (1993: 24 n. 2). The issue is ultimately whether an individual reader perceives incongruity as a sign of editorial or authorial activity, and how that individual then proceeds to interpret that incongruity.

If one believes the sources are ultimately indiscernible outside of more concrete evidence such as that provided by manuscripts, or that there may not even be sources, and 'sacrilegiously' suggests that perhaps Zechariah is the work of a single hand (stranger things have happened), the object of study must be changed. This study seeks to understand the Masoretic Text of Zechariah.[2] The object of study becomes,

---

1.   See also Nogalski's criticism of House on this comparison (1993b: 11 n. 51).

2.   The closest commentator to this position is Rignell, who views the Masoretic Text as 'extremely reliable' (1950: 13). He reviews and criticizes redaction critics' search for the original text of Zechariah, and changes of the received text, as a very subjective enterprise (1950: 10-14, esp. 12).

From a historical perspective, since our principal manuscripts come from the tenth century, perhaps we are 1500 years away from the historical time period we should be studying, if we are attempting to be 'objective, scientific' historians. Perhaps we should be citing mediaeval parallels to portions of the Hebrew Bible rather than ancient Near Eastern ones; or at least be looking at mediaeval politics which would cause redactions and/or emendations (especially so for differences in pointing) rather than just ancient Israeli, Persian or Greek politics.

ultimately, that of individual readers, namely, myself as reader and author. The object of study is never truly a historical text, but the combination of this text, the Masoretic Text, with a living individual, me.

Zechariah 1–8 gives the overall effect of a concise self-contained unit and few scholars posit extensive editorial activity in these chapters.[3] Historical-critical issues do not play a large role in this study for two reasons. First, I do not have the confidence of others in dating these eight chapters, or portions thereof, and cannot establish any datum from which to start dating these chapters. My principal historical methodology, unsophisticated as it is, is to view the last date in a book, or historical index, as the most recent the work is likely to be. This dates almost the entire Hebrew Bible to the Second Temple period (the recent historiography of P.R. Davies, G. Garbini, T. Thompson, *et al.*, provide more scientific historical proof that the entire Hebrew Bible may be the product of the Persian period; see Garbini 1994: 180).

Far too much credit is accorded to the hypothesis that traditions were passed on and modified through time. I think this assumption is steeped deeper in religious conservatism than historiography. Yet even this assumption is subject to criticism, as the author could be post-dating the work much like science fiction. Thus, texts are not dated here because I do not feel they are readily datable. While I acknowledge that traditions *may* have been passed down and later recorded, I remain dubious. All that can confidently, and competently, be stated is that these chapters were written after the fourth year of Darius.[4] With the exception of Bauer (1992: 293-96), commentators are, overall, very confident and unanimous in dating Zechariah 1–8 to between 520 and 516 BCE, because of the common belief that the temple is not yet complete when Zechariah 1–8 is written. The central reason one dates Zechariah 1–8 between 520 and 516 is dependent on the mention of Darius in the text

---

3.   For various views on the redaction of Zechariah, see Wolfe (1935: 117-25); Sinclair (1975: 36-47); Fohrer (1968: 463-64); Seybold (1974a: 23), Stockton (1978: 227-28); and Redditt (1992: 258-59).

4.   For various views on dating Zechariah, see Ackroyd (1958: 14-15, 21); Whitley (1954: 61); Waterman (1954); Morgenstern (1949: 377-83, 400-408); Berquist (1989: 139-56); Robinson (1951); Japhet (1982: 79); Galling (1964: 123); and Bauer (1992: 293-96), who interestingly dates Zechariah to Darius II instead of Darius I. Ackroyd's comments conform to the evidence best: 'if the dates are followed exactly…then no precise correlation can be established on our present evidence with the events taking place in Babylonia' (1958: 21).

and assumptions surrounding the genre of prophecy, namely, that prophecy is not a form of historical fiction—which would allow one to date it much later than 516. Associated with this assumption is the type of audience that listens to prophecy (I would prefer to say 'reads' prophecy) and its intended effect on the listeners ('readers') (cf. 'The Fabricated Audience' below). Still, with the debate unsettled concerning the dates of both these works, who can really say definitively whether they were written by the same author or not? Even on stylistic grounds an author may use different genres to communicate his point, as Lodge does in his work *Changing Places* (1974). G. Garbini's statement is pertinent: 'we need to consider the extreme difficulty of identifying today how much in post-exilic Hebrew literature dates back to the Persian period and how much to the Hellenistic period' (1994: 184).

Secondly, I do not understand reading books in any way but their final form. Regardless of the historical circumstances which contributed to the book's present shape, all readings are modern readings. From a modern perspective the text exists only in its physical final form; all other theories of the history of the text are hypotheses. This ties into the lack of confidence in apportioning different sections of the book to different hypothesized histories for those respective portions of the book.

I take the view that prophecies are 'poetic historical fiction' (precursors to Robert Graves?) rather than seeing them as oral creations later put to writing.[5] Specifically relative to visions, such as are contained within Zechariah, are Amsler's comments: 'Incontestablement, le récit de vision est une construction littéraire' ('The vision account is unquestionably a literary construction') (1981: 360; see his comments on the literary nature of visions, 360-62). He bases this on: (1) the time difference between a vision and the narrative account of it; (2) the literary excellence of the visions; and (3) the metaphorical nature of the visionary material (360-61). Similarly, Blocher says, 'Zacharie, en tout cas, nous a laissé la plus "livresque" des prophéties' ('Zechariah, in any case, is the most "literary" of the prophets we have') (1979: 264).

---

5. On prophets as poets (or not) see Petersen (1981: 91); Mitchell (who notes that 'The Versions give Zechariah the credit of being a poet as well as a prophet'; 1980: 83, 99-100); and the Meyers (1987: lxiii-lxvii) who conclude 'that Haggai–Zechariah 1–8 must be formally characterised as prose or "oracular prose"' (1987: lxiv).

Especially relevant to the literacy/orality debate is Carroll's and Auld's series of debates with Williamson and Overholt in *JSOT* 27 and 48.

The transition to this type of thought from a more traditional under-standing of the prophets is simply the change from presuppositions of orality to presuppositions of literacy for the prophets. The only defini-tive historical presupposition of this work is that the Hebrew Bible forms the principal intertextual interpretative key. The principal reading strategy is to view Zechariah 1–8 as literature, in the modern sense of the term, and try to make sense of it as such. Zechariah 1–8 may be an ideologically exclusivist[6] and sexist work deserving critique in these respects, but it still functions in many ways as literature. Interpretative analogues are sought in other literature, rather than attempts being made to construct a historical situation as *the* datum from which to interpret Zechariah 1–8.

My cautions in assigning historicity to a text is entwined with senti-ments best summed up by Byatt:

> She had sat in Sunday school, hearing a fly buzzing against a smeared high window in the vestry and had hated the stories of St Paul and the other apostles because they were true, they were told to her as true sto-ries, and this somehow stopped off some essential imaginative involve-ment with them, probably because she didn't believe them, if required to believe they were true. She was Hamlet and his father and Shakespeare: she saw Milton's snake and the miraculous flying horse of the Thief of Baghdad, but St Paul's angels rested under suspicion of being made-up because she had been told they were special because *true* (1994: 163).

I am worried, like Gillian Perholt (the character to whom this sentiment is attributed), that the emphasis on the historical nature of biblical texts robs them of their fairy-tale-like magic. Angels can possess the ethereal character of djinns, but are so often relegated to the role of Yahweh's messengers in biblical commentaries. There is no doubt that they func-tion in this capacity, but they are so much more (for example, the angel that ascends the flame in Judg. 13.20 is as marvellous as a djinn bursting

---

6.   I object to the use of the term 'universalistic' to describe an ideology such as is described in Zechariah. Why is allowing another to succumb to one's ideology called 'universalism'? This is a theological hijacking of an English word. The *Oxford Encyclopedic English Dictionary* lists the term 'universal' as meaning 'of, belonging to, or done etc. by all persons or things in the world or in the class con-cerned; applicable to all cases' (1991: 1579). Yet the same dictionary lists a univer-salist as 'a person who holds that all mankind will eventually be saved' and 'a member of an organized body of Christians who hold this' (1579). This is ideologi-cal imperialism and should be labelled as such. One would think a universalist would hold to basic tenets applicable to all of humanity (if there are any).

from a bottle). Unfortunately, these aspects of the text cannot be researched as they are in the realm of fantasy: 'fantasy is entertaining, enjoyable, and inspiring on a multitude of levels. I can analyze many of the levels, but I cannot analyze the enjoyment and the inspiration without losing them' (Miscall 1992: 47).

The Literary Unit

The lively debate over how to ascribe meaning to a work has led Culler to conclude that the 'attempt to derive meaning from linguistic structures or linguistic conventions must contend with the fact that speakers can mean different things by the same linguistic sequence' (1988: 146). To determine meanings for a text a reader must frame the work she wants to interpret. To frame the book of Zechariah a reader decides which books, archaeological data and other information are relevant and needed to understand the meaning of the book of Zechariah: the reader frames the context in which she will understand the book of Zechariah. This is the paramount step of all interpretative activities because 'meaning is context-bound, context is boundless' (Culler 1988: 148). How to frame a work is not an easy decision. In Culler's words, 'Contextualization is never completed; rather one reaches a point where further contextualization seems unproductive' (1988: 148). Even the mental images a reader creates are a framing device (Henry 1990: 96). But when does further contextualization become unproductive, and who decides it is unproductive? It is very difficult to determine when further contextualization is unproductive, as every new context that is read often further illuminates the text under consideration. Fish claims it is interpretative communities which decide whether interpretations are productive or not. Ultimately, though, this decision rests with the individual reader who may cling to a reading of a text in the face of outright opposition from all interpretative communities. An ideal reader will have read the entire corpus of books the author of a text has read, and have undergone identical life situations. But this type of reader does not exist. Is contextualization unproductive when the text seems to resist some reading enforced on it by the reader? Since deconstruction has shown that all readings will be resisted in some way by the text, what types of resistance are acceptable, and which unacceptable? Interpreters must make decisions and then offer them to their public for acceptance or rejection. Interpretation is a lot like poetry. The question to then ask when the reading is finished is '*Do you like it?*'

This enquiry limits itself to Zechariah 1–8. This is perhaps an unjusti-fied excision of these eight chapters from their larger frames. One need only consult the titles of most commentaries to realize the scholarly consensus surrounding the division of the two portions of the book.[7] A multitude of frames can be identified for Zechariah 1–8: Zechariah 1–8 on its own; the entire book of Zechariah (Baldwin 1972: 68-70, 82; But-terworth 1992); the Haggai–Zechariah 1–8 corpus (Meyers and Meyers 1987; esp. lii-lxvii); the Haggai–Zechariah–Malachi corpus (Pierce 1984a, 1984b; Bauer 1992: 16-23); the larger literary unit of the book of the Twelve (Conrad 1999; House 1990; Nogalski 1993b; 1993c); the latter prophets; the Hebrew Bible[8] *et cetera ad infinitum*. Zechariah's relationship to all of these frames is worthy of study. Should the reader view elements of Zechariah as allusions to other biblical texts such as Isaiah, Ezekiel, Jeremiah and Deuteronomy? Should she limit herself to an examination of Zechariah's place in the book of the Twelve? Should she read Zechariah on its own? Should she look at similar ancient Near Eastern texts for parallels? Simply put, *what books must she read to read Zechariah and how do these changes of context change her response when she reads Zechariah?* Still, one must limit oneself in some way and Zechariah 1–8 is this thesis's primary object of inter-pretation. This is a very subjective decision chosen primarily because it is the visionary[9] material which is principally examined with an interest to close-read this material in its immediate context.

The problem of dismembering chs. 1–8 from chs. 9–14 still exists. While the majority of scholarship accepts this division, I am not taking Zechariah 1–8 as my object of study because of any historical views on

7. For a history of scholarship on the issue of dividing Zechariah 1–8 from 9–14, see Baldwin (1972: 62-70); Coggins (1987: 60-69); or Mitchell (1980: 232-44).

8. This is not a new observation. Mitchell, writing in 1912, says of Zechariah, 'his prophecies show that he was acquainted with nearly all the prophetic *books* and borrowed liberally from several of them' (101; emphasis mine). See Mitchell for a list of examples where Zechariah employs the style of earlier prophets (1980: 100-102).

9. I reluctantly use the term 'vision' throughout this work because the Hebrew term for vision (חָזוֹן) is conspicuously absent from the peculiar events described in Zech. 1–8 (In the whole of Zechariah it only occurs in 13.4 as חֶזְיוֹן). My use of the term does not distinguish oracular and visionary material, and I use 'vision' to des-ignate the entire prophetic episode; for example, in my terminology Zechariah's first night vision includes all of Zech. 1.7-17.

Zechariah 1–8 coming from a different source than Zechariah 9–14. Rather, I am studying Zechariah 1–8 as one might study an act or a scene from Shakespeare.

Zechariah 1–8 is divided from 9–14 on stylistic grounds. This thesis does not intend to imply any historical differentiation between the two sections, nor to disagree with those who see them as two distinct entities. The debate surrounding the unity or disunity of these books has taken many forms: structure (Butterworth 1992); thematic unity and literary connectors (Pierce 1984a; 1984b); phraseology, themes, style and physical evidence (Baldwin 1972: 66-69); shared symbolism and symbolic clusters (Ruffin 1986);[10] and statistical linguistics (Radday and Wickmann 1975; Radday and Polatschek 1980; Portnoy and Petersen 1984). Baldwin and Ackroyd are very honest about these issues of dating and unity:

> Such a bewildering variety of views on both date and unity leaves the reader at a loss to know what to believe. The very fact that there is such diversity undermines confidence in the methodology used. As P.R. Ackroyd observes, 'It may be wondered whether the attempt to date is the most useful approach to the material'. Historical allusions are vague and defy attempts to refer them to specific people or events. Moreover, the author makes free use of his sources' (Baldwin 1972: 68; quoting Ackroyd [Ackroyd's original is from *Peake's Commentary on the Bible*]).

Following this advice, I do not attempt to date Zechariah or to prove or disprove its unity. Zechariah 1–8 is studied rather than 1–6 because of the numerous interconnections between the visions and both 1.1-6 and chs. 7 and 8. I am persuaded by the Meyers' arguments on the unity of Haggai–Zechariah 1–8, just as I am persuaded by Pierce's arguments for the unity of the Haggai–Zechariah–Malachi corpus, but do not set either of these corpora as my principal object of study because I feel the works are still significantly different enough stylistically to set the visions and their immediate context as my object of study. The primary

10. Ruffin examines the role of symbols over the course of the entire book in an attempt to determine 'if there is a coherent message communicated by the book as a whole' (1986: 1). He links ethics and anatomy, agriculture and leadership, as well as elements and protection or purification to show the variations of meaning conveyable through symbols and how abstract concepts become attached to symbols. This presents a reading with multiple levels of meaning interacting simultaneously. While I do not believe that Ruffin succeeds in *proving* that Zech. 1–14 is a unity, he does provide some very interesting readings of Zechariah's symbolic world.

object of study is the booklet of visions, Zechariah 1–8, with its often noted three sections based on the dates given in 1.1, 7 and 7.1 with their corresponding differences of genre. All of these interconnections suggest Zechariah 1–8 is a literary unity, the reading of which as a unity fills in gaps that reading the individual portions does not provide.[11]

How about Using the *pisqot* to Divide the Text?

Unfortunately, no one seems to really know the function of the *pisqot*. Yeivin notes that this practice dates from the third century or earlier and quotes the halakic midrashim's explanation of the phenomena, 'Why were the *pisqot* introduced? To give Moses time to reflect between each *parashah*, and between each subject' (Yeivin 1980: 41). Obviously nobody has known the function of the *pisqot* for some time. Likewise, it is difficult to make any significance out of its occurrence here.

Everywhere else the *petuhot* occur in Zechariah 1–8 they precede divine speech marked by היה דבר־יהוה...לאמר (4.7-8; 7.3-4; 7.7-8; 7.14–8.1) or כה אמר יהוה צבאות (8.6-7; 8.19-20). Perhaps whoever added the *petuhot* to Zechariah 1–8 used them to mark the speech of the deity, and thus 2.10-17 is the speech of the deity. While a change of speaker does occur sometimes after a *petuhah*, unfortunately, *petuhot* do appear in the middle of reported speech (Jer. 19.5-13; Ezek. 2.5-8; Hos. 2.15-16; 6.11–7.8; Mal. 4.4-5) and cannot be used to definitively determine a change of speaker.

The *pisqot* in Zechariah are as follows:

> 1.6 ס 1.17 ס 2.2 ס 2.4 ס 2.9 פ
> 2.11 ס 2.13 ס 2.17 ס 4.7 פ
> 5.8 ס 5.11 ס 6.8 ס 6.15 ס 7.3 פ
> 7.7 פ
> 7.14 פ
> 8.3 ס 8.5 ס 8.6 פ
> 8.8 ס 8.13 ס 8.17 ס 8.19 פ
> 8.22 ס 8.23 ס

One cannot divide the text into pericopes solely on the evidence of the *pisqot*, as this would break up the narrative in the middle of 'stories'. One cannot divide the text on the basis of the *petuhot*. This would create textual divisions suggested by the layout above (that is, 1.1–2.9; 2.10–4.7, etc.). This is unacceptable as it divides stories unnecessarily and without just cause. An example is the *petuhah* at 4.7. This occurs in the middle of the pericope concerning Zerubbabel, as well as in the middle of the larger narrative concerning the lampstand. This divides the text at a point which appears intricately related to its context. (Though many divide 4.6b-10a from

---

11. See below for examples of how reading throughout these sequences creates a story in the mind of the reader based on the composite material provided by all three sections of the text.

ch. 4 [for example, Meyers and Meyers 1987: 265-72], 4.6b-10 is usually treated as a unit.) The division after 7.3 entails a change of implied speakers, but it still concerns the same topic (fasting). The material which follows the division at 2.9 is of a different nature though, and the *petuhah* may exist here to divide the text.

The *setumot* are even more perplexing. While the divisions at 1.6, 17; 2.4, 17; 5.11; 6.8, 15; and 8.23 roughly adhere to modern commentators' division of the text, one would expect a *setumah* at 3.10; 4.14; and 5.4 if its role was to divide the visions from one another. Furthermore, the purpose of the *setumah* divisions at 2.2, 11, 13; and 5.8 is confusing. This said, the *setumah* divisions at 8.3, 5, 8, 13, 17 and 22 do divide oracles which deal with different subject matter and appear to fulfil some type of role in discerning the oracles.

The *pisqot* thus appear in places to divide the text where modern commentators' expect divisions, but also occur in places where it seems odd for a division to take place. They are therefore not very reliable for dividing the text.

The Genre of Zechariah 1–8

The division of Zechariah into two portions is not meant to make any historical implications such as supporting, or denying, claims that Zechariah 9–14 was written earlier or later than Zechariah 1–8. With the scant evidence available for this time period, for all we know, and if commentators were more honest, for all they know too, Zechariah could have written the whole book, or may never have even existed. The use of the word 'Zechariah' in this thesis refers to a character in a book who is the implied author of that book (see the section 'The Implied Narrator of Zechariah 1–8'), but is not intended to suggest anything more beyond that. Who knows if there ever was a real Zechariah and if he wrote this book? Perhaps 'Zechariah' is a pseudonym. Even if he is the actual author, it is difficult to believe such bizarre events befell him. As Selden says, 'history is always "narrated"...the past can never be available to us in pure form, but always in the form of "representations"' (1989: 105; see his discussion of New Historicism, 103-10).

In the light of this, we must consider what kind of representation we are dealing with when attempting to write history. Attributing the actions in these texts to the characters therein is to succumb to the textual world: to accept it at face value. Fair enough, it may have happened. But it more likely did not. Judging by the surreal nature of the story, is the reader expected to believe these events actually occurred, which is implicit in trying to extract history from a text? Reading Zechariah as history is akin to viewing Dali's 'Sleep' as landscape painting. This does not belittle the value of Zechariah 1–8, rather, it questions whether history is the proper object of study in examining this text.

Carroll's comments on Jeremiah, which he sees as ahistorical and very intertextual, are analogous to the situation in Zechariah:

> there are so many citations from other parts of the Hebrew Bible that any reading of the book as history or the reportage of actual events in the period set by 1.1-3 strikes me as a complete misreading of the text. Social reality models are irrelevant here. The text is too convention-bound, too stereotypical for them to do sufficient work. The book is a supplementation of other books (a kind of *Ergänzungstext*) and the social dynamics of its production will have to be found in terms other than historical reportage of the sixth century (1990: 40).

To make the decision about how to read this text demands that the reader make assumptions about the genre of the text. Robert Carroll's statements about genre, Jeremiah and comparative history are also appropriate to Zechariah:

> If it is a commonplace in classical and ancient historical studies that such writers [Herodotus, Homer, Livy, Plutarch, Thucydides, and Xenophon] are a mixture of history, myth and inventive writing, why should biblical scholars imagine that the Bible escapes such classifications (1990: 41; material in parentheses from previous sentence).

The decision as to which genre to attribute to this text is another framing choice that will affect the interpretation, because assumptions about genres follow this interpretational choice. 'Genre' is an evasive term that is practically useless because of the difficulty of defining genres: whenever one tries to determine a genre, there are always elements of a given text which refuse to conform to that definition of genre, or the definition for the genre is so broad it is useless. Who can authoritatively and convincingly argue for and declare the genre of Zechariah? Amsler identifies four genres in Zechariah 1–8 (1972: 227-30). Some, like Hanson, might say 'early apocalyptic,' but that implies there is a consensus on how to define 'apocalyptic' (Petitjean 1966: 57 n. 68, 69). Others might say 'late prophecy', but what is prophecy, and what is a prophet? Petersen has shown how 'each society in which prophets are read and pondered has tended to inject its own value structures and models when speaking about Israel's prophets' (1987: 1). His proof is that

> In late eighteenth-century Germany, prophets were understood to be romanticists, expressing the spirit of natural poetry. In nineteenth-century

England and Holland, prophets were understood as sober rationalists
expressing strict moralisms, and in the 1960s in the United States,
prophets were often viewed as counterculture figures...prophets have
been understood as priests, charismatics, ecstatics, poets, theologians,
politicians—the list could go on almost without limit (1987: 1).[12]

Petersen concludes, 'we need to admit that it is unlikely that we will
ever achieve consensus on a single notion on the nature of prophecy'
(1987: 17). I personally like Davies's view that a prophet is anyone
who calls himself or herself a prophet and can get at least one person to
believe them (personal communication). More specific to this discussion of genre is Carroll's comment, 'As for the genre of a prophetic
book as a whole, who will agree on deciding what that might be?'
(1990: 42). Further, 'What I do hold to be the case is the difficulty
(extreme at times) of determining which elements in a given text of the
Bible have a claim to be regarded as historical and which as literary,
ideological or fictional' (Carroll 1990: 44).

Zechariah's genre roughly adheres to the category of magic realism,
surrealism or perhaps fantasy literature. All literary works ultimately
define their own genre as they appropriate the style(s) of another genre
or other genres. The most important assumption that will affect interpretation is probably related to the reader's assumptions surrounding
what is a prophetic book. The closest this book comes to defining
Zechariah's genre is to call it a pastiche of earlier work: it is a composite work which incorporates a mix of genres and traditions (oracles,
visions, historical summaries and priestly and prophetic inquiries).

While some commentators see the mixture of oracles and visions in
Zechariah as indicative that the material contained in Zechariah must
have originally come from separate collections (Meyers and Meyers
1987: lxxi), the prevalent view is to approach the visions and oracles as
parts of a unified work:

> The varied literary genres within each prophetic work are interwoven
> into a coherent whole... Not only have we found no cause to recognise
> an independent context for each, but also we have found good reason to
> view the visions and the oracles as integral parts of a whole. The mixing
> of genres is a sign of artistry rather than of differentiation of authorship
> or setting (Meyers and Meyers 1987: xlv).[13]

12. Petersen also lists six views on prophets 'that have been influential in the
twentieth-century critical discussion of prophecy' (1987: 10-16).

13. Bergdall (1986: 25) and Halpern (1978: 168) also do not view this change of

Meyers and Meyers elaborate on this in a later work.

> Although it would be convenient to separate the oracles and consider
> them as a discrete component of Part Two, their integral relationship
> with the visionary units invalidates such a separation... The ideas
> expressed by the oracles are based upon and also amplify themes found
> in the visions with which they are associated. In other words, vision and
> oracles complement and supplement each other (*ABD*: VI, 1064).

The Literary Nature of Zechariah 1–8

Janet Tollington examines the evidence surrounding writing and written
texts in the Tanakh and makes a strong case for the existence of writing
in ancient Israel beginning with the monarchy (1993: 18). She analyses
terms relevant to literacy in the Tanakh and concludes that, 'the higher
strata of Israelite society appear to have been literate from the begin-
nings of the monarchy, maybe even earlier, and...the necessary writing
materials were available' (1993: 18). Relative to prophetic texts, she
suggests 'it is a possibility that the preaching of the classical prophets
could also have been put down in writing at the time it was uttered, or
soon after, either by the prophets themselves or by those who heard
them' (1993: 18). While she does not definitely conclude that these collections must have been written, she postulates that it is just as feasible
that they were preserved in written form as the consensus position that
they were transmitted in oral form (1993: 19). She concludes:

> The truth is that we do not know; but the scant evidence found in the Old
> Testament permits the hypothesis that the Israelites placed greater reli-
> ance on written documents than on oral tradition throughout the mon-
> archic age. This is a subject which merits deeper study but I feel justified
> in concluding that Haggai and Zechariah probably had access to some
> legal, cultic and prophetic literature and were not dependent only on

genre as indicative of different authorship. Halpern (1978: 190). Harrelson (1982:
119) and Petitjean (1966: 60) see Zechariah as merging Mesopotamian temple reno-
vation rituals and the traditions of Israel. Wallis sees parallels between the Egyptian
'Dramatischen Ramesseum-Papyrus' and Zechariah 1–8 (1978: 382ff.). Seybold
believes the world of myth underlies much of Zechariah's imagery: a combination
of Babylonian New Year myth, the symbolism of the court, and the symbolism
(myth?) of the earlier temple underlie Zechariah (1974b: 93-94, 99, 101). G. Fohrer
believes Zechariah's 'images and ideas derive primarily from three realms: Israelite
conceptions...myth and fairy tale...and foreign cults' (1968: 462). These are yet
other ways of intertextually reading Zechariah.

what was remembered and repeated of Israel's religious heritage. However, the availability of texts implies nothing about the use to which these prophets may have put such material (1993: 19).

Meyers and Meyers state it more strongly, 'Zechariah's persistent mention of what appears to be a written corpus suggests that the Primary History (Genesis through 2 Kings) together with a prophetic corpus already constituted a body of sacred writings' (*ABD*: VI, 1062).[14] The existence of this corpus allowed these authors to significantly engage in dialogue with these earlier texts when they wrote (Tollington 1993: 245).

The complexity of the book of Zechariah has led some to conclude that it was literature from its inception. Barton speaks at length of this matter:

> A question which this often raises in the minds of students of apocalyptic, but one which is equally useful in studying the prophets, is whether in some cases the vision is not a 'genuine' vision at all, but a literary convention deliberately and consciously adopted by the prophet. If so, then the 'prophet' or apocalyptist is to be seen more as a writer than as a speaker. This question arises already with Ezekiel and Zechariah, for their allegorical visions seem to lack the immediacy and directness of the brief vision reports in Amos or Isaiah (*ABD*: V, 494).

He says further, 'prophecy gradually turned from a spoken into a written phenomenon' (*ABD*: V, 494).

Davis takes a much stronger line:

> In current opinion Zechariah wrote his prophecies...the book of Zechariah would be his own and its arrangement his own. The theory that it was left to the disciples of Zechariah to cherish his words, gather the fragments of his discourse from sentiments of love and piety, throw them together in wild confusion and publish them without his supervision is not 'according to analogy'. It was not the manner of the prophets. Jeremiah dictated his to an amanuensis (Jer. xxxvi. 2, 4, 18, 32); Habakkuk was told to write his (Hb. ii. 2.); Ezekiel seems to have written his (Ezek. i. I, 4 *et passim*). Why not Zechariah too? (1920: 263-64).[15]

14. See Clines (1990) for a discussion of the existence of the primary history.

15. Likewise North, 'The artificiality and structure of First-Zechariah's visions, with their interpreting angels, suggest that we have here a literary composition intended to be read silently rather than aloud' (1972b: 71; similarly Marks 1987: 210).

Speaking of the authors of Haggai and Zechariah, Tollington says, 'Their prophecies were recorded as literature at an early stage of their history, perhaps even from the outset, with a consequence that they show little sign of having been significantly altered by editorial or redactional expansion' (1993: 245). Further, 'Zechariah...conveyed a major proportion of his message through literature rather than by oral ministry' (1993: 247). She suggests that the writer of Zechariah may have had access to texts of the earlier portions of the Tanakh, rather than basing his work on oral traditions.

Chapter 3

BUILDING FOUNDATIONS TO READ ZECHARIAH:
METHODOLOGICAL PRESUPPOSITIONS

There are many elements of Zechariah which are confusing. They are
difficult to catalogue because many of them overlap with each other and
are thus difficult to reduce to one category; that is, many textual elements fit into more than one of the categories of incoherence presented
here. Nevertheless, categorizing these confusing elements allows one to
speak of this incoherency, rather than to only experience it.

The Nature of Language

Language delivers its judgment to whoever knows how to hear it.
Lacan 1988: 39

Central to this thesis is Bakhtin's conception of language. Heteroglossia stands at the heart of Bakhtin's conception of language. While
heteroglossia occurs both between different languages and within a
given language, I am primarily concerned with its intralinguistic nature:[1]
the synonymous presence of different languages in a speech utterance.

> At any given moment of its evolution, language is stratified not only into
> linguistic dialects in the strict sense of the word (according to formal lin-
> guistic markers, especially phonetic), but also…into languages that are
> socio-ideological: languages of social groups, 'professional' and 'gen-
> eric' languages, languages of generations and so forth. From this point of
> view, literary language itself is only one of these heteroglot languages—
> and in its turn is also stratified into languages (generic, period-bound and
> others). And this stratification and heteroglossia, once realized, is not
> only a static invariant of linguistic life, but also what insures its
> dynamics: stratification and heteroglossia widen and deepen as long as

---

1. An obvious interlinguistic heteroglossia occurs in Zechariah with Babylonian loan-words like the months שְׁבָט and כִּסְלֵו (1.7; 7.1).

language is alive and developing. Alongside the centripetal forces, the centrifugal forces of language carry on their uninterrupted work; alongside verbal-ideological centralization and unification, the uninterrupted processes of decentralization and disunification go forward... Every utterance participates in the 'unitary language' (in its centripetal forces and tendencies) and at the same time partakes of social and historical heteroglossia (the centrifugal, stratifying forces)' (1990: 272).

Furthermore, there is an 'intra-language dialogue' (Bakhtin's term; 1990: 273) constantly occurring:

any concrete discourse (utterance) finds the object at which it was directed already as it were overlain with qualifications, open to dispute, charged with value, already enveloped in an obscuring mist—or, on the contrary, by the 'light' of alien words that have already been spoken about it. It is entangled, shot through with shared thoughts, points of view, alien value judgments and accents. The word, directed toward its object, enters a dialogically agitated and tension filled environment of alien words, value judgments and accents, weaves in and out of complex interrelationships, merges with some, recoils from others, intersects with yet a third group: and all this may crucially shape discourse, may leave a trace in all its semantic layers, may complicate its expression and influence its entire stylistic profile. The living utterance, having taken meaning and shape at a particular historical moment in a socially specific environment, cannot fail to brush up against thousands of living dialogic threads, woven by socio-ideological consciousness around the given object of an utterance; it cannot fail to become an active participant in social dialogue (1990: 276).[2]

Bakhtin discusses this further:

2.   Many others have spoken about how in one way or another, readers cannot help but bring with them their previous reading experience (for example, Culler 1980, Holland 1980, Fish 1980a; 1980b; see Tompkins 1980). Holland focuses on the reader's psychological processes and how the individual's construction of their identity, complete with defence mechanisms, interacts with the text (1980). Culler discusses how readers bring their knowledge of the 'operations of discourse' and how there is inevitably a gap between the writer's knowledge of discourse and the reader's (1980). Fish proceeds along similar lines and speaks of the backlog of language experience (semantic and syntactic) in both the writer and the reader which is united in the reading act (1980b: 84-87). For a lively debate surrounding the roles of readers and authors in the interpretation of texts with the example of a celebrated author *au courant* with literary theory (Umberto Eco) see Collini (1992).

> Every type of intentional stylistic hybrid is more or less dialogized. This
> means that the languages that are crossed in it relate to each other as do
> rejoinders in a dialogue; there is an argument between languages, an
> argument between styles of language. But it is not a dialogue in the nar-
> rative sense, nor in the abstract sense; rather it is a dialogue between
> points of view, each with its own concrete language that cannot be trans-
> lated into the other (1990: 76).

This dialogism wages its war in individuals, as all language is the prop-
erty of individuals.

> As a result of the work done by all these stratifying forces in language,
> there are no 'neutral' words and forms—words and forms that can
> belong to 'no one'; language has been completely taken over, shot
> through with intentions and accents. For any individual consciousness
> living in it, language is not an abstract system of normative forms but
> rather a concrete heteroglot conception of the world. All words have the
> 'taste' of a profession, a genre, a tendency, a party, a particular work, a
> particular person, a generation, an age group, the day and hour. Each
> word tastes of the context and contexts in which it has lived its socially
> charged life; all words and forms are populated by intentions (1990:
> 293).

To digress, another aspect of heteroglossia which is pervasive in this
study, and in all biblical studies, is the interlinguistic heteroglossia
occurring between the native language of the interpreter (be it English,
French, German, modern Hebrew, etc.) and ancient Hebrew. Impossible
to chart, this heteroglossia is constantly occurring in the field and is
being perpetuated with every word study an interpreter performs. We
are not 'discovering' ancient Hebrew, rather we are constantly grafting
new signifieds onto the signifier.

To return to the discussion at hand, while Bakhtin emphasizes the
socio-linguistic aspects of language, it is his philosophy of language as
a living organism, as a 'historical becoming' (Bakhtin's term; 1990:
288), which bears most heavily on the reading strategy employed here.
There are similarities between Bakhtin's theory of language, reader-
response criticism, and Lacan's theory of language that stresses 'the
priority of the signifier in relation to the signified' (1988: 42).

Lacan's treatment of the symbolic chain and how signifiers are constantly in flux is most pertinent here. To Lacan, all socialized humans
are part of the symbolic order. Children emerge from the mirror stage

into language (which is the symbolic order?).[3] After this emergence, the symbolic order structures their unconscious and forms their selves: 'it is the symbolic order which is constitutive for the subject' as the subject is oriented by 'the itinerary of the signifier' (1988: 29; see Eagleton 1985: 165-67; and Wright 1982: 154-56). Every time a subject hears, speaks, reads or writes a signifier, that signifier is minutely altered in the mind of the subject: as with Bakhtin, signifiers are constantly in flux. Lacan speaks of the repetition automatism:

> For we have learned to conceive of the signifier as sustaining itself only in a displacement comparable to that found in electric news strips: this because of the alternating operation which is its principle, requiring it to leave its place, even though it returns to it by a circular path (1988: 43).

This is partially because 'the signifier is a unit in its very uniqueness, being by nature symbol only of an absence' (Lacan 1988: 39). The subject attaches the various denotations and connotations to the signifier, the contexts in which it occurs, the syntactical rules surrounding its use, synonyms, antonyms, words which commonly occur with that signifier, words which cannot occur with the signifier: all the rules which govern language that a native speaker is consciously or subconsciously aware of, as well as all of the previous accretions of that signifier on the mind of the subject. Each morpheme, lexeme, word or phrase, genre, idiom, collocation, grammatical marking and concept of the text is a victim of overdeterminacy.[4] Every aspect of the subject's experiences with the signifier may be condensed into that signifier in the mind of the subject. As with all psychological processes, some of the previous experiences with the signifier will be repressed. All aspects

---

3.   Lacan's language is very rich. Bowie says the problem of understanding Lacan is that his terms are not static while they mutually define each other and change in implication (1987: 105). Eagleton phrases it thus: 'All desire springs from a lack, which it strives continually to fill. Human language works by such lack: the absence of the real objects which signs designate, the fact that words have meaning only by virtue of the absence and exclusion of others. To enter language, then, is to become a prey to desire: language' (Eagleton 1985: 167; see Lacan 1988: 52). My presentation of Lacan here leaves the role of desire in language grossly unaccounted for. I feel justified in this in that I am not attempting to present a Lacanian interpretation, rather I am merely trying to use only a part of Lacanian theory as a prop in my theory—to help me in a task I have undertaken: to help me obtain an object I desire.

4.   Derrida's discussion of the trace and its effects on conceptions of temporality and presence deals with many themes mentioned here (1976: 65-73).

of the text invite intertextual couplings, and we should allow these lexia free rein to engage in their textual escapades. Eagleton gives a very practical example which emphasizes the fluidity of the signifier:

> If you dream of a horse, it is not immediately obvious what this signifies: it may have many contradictory meanings, may be just one of a whole chain of signifiers with equally multiple meanings. The image of a horse, that is to say, is not a sign in Saussure's sense—it does not have one determine [sic] signified tied neatly to its tail—but is a signifier which may be attached to many different signifieds, and which may itself bear the traces of the other signifiers which surround it. (I was not aware, when I wrote the above sentence, of the word-play involved in 'horse' and 'tail': one signifier interacted with another against my conscious intention.) The unconscious is just a continual movement and activity of signifiers, whose signifieds are often inaccessible to us because they are *repressed*. This is why Lacan speaks of the unconscious as a 'sliding of the signified beneath the signifier', as a constant fading and evaporation of meaning, a bizarre 'modernist' text which is almost unreadable and which will certainly never yield up its final secrets to interpretation (Eagleton 1985: 168).

Reading Foundations

This work is heavily influenced by theories of intertextuality,[5] reader-response criticism and Bakhtin.[6] Reader-response theory, and the inter-textual theory that grew out of it, explain how readers connect two or more texts in their construction of meaning for a text. When people read they collect phrases until they reach a point where the drive to make sense out of a text is frustrated by some kind of aberration in the text, be it lexical or syntactical, which readers find difficult to amalga-mate into coherent readings.[7] The aberration is an aspect of the text which is not explained by the interpretational strategy of the reader. When someone admits a text is difficult to understand, she is discussing portions of the text which refuse to conform to her reading strategies. The reader recognizes a similarity between the text being read and some external 'text' (this is not limited to textual similarities—'element',

5.   For a useful anthology on intertextuality see Still and Worton (1990: 1-44).

6.   Still and Worton also draw connections between Bakhtin and intertextual theory (1990: 4, 15-17). Landow shows the interrelation of Bakhtin, intertextuality, hypertextuality and many other literary theorists (1992: ch. 1).

7.   Writers who speak of this are legion. See esp. Culler (1980); Fish (1980a; 1980b); Iser (1980); and Riffaterre (1990: 57-59).

'phenomenon' or 'stimuli' could be substituted for the 'text' in single quotation marks). As Riffaterre notes, 'These perceptions, this reader response to the text, cannot be explained by linguistic structures, since these are observed in non-literary and literary utterances alike' (1990: 56).[8]

Some terminology will be necessary for this study. This terminology has been eclectically chosen from theorists more for its straightforwardness and adherence to more common uses of English rather than for the sophisticated nuances that attend these terms in the theoreticians who coined them. Obviously, this is an appropriation of the work of the theorists and a hostile takeover as well, since it disregards *substantial* portions of their theoretical work. Still, these terms are employed so that those familiar with the theory will recognize them (and hopefully the work set for the terms) and in order to avoid alienating those unfamiliar with the literature on intertextuality.

Hypertext is a term drawn from Genette which is 'the latecome text' (Still and Worton 1990: 23). It is like Kristeva's *Focussed* text. It refers to the text which is under consideration. Unfortunately, like Lacan's sliding signifiers, this is a very mobile term which shifts as the object of study changes. Hypertext is the text being studied which is perceived as re-using and recycling material from the pre-texts. These pre-texts are then sought by the reader to furnish an interpretation.

Pre-text is Still and Worton's term which is not precisely defined in their work, but which refers to the perceived 'original' text. They claim Genette's hypotext (that which the hypertext has drawn from) is the 'pre-text' (Still and Worton 1990: 23). 'Pre-text' in this thesis refers to a text from which the reader perceives the author to have drawn material in the production of the hypertext. It is the corpus of literature to which an intertextual connection is made; that is, if Zech. 3.2 is perceived to quote Amos 4.11, then Amos 4.11, its immediate context, and any other parts of the book of Amos which this reader connects with Zech. 3.2, is the pre-text (and not merely Amos 4.11).

Most theories of intertextuality stress the importance of reading both the hypertext and the pre-text in the light of each other. While I embrace the emergent idea that the intertextuality of Zechariah and, say, Isaiah are mutually illuminating, my principal concern is with interpreting Zechariah, and I will limit myself to only investigating that half of the

---

8. Likewise Frow seeks 'to break down the limits between the textual and an apparently external and non-textual ("contextual") domain' (1990: 54).

intertextual equation. Perhaps in a later foray I will venture into Zechariah's implications on the 'pre-texts'. Actually, once I have read Zechariah any reading of the pre-text is ultimately influenced by Zechariah as I cannot delete from my consciousness the experience of having read Zechariah.

Furthermore, the term 'pre-text' is itself somewhat at odds with most intertextual theories, which are primarily ahistorical. Obviously the use of the term 'pre-text' is a historical assumption regarding which text precedes the other. In the light of the constant debate over the dating of biblical books, I am persuaded by many others (for example, Eslinger 1992: 52-53) that it is impossible to discern on the available evidence in what order the biblical books were actually written. I cannot even confidently assign a century to most books in the Hebrew Bible, but following Davies and others lean towards dating the entire corpus after 520 BCE. Therefore my use of the term 'pre-text' does not imply any actual historical precedence for the texts under consideration. Rather, I follow Eslinger's criticism and suggestion that biblical scholars use the 'sequence of the Bible's own plot' to engage in

> a self-consciously literary analysis of the textual interconnections in biblical literature. In it, we continue to use the indications of sequence that historical-critical scholarship has (improperly) relied on, but in full awareness of this reliance and without the conceit that we use a 'scientific' historical framework independent of it (1992: 56).

As Childs has said, 'A reconstructed depth dimension may aid in understanding the interpreted text, but it does not possess an independent integrity for the exegetical task within the context of the canon' (1987: 43). Later he says:

> to assume that the prophets can be understood only if each oracle is related to a specific event or located in its original cultural milieu is to introduce a major hermeneutical confusion into the discipline and to render an understanding of the canonical Scripture virtually impossible (1987: 48).

Van Wolde's comments are also pertinent to this discussion: 'it is not the chronology of texts that should occupy the centre of attention, but the logical and analogical reasoning of the reader in interaction with the text' (1989: 43).

> The intertextual approach starts from the assumption that a writer's work should not be seen as a linear adaptation of another text but as a complex of relationships; the principle of causality is left behind... The text, here,

is the directing instance because it offers certain possibilities, and the
reader is the instance that assigns meaning by using these possibilities
and relating them to his own *stream of interpretants*, i.e. the residue of
previous processes in which he has assigned meaning (1989: 47).

I am not claiming that my work is ahistorical, but do confess that the
history I do is extremely conjectural. Nevertheless, our concepts of the
past influence our present and our future, and history is thereby important as an object of cultural affectation. When I use the term 'pre-text' I
do not claim to be making historical conclusions regarding the compositional history of the biblical books, but am only using the plot of the
Bible as a heuristic device.

Connective is Riffaterre's term for any textual element, be it lexical
or syntactical, which links the pre-text and the hypertext.[9] He describes
connectives as 'signposts' which 'belong equally in text and intertext,
linking the two, and signalling in each the presence of their mutually
complementary traits...[they] combine the sign systems of text and
intertext into new semiotic clusters' (1990: 58). Some theorists call the
connective the *intertext*. The connective is the similarity, whatever it be
(morphological, syntactical, lexical [including cognates, synonyms, an-
tonyms], mythological, grammatical—practically any aspect of language and that which it entails), that causes the reader of the hypertext
to think of the pre-text. Examples of connectives could include a word
or phrase which occurs in both texts, a similar physical layout of the
text, or a similar mythological theme (for example, a quest for immor-
tality).

Many have tried to describe exactly what triggers the intertextual
recognition (see Still and Worton [1990]). It is connections which lie at
the centre of all interpretational activity, whether they are intra- or intertextually based, literary or historical (thus Freud's theory of free association is truly the master trope of all interpretation). Simply put, it is the

9.   A principal difference between my use of the term and Riffaterre's is his
obsession with the ungrammaticality of the connective, that is, the connectives'
failure to follow the grammatical expectations of the reader triggers this recognition
to Riffaterre (1990: 58; 71-76). I believe this is partially the case, but many other
factors also trigger intertextual recognition. I think Riffaterre focuses on the
ungrammaticality of connectives so much because of his quest to establish the
mechanisms of intertextual recognition. That said, he does not only use this crite-
rion to define the connective.

recognition by the subject of some similarity between two elements
which instigates the 'recognition', or attribution, of an intertext.

Matrix Formation: A Metaphor of Reading

The foregoing discussion has laid the theoretical groundwork that
underlies the 'system' of interpretation (mis)used in this thesis. Actually, I have difficulty in using the word 'system' for interpretative activities, as I believe it implies an order to interpretation which does not
exist; interpretation is an act which chases many disordered thoughts
and then poses as an orderly process when it is frozen in print. As the
quote from Borges which began this Part asserts, this is necessitated by
the medium of language. The subjugation of the reader to the symbolic
order both allows and dictates this infinite transference: the reader is
slave to the liberating word. When she attempts to recall her reading
experience, she will always have more than one thought which never
reaches the page. Further, every recollection engenders new associations. Many (all which are not repressed) are visible to the reader when
she attempts to describe her personal experience of a word (or, for
Borges, a letter). Unfortunately, she will always fail in her task to
describe this ineffable experience of reading. She is simultaneously
conscious of all previous experiences which she relates to that reading
experience and frustrated at the impossibility of sharing it.

The interpretation enclosed herein combines numerous interpretational activities. Perspectival narrative criticism, centred around close
reading, is used to examine the rhetoric of Zechariah. This becomes
part of an interpretational process that Miscall calls labyrinth building:[10]

> Labyrinth is also an allegory for reading. Reading, as I pursue it, is a pro-
> cess of building and (de)constructing a text, a Labyrinth; it is not a speci-
> fically directed procedure, 'the method,' to reach a set entrance, center or
> exit that can serve as the one meaning or interpretation of the text. It is
> more a reader-directed process, in which the reader decides which tex-
> tual threads to pick up and follow, how far to follow each one and
> whether to tie them all together at some end or center or just leave them
> lying on the page (1991: 107).[11]

10. See Miscall (1991; esp. 103-107) for his development of this reading model.
11. He proceeds to create a labyrinth of interpretation by tracing the theme of
'light' (אור) and words related to it (by synecdoche, synonymity or antonymity) in
Isaiah.

While Miscall's metaphor for the readerly process is apt, the term 'matrix' is here substituted for 'labyrinth' to avoid the connotations of stability inherent in the word 'labyrinth', as well as for the extra dimension 'matrix' implies for the connecting process (this is perhaps pedantic as Miscall deftly uses the term 'labyrinth' as an allusion to Theseus). No matter how hard interpreters try to maintain a stable interpretation, there are elements which will not fit into a pattern, and which may openly oppose previously made connections. As Miscall has observed, there are too many 'verbal threads' which could be followed, and readers must decide which ones they will follow and which they will ignore (1991: 108, 117). Vorster says similarly, 'proponents of intertextuality focus on texts as networks pointing to other texts... In the place of an object which has meaning has come a network calling for reaction by the reader' (1989: 22). Vorster draws attention to how text types (for example, birth stories or apocalyptic texts) draw the reader to read that text 'within the range of that intertext' (1989: 21-22). That is, the text type makes the reader think of other texts of a similar type.

The reader starts to create a matrix when she begins to read; every utterance in the story to which the reader attributes meaning is a node. Henry states, 'Many of the objects referred to in a given text are repeated and nuanced throughout the novel or poem, or over a series of poems by an author, building upon simple analogies to create in essence a new meaning for a word' (1990: 98). This is an example on the intratextual scale that reflects the process that Bakhtin discusses on the larger scale of the living subject. This is the process which intertextual theory, reader-response theory and Lacan's symbolic chain attempt to account for: the past life of the subject/reader which encounters the text. Each interpretative choice is a path between the nodes. The nodes join together to form the matrix. The matrix, which is the connection of all these nodes together, is the interpretation. The act of connecting together two points or nodes in the text (or texts) interprets the text in the light of this decision. Each node of the story alters the matrix: some nodes add portions to the matrix, some destroy previously built portions of the matrix, and some condition and limit aspects of the matrix.

The matrix is constantly in mind, and in flux, as the reader builds the story, and conditions how the reader understands each event as it occurs: she reads in light of the created matrix, which, in turn, is constantly transformed by the nodes she reads. Many elements form sub-matrices within the overall matrix. After a reader has made an interpretative decision by connecting two or more nodes, the cognizance of the other choice leaves an impression in the reader's mind. The other choice never completely disappears—it is simply marginalized. If enough evidence accrues for the marginalized choice as the reader continues to read the text, then the interpreter changes their interpretative option and the dominant choice becomes the marginalized and vice versa—the reader may still disconnect the nodes, and in some cases may connect one or more of those nodes elsewhere. Even after this connection is effaced, a trace of the earlier path between the nodes constantly threatens to rearrange the matrix and return it to its previous shape. Both options may even exist simultaneously and address different aspects of interpretation. One could then speak of parallel matrices that compete for domination as 'authoritative'. These competitions take place on many inter- and intratextual levels. Sometimes, mutually exclusive choices are held in the interpreter's mind and the matrix oscillates between two patterns. Multiply this by the number of interpretative options in all texts and there emerges a staggering number of possible interpretations. The implications of other elements in the story are changed, and entirely new matrices arise when only one option is changed, as the changes can affect the entire text. This is similar to those matrices one can buy at fairs or markets which change their shape from a cube to a star to a rectangle and back again. Unfortunately, unlike for Odysseus, our shapeshifter will never reveal its true shape even if we clasp it forever.

Rather than limit itself to the intratextual scale of Zechariah 1–8, as Miscall does with the book of Isaiah, this study will also investigate this process on the much larger intertextual scale. This decision is made because of a belief that the inter- and intratextual drives present a false dichotomy and both represent the same acts which occur in the reader's mind. This matrix building is analogous to Bakhtin's and Lacan's view of words (here nodes) as constantly in flux. There is a symbolic order which surrounds all nodes and consciously and subconsciously links these nodes to words and syntax. There is a symbolic universe which surrounds every node and which may enter a text through the presence of that node in the hypertext. Nodes are like Borges's Aleph described in the opening quote to Chapter 1. As a demonstration of a node I will relate a personal example. On re-reading Landow after writing this sentence, I noticed that Landow also draws this analogy between intertextual reading theory and Borges's Aleph. I had read Borges before reading Landow. This recollection of Borges while writing this work and dealing with the joint issues of intertextuality and reading, two areas that Landow deals with, may betray a repressed aspect of my symbolic order which has subconsciously remembered Landow's use of Borges.

Of course, the paths readers choose to lay between textual points and the points they choose to highlight are an extension of their existential position in the universe: the paths reflect the combination of life experience that merged to create the social entity the individual reader is, and the symbolic order which composes that individual. They reflect the context in which the reader chooses to evaluate textual statements. Reading other texts changes the matrix and engenders a reading different from a reading which fails to consult other texts. Neither reading is privileged, they are just different. Other texts are consulted because readers raise questions unanswered in the text; for example, if a text declares 'Yahweh was angry with your fathers' some readers want to know when Yahweh was angry, even though this issue may not be central to the text in which the phrase occurs. Another way other texts enter the hypertext is through the symbolic order which surrounds every word. The matrix is constantly in flux and ultimately based on the reader's decisions and assumptions: it will either disintegrate, be modified or be upheld by the further combination of the text of Zechariah, other texts and the reader.

In essence, various meanings for textual elements oscillate in a reader's mind and make it difficult to confidently proclaim any element in the text has any specific meaning. In effect, all of the textual allusions are grafted onto the mind of the reader in the reading process and emerge whenever connections are possible, but are hardly ever removed (I won't here delve into Freudian concepts like repression, displacement or projection which are applicable to the language game as it is an act of the psyche). A powerful example of this is found in Calvino (1993). There, one of the characters muses on such a mundane word as 'isosceles':

> the word 'isosceles', once I had associated it with Irina's pubes, is charged for me with such sensuality that I cannot say it without making my teeth chatter (1993: 85).

Calvino has demonstrated in these 27 words of a character what the pages of theorizing above have strained to establish. Now the word 'isosceles' is part of the reader of this text's symbolic order; and so the process continues. Once a node is activated, it constantly waits (at the door?) to spring up and inject its implications into whatever reading situation is encountered.

As Landow has written, drawing from Bush's works on the memex, this type of construction of the interpretational process allows four different objects of enquiry and changes the conception of the word 'text':

> *texts* refers to (a) individual reading units that make up a traditional 'work', (b) those entire works, (c) sets of documents created by trails, and perhaps (d) those trails themselves without accompanying documents (1992: 17).

It depends on what a researcher's object of enquiry is as to which definition of 'text' she or he uses. The final product may not be an interpretation which makes complete sense and may confuse the reader at some times, but this interpretation reflects the reading process far more clearly than more traditional forms of interpretation.

In a nutshell, pre-texts enter the hypertext: (1) through readers' cognisance that they do not fully understand the text and need some external text of which they are as of yet unaware;[12] or (2) through readers' conscious or subconscious knowledge of the world and their personal and/or social symbolic orders which cluster around nodes (or words). Hubbeling says similarly,

> the meaning of a certain symbol is connected with the meanings of other symbols and [that] it depends also on the interpretation of a whole culture and religion... Meanings of words, sentences, propositions, activities, etc. and thus of symbols too depend also on their consequences! The meaning of a certain symbol can therefore never be considered by itself alone (1985: 83).

Readers carry their entire history with them when they read, and the words on the page interact with the words in their mind to produce a matrix. Reading occurs on horizontal and vertical planes.[13] On the horizontal axis is the text which a reader progressively reads in a linear fashion. The reader's mind occupies the vertical axis and attaches any number of elements to each node (that is, any unit of meaning) in the horizontal axis of the text. It is not only the precise connective which enters the hypertext this way, but the entire context in which the connective occurs. Mettinger phrases it this way:

12. See Riffaterre (1990: 56-58).
13. See Mettinger (1993: 258-65).

the allusive signal sometimes triggers a memory of an earlier text that may refer not just to one single point in that text but to one or more of its larger sections as a unit. There are cases when the marker allows a large portion, maybe even the totality of the echoed text, to become part of the semantic structure of the new poem (1993: 264).

As Landow says, reading and writing are not non-linear; rather, they are 'multilinear' or 'multisequential'.

With a text like the Bible for which concordances exist, readers not only carry their personal experiences, but can set out to add to the symbolic chain which surrounds a word by looking at its other manifestations in the biblical text. When the reader has examined the occurrences of a word in other biblical texts and then returns to the original hypertext, she brings with her all the other connotations of this word in the other texts, as well as all the other words with which that word was associated in the other biblical texts. This creates another symbolic chain that attaches itself to each word for which the reader consults a concordance.[14] The reader uses a tool to create Landow's category c—a set of documents created by a trail, and a symbolic order for the word or phrase consulted. The use of a concordance is an intertextual step. Surprisingly, given how central the concordance is to biblical studies, few have written on the processes which occur in the reader when consulting a concordance or the methodology inherent when using a concordance.[15]

Reading Imagery

There is another layer of interpretation that lies beyond the linguistic layer of the text. It is not just the lexical items and the symbolic order which surround these lexical items, that a reader links together to form a matrix. In the words of Henry, 'Exploring a literary work by word, sentence, verse, or phoneme facilitates the kind of intellectual processes

14. See the section 'Snatching Texts from the Fire' for an example of this kind of process.

15. Taking a different angle of approach, Henry critiques the use of concordances and awaits the day when 'an image generating system' will replace them: 'while a concordance can produce each appearance of a word and the other words around it, an image generating system will create with fluidity a more primal context for those occurrences, allowing access to the visual component of symbolic thought' (1990: 98).

that seem to stimulate the discovery of new meaning, but it does not mimic or capture those processes' (1990: 100).[16] The processes *are* the meaning. Moreover, 'Language, however, does at times create pictures in the mind, and...those pictures or images are of fundamental importance in deciphering and understanding a literary work's meaning' (Henry 1990: 95).

Miscall develops this type of idea: 'images are textual elements that are to be seen, visualized or imagined rather than just thought or conceptualized' (1991: 104). Further, 'a particular image can entail rhetorical or logical development. For example, light includes fire by synecdoche since fire produces a type of light; the same applies to sun, moon and stars which produce light' (Miscall 1991: 104).

The mental picture created by the reader becomes itself an interpretational entity which the reader uses to interact with the text. This is interpretation at the level of thought processes, rather than the more canonically accepted interpretational practices of the community (see Henry 1990: 93-95, 100-101). Some meaning is 'derived by visually reconstructing the scenes and placing one upon the other as images' (Henry 1990: 99). Once a mental picture is imagined, it interacts and merges with other mental pictures. Once these mental images are formed, they are nodes in the matrix and interact with the matrix (which is composed of lexical items and other mental images). The lexical symbolic order from which the mental picture is created surrounds the image so that it carries its original context with it. When a reader recalls the image, she imagines: (1) a mental picture of the image; (2) the words which combined to form that image; (3) the semantic fields of those words; and (4) the context which the reader has attached to the words that the reader combined to form the images. Words create images which affect the interpretation of the words that are read subsequently. Every symbol conceives another symbol and thought before the previous pattern in a ceaseless string of births.

Northrop Frye said that 'Eros is still the driving force of the poetry and Eros does not care how casual or inappropriate any given metaphor

---

16. While computer technology has not developed this far yet, the day in which multimedia computer art is accepted as interpretation is eagerly awaited. While Henry outlines how to begin thinking of programmes which will facilitate this process (see 1990: 95-98) his goal is to understand the act of reading (an unattainable goal, in my opinion). This is an alternative medium of interpretation which should stand alongside commentary or monographs.

may be: he only wants to get as many images copulating as possible' (1985: 590). The sheer quantity of relationships between all the visions and oracles in Zechariah makes that book, as assessed by Frye's metaphor, orgiastic. Interpretation is then an orgy of signs which impregnates the reader with meanings. The new entity which is the product of this copulation is the interpretation in the reader's mind. This interpretation continues to grow after it is implanted in the womb of the interpreter's mind. When two images merge, they bring with them their respective symbolic orders. Yet, as in genetics, choices are made between which aspects of those symbolic orders will be passed on and compose the interpretation: they are repressed in the mind of the reader. The lexical symbolic order is united with the imaginary order. The verbal and visual or imaginary planes merge in the interpreter's mind and continually interact with and modify each other.

This chapter has established, at some length, the presuppositions which this reader brings to Zechariah 1–8. The object of inquiry is the Masoretic Text of Zechariah 1–8, which is believed to be literature from its inception. I attempt to make this text mean on two levels. First, the text will be examined on the intratextual level to see what kind of text it is, how it functions as literature, and what kind of meaning can be constructed when one forms a matrix which is controlled by this frame. Next, a close reading will be performed on one particular pericope (1.7-17) to see how the expanded frame of the minor prophets changes the interpretation. Finally, an intertextual reading will be pursued on various elements in the text of Zechariah to see how that frame produces a matrix different from the matrix produced by the other two frames. It is a fine line between the frame of the minor prophets and the 'intertextual' frame which includes the entire Hebrew Bible as both are ultimately intertextual readings. The goal is both to determine what kind of readings a reader versed in intertextual theory and narrative criticism produces for Zechariah 1–8, and to examine how the text resists certain reading strategies. It is hoped this will shed light on what type of booklet Zechariah 1–8 is.

THESIS

Chapter 4

READING ZECHARIAH ON ITS OWN GROUNDS:
AN INTRATEXTUAL ANALYSIS OF ZECHARIAH 1–8

[T]he Bible may be a holy book, but it...does the most devilish things
with language.

Burgess 1993: 21

The Implied Narrator of Zechariah 1–8

It is difficult to determine precisely who narrates Zechariah 1–8. The
book begins with an external unidentified narrator, who speaks in the
third person about Zechariah and Yahweh (1.1). Although all the commentators I have read identify this first-person speaker as Zechariah
even though the name Zechariah only occurs in these introductory formulas (1.1, 7; 7.1, 8), there is the possibility that an unnamed narrator
receives these *Nachtgesichte* ('visions').

The formula used in v. 1, לאמר...(*x*) דבר־יהוה אל־ (ויהי) היה ('The
word of Yahweh came to [*x* = proper noun *or* first-person pronominal
suffix] saying'), always introduces Yahweh's first-person direct speech
throughout the Tanakh (excluding Zechariah) which is directed to the
individual identified in the formula.

The formula לאמר...(proper noun *or* first-person pronominal suffix)
היה דבר־יהוה אל־ in the Tanakh

See Gen. 15.1; 1 Sam. 15.10; 2 Sam. 7.4; 1 Kgs 6.11; 16.1; 17.2, 8; 18.31; 21.17,
28; Isa. 38.4; Jer. 1.4, 11, 13; 2.1; 13.3, 8; 16.1; 18.5; 24.4; 28.12; 29.30; 32.26;
33.1; 33.19, 23; 34.12; 35.12; 36.27; 37.6; 43.8; 49.34; Ezek. 3.16; 6.1; 7.1; 11.14;
12.1, 8, 17, 21, 26; 13.1; 14.2, 12; 15.1; 16.1; 17.1, 11; 18.1; 20.2; 21.1(H), 6(H),
13(H), 23(H); 22.1, 17, 23; 23.1; 24.1, 15; 25.1; 26.1; 27.1; 28.1, 11, 20; 29.1, 17;
30.1, 20; 31.1; 32.1, 17; 33.1, 23; 34.1; 35.1; 36.16; 37.15; 38.1; Jon. 1.1; 3.1; Hag.
2.10; 2 Chron. 11.2; and 2 Chron. 12.7. For almost all of these references, the individual identified in the formula as the recipient of the message is the individual

addressed in the following verses. Possible exceptions are Jer. 18.5; 33.19; 34.12; Ezek. 12.21 and 18.1, in which an individual is identified in the formula as the addressee, but plural verbal forms and pronominal suffixes are addressed by Yahweh. In Jer. 18.5 Yahweh begins his speech by addressing the house of Israel, but addresses the prophet in the masculine singular imperative in v. 11. Since the prophet is not commanded to recite these words to the house of Israel, the effect is much like a soliloquy with a trumped-up actor (Yahweh) performing for the benefit of the prophet in order to display his concern for Israel. At the narrative level, the prophet is thereby ultimately still the recipient of this message. At the level of the book, this betrays the literary nature of the work—the author has left the realms of narrative realism in favour of character portrayal. Alternatively, since the only other audience present is the potter, the potter and Jeremiah together represent the house of Israel and are thus addressed in the plural.

In Ezek. 12.21-25, the passage most analogous to Zechariah, a similar phenomenon occurs: Yahweh addresses the prophet with a second-person plural pronominal suffix and then charges the prophet to speak to the people (them). Perhaps the plural masculine suffix represents the proverb in the land, and is plural because the proverb is an aspect of language that is collective rather than being the speech of the prophet. That indeed an individual is addressed in this section is made clear in Ezek. 12.23 where the prophet is addressed in the singular.

While Ezekiel 18–19 also concerns a proverb among the land, an extended speech is delivered concerning Israel which addresses Israel with second-person plurals. But Yahweh is still pictured at the end of this speech as speaking to the individual prophet when he addresses the prophet in the singular imperative in 19.1.

In Jer. 33.19 and 34.12, Yahweh addresses a plural audience after the formula. The context of 33.19 places Jeremiah inside the court of the guard receiving what appear to be secret revelations from Yahweh (33.3). Much of the material in ch. 33 appears in the middle of a speech from Yahweh to Jeremiah which is intermittently interrupted by references to a plural addressee (33.10, 20-22). The passage is confusing. In 33.23-24 the text portrays Yahweh as addressing the singular (Jeremiah) again, so it is difficult to know what to make of the section 33.19-22. Perhaps it is another soliloquy. Jeremiah 34.12-22 has many of the same problems. These 'soliloquies' are intrusive and make it difficult for the reader to discern what is going on. Perhaps a clue is found in the phrase כה אמר יהוה which precedes these changes of expected addressee in 33.20 and 34.13. While the phrase does not identify another audience, that this phrase often occurs at a change in audience may identify it as a significant enough disjunctive clause to suggest a change in audience in these passages (cf. Jer. 2.2; 28.12-13; 29.31).

In these instances it is perceivable that the prophet represents the people of Israel and/or Judah and Yahweh thus addresses the prophet in the plural. If Yahweh addressed the prophet in the second-person singular, one might interpret Yahweh's speech as dealing with personal matters pertinent solely to Zechariah, rather than the collective Israel and Judah, that is, the reader might think Yahweh had a personal gripe with the recipient of the message.

Obviously, this formula is not used exactly the same way throughout the Tanakh. Still, in all the cases outside of Zechariah, Yahweh is readily identifiable as the speaker. In an overwhelming majority of the examples, and a case can be made for all the examples, the recipient of the message conforms to the expectations implanted by the formula.

Jeremiah 32.6-8 is an example of how one would expect this formula to introduce first-person speech. There, Jeremiah is pictured as the speaker at the beginning of the narrative (32.6). He then reiterates the speech Yahweh said to him in 32.6, and then returns to first-person speech in 32.8.

Ezekiel 1.3 is an example of how one usually expects this formula to be used with first-person speech. There the formula is very similar,

היה היה דבר־יהוה אל־יחזקאל בן־בוזי הכהן בארץ כשׂדים על־נהר־כבר
ותהי עליו שׁם יד יהוה

> ('The word of the Lord came to the priest Ezekiel, son of Buzi, in the
> land of the Chaldeans by the river Chebar; and the hand of the Lord was
> on him there' [NRSV])

but lacks the key construction לאמר ('saying'). Here first-person speech follows the formula, but first-person narration precedes the formula (1.1-3). With the absence of לאמר the reader does not expect the direct speech of Yahweh to follow the formula. This conforms to 'naturalized' expectations (see the paragraph below for a discussion of naturalized conventions).

The occurrence of לאמר is particularly troubling in Zech. 1.1. Joüon says 'the infinitive לֵאמֹר, *dicendo, by saying, saying* [which he also translates as *in saying*; 1991: 337] is an extremely common and very widely used phrase...which introduces direct speech and serves a useful device in the absence of punctuation marks' (1991: 438).[1] In a study directed towards the identification of direct discourse in Hebrew literature, Meier says, 'the unique contribution that לאמר makes to syntax is to identify unequivocally the very next word as DD [direct discourse]' (1992: 326). He say further, 'the infinitive לאמר comes close to being an unequivocal marker of immediately following DD in biblical Hebrew' (1992: 94). It is so pervasive that his concerns are with why it 'does not mark all DD' as 'it is exceptional for לאמר to appear without a following quotation in the some 935 times it appears' (1992: 94, 20). Thus the formula היה דבר־יהוה אל־זכריה...לאמר ('it was the word of

---

1.   Waltke and O'Connor similarly say לאמר is 'used to introduce direct discourse after verbs of saying and of mental activity (thinking, praying, etc.)' (Waltke and O'Connor 1990: 36.2.3e).

Yahweh to Zechariah…saying') leads the reader to expect Yahweh to speak to Zechariah in v. 2. Meier supports this view, 'it is normal for the phrase היה דבר יהוה to conclude with לאמר when DD follows' (1992: 22). Chatman, following Culler, calls this type of expectation of conventions 'naturalizing' them: 'To naturalise a narrative convention means not only to understand it, but to forget its conventional character, to absorb it into the reading-out process, to incorporate it into one's interpretive net, giving it no more thought than to the manifestational medium' (1983: 49).

לאמר is a naturalized convention. In an aberrant manner, the speaker of v. 2 refers to Yahweh in the third person and addresses his or her speech to a second-person *plural* audience (*your* [pl.] ancestors [אבותיכם]). This creates the impression, contrary to the expectations based on the formula's usual function, that Yahweh is *not* the speaker of v. 2. This leads some to suggest v. 2 is an interpolation (Petersen 1984a: 129; Mitchell 1980: 86, 110; Mason 1977a: 32).[2] But one need not appeal to redaction criticism to explain this phenomenon since this does not absolutely defy the norms: one can understand v. 2 as Yahweh's third-person self-referential speech. Yahweh frequently refers to himself in the third person throughout the Tanakh (see Gen. 18.14; Exod. 34.6-7; 2 Sam. 7.5, 8, 11; Isa. 18.13, Jer. 4.4, etc.). In fact, so often that Meier concludes, 'pronominal referents may be illusory guides to sorting out who speaks what words. If God can speak of himself in the third person…or use the first person plural…pronominal shifts by themselves are a shaky foundation for distinguishing divine from human speech' (1992: 208). Yahweh even clearly refers to himself in the third person within the confines of Zechariah 1–8: Yahweh says to the Satan/adversary in 3.2 'Yahweh rebuke you' (ויאמר יהוה אל־השטן יגער יהוה בך). It is thus not aberrant, in Zechariah or in the Tanakh, for Yahweh to refer to himself in the third person.

But some see a problem with Yahweh speaking in the third person and thus read this speech as the messenger of Yahweh's speech (for example, Day 1988: 110). This type of emendation is an example of the norms confusing commentators, who subsequently emend the text to make it adhere to their conceptions. A similar example is ויאמר ('and he

---

2.   While Petersen believes v. 2 is an editorial insertion, he maintains v. 2 is Yahweh's speech to Zechariah in the present structure of the text, rather than Yahweh's speech to the audience to which Zechariah is commanded to pass on Yahweh's speech in vv. 3-6 (1984a: 130).

said') Zech. 4.2b which many commentators read with the *qere* as וָאֹמַר
('and I said') to adhere to the usual convention in the visions of the
conversing messenger asking Zechariah a question and then Zechariah
providing the answer. The *qere* reflects the same process, but is just
older. Some readers, ancient and modern alike, do not like variation in
their literature and so change the text to limit variation rather than allow
the text to possess a quavering voice.

The use of the second-person plural in a speech that the form dictated
should be directed to Zechariah is not as problematic as it may initially
seem. One could interpret the use of the plural in 1.2 as indicative of
Zechariah as the representative of the people with whose ancestors
Yahweh was angry. Zechariah stands as a metonym for the people
Yahweh is angry with. Yahweh says he was angry with your, in the
plural, ancestors, so the reader does not think Yahweh was angry with
only Zechariah's ancestors. Rather, Yahweh was angry with the ancestors of the group of people, of whom Zechariah is a part. Strangely,
after defying the reader's expectations in 1.2, the text reverts to conventional norms in v. 3 and addresses a singular audience (וְאָמַרְתָּ) suggesting that Yahweh is indeed speaking to Zechariah throughout this
passage and lending support to the theory that Zechariah is a metonym
for the people whose ancestors Yahweh is angry with. Alternatively,
one could read Zech. 1.2 with Mason and interpret this strange mixture
of an introduction to Yahweh's speech (1.1) interpolated by Zechariah's
speech (1.2) as a combination of Yahweh's speech to Zechariah with
Zechariah's speech to his contemporaries (1977a: 32). Or one could
read v. 2 as a narratorial intrusion by the third-person narrator who
speaks in v. 1. But 1.2 is a bizarre place for an intrusion by either the
narrator or Zechariah. While in the final analysis the formula can be
seen or made to adhere to conventions, the strange mix of both referring
to Yahweh in the third person and addressing a plural audience plants
an uneasiness in the reader surrounding the trustworthiness of this formula. Here it is important to note that in none of the exceptions to the
usual function of the formula (Jer. 11.1-5; 34.12-22 Ezek. 12.21-25 or
18.1-4) are both the speaker and the audience unspecified. In fact, it is
never in doubt that Yahweh is the speaker, only the number of the audience is in doubt elsewhere. The formula alerts the reader to the fact that
all may not function as expected in the text to follow; not even the
grammar is stable.

While the use of this formula in Zech. 1.2 troubles the reader, its use

in 1.7 absolutely defies narrative conventions. When one sees the intro-
duction in 1.7, which contains the same formula ('it was the word of
Yahweh to') one again expects Yahweh to speak in v. 8. Likewise
Meier:

> The transformation of a rubric into a DD [direct discourse] marker is
> evident in Zech. 1.7 where Zechariah's autobiographical discourse is
> disconcertingly introduced as a divine oracle... One anticipates God's
> words but hears the prophet's instead. Because the phrase היה דבר יהוה
> functions as both a rubric and a DD marker in Hebrew, the secondary
> insertion of לאמר, transforming it from the former to the latter is an easy
> process in textual transmission (1992: 23).

First-person speech does indeed follow in 1.8-17, yet in a blatant
affront to expectations it is Zechariah who speaks. Though the formula
predominantly precedes the speech of Yahweh, rather than a vision, it is
the formula's previous association with visions (see Gen. 15.1; Jer. 1.11,
13; see also the near parallel in Ezek. 1.3), and the events which follow
in 1.8-17, that betray that it is not Yahweh but the prophet speaking in
v. 8. That the form is accompanied by a vision confirms the reader's
'stylistic' expectations, while defying the reader's syntactic expectations. Niditch discusses the use of this formula in Zechariah:

> What is interesting is that the introductory rubric has become frozen, an
> entity which exists on its own in tradition; it is used to indicate that a
> vision has taken place even once the syntax and literal meaning of the
> rubric is not ideal for the continuing syntax of the vision (1983: 129).

Zechariah 4.8-10, and 6.9-15 may also abrogate these conventions.
Verse 4.8 abrogates the norm if one interprets the speaker, who is the
one sent (v. 9), as an individual other than Yahweh. Zechariah 6.9-15
abrogates the norm if one identifies the one sent (Zech. 6.15) as neither
Zechariah nor Yahweh. That would make the speaker the conversing
messenger identified in 6.4. Alternatively, Yahweh is still the speaker,
but he is dictating a speech for Zechariah to deliver. By this reading
Zechariah declares he is indeed the one sent to them, as Yahweh has
dictated.

For the most part, Zechariah definitely narrates from 1.8 to 6.15
(Rudolph 1976: 74). In 7.1 it appears that an external narrator has re-
appeared as the formula recurs, but without לאמר. This use of the formula is not abnormal, as often words of the original speaker (the individual narrating the incident) interject between the formula and the
words which Yahweh has said when לאמר is absent (see 1 Kgs 13.20;

Jer. 1.2; 25.3; 42.7; 46.1). This switch to third-person narration returns the reader to the level of the narrator, rather than the level at which Zechariah was narrating his first-person account in 1.8–6.15.[3] When the narrator then alternates statements which declare that 'the word of Yahweh came to Zechariah' (היה [ויהי] דבר־יהוה אל־זכריה; 7.1, 8), 'the word of Yahweh Sebaoth came to me saying' (ויהי דבר־יהוה צבאות אלי לאמר; 7.4; 8.18) and the unattributed 'it was the word of Yahweh Sebaoth saying' (ויהי דבר־יהוה צבאות לאמר; 8.1), the impression is created that the narrator and Zechariah are the same individual.[4] The possibility that Yahweh continues to reveal the divine matters to Zechariah while Yahweh Sebaoth speaks to an unnamed narrator exists, but it seems more natural (for whatever natural is worth—the word 'natural' really means 'this reader is inclined' + the rhetorical force of the word 'natural') to read these characters as the same individual: Zechariah. By this reading, the recipient of 8.1 is unspecified because specification is unnecessary: it is obvious by this stage in the narrative that Zechariah is the 'I' of the narrative and is the recipient of the word of Yahweh (Sebaoth). The continued use of the first person to designate Zechariah's speech throughout the 'visions' is further reason to associate the use of the first person here with the character Zechariah.

Within the vision sequence a similar phrase occurs (ויהי דבר־יהוה אלי לאמר; 4.8) to those in 7.4 and 8.18. This false objectivity to the narrator suggests that while 1.1-7 is not obviously narrated by Zechariah as are 1.8–8.23, the mixture of objective and subjective narrators allows one to read back into 1.1's introductory formula, היה דבר־יהוה אל־זכריה ('it was the word of Yahweh to Zechariah') the same implications this

---

3. Working with Zech. 9–14, a text similar to Zech. 1–8, Larkin examines the alternation of first-person and third-person divine speech. To her, 'first person divine speech in Zech. 9–13 almost always seems to be primary in that any third person speech which follows it is likely to relate to it as interpretation to revelation' (1994: 64). It is outside of the scope of this work to examine examples of mantological exegesis in Zechariah 1–8, but here is an example of a commentator using the alternation of first- and third-person speech to indicate an activity other than heavy handed redaction.

4. NRSV amalgamates the two entities when it translates ויהי דבר יהוה צבאות as 'The word of the LORD of hosts came to me'. The translators have added 'to me' to 8.1 thereby defining the recipient of the message and equating the narrator with Zechariah. Presumably they did this because when the formula is used with Yahweh of hosts (rather than the form 'Yahweh') the narrator speaks in the first person (7.4; 8.18).

introductory formula possesses elsewhere in the book (1.7; 7.1, 8; 7.8 is slightly different having a *waw* consecutive imperfect instead of the perfect form of the verb 'to be', but this difference appears insignificant) and to see it as introducing Zechariah's speech. The individual originally perceived to be an external narrator in 1.1-7 is actually Zechariah. Zechariah, under the guise of the narrator, is relating the speech of Yahweh Sebaoth to Zechariah, that is, to himself, in Zech. 1.1-7. But this is an observation only progressively realized as the text is read. By the end of the work the reader has realized that Zechariah is the narrator/implied author. ('Progressive realization' appears to be one of the compositional techniques of Zechariah and is also seen in the identification of the man who stands between the myrtles [see the section 'Excursus: Reading in the Frame of the Minor Prophets'].) That the work is eponymous also suggests this, or at least suggests that whoever named the book may have read it this way. The author, of course, possesses the prerogative to modify linguistic norms for the 'sake of their artistic expression'. The use of this formula in Zechariah appears to be one such case of the artist asserting his prerogative.

Zechariah is thereby the implied narrator of 1.8–8.23, the filter through or perspective from which the entire book is narrated. This makes Zechariah 1–8 monologic. Zechariah 1–8 is an undivided utterance from a single voice: the implied narrator Zechariah. This makes the problem of its incoherence particularly acute: it is a single voice spouting incoherent statements.

Other Grammatical Problems in Zechariah 1–8

Three other grammatical abnormalities are 2.12, 4.12 and 6.6. Petersen says 6.6 'is problematic on several counts. It commences with a relative clause, apparently referring to a noun or noun clause which has been lost from the original Hebrew text...[and] the first verb is not extant in the MT but is presumed to be either *yāṣᵉû* or *yōṣᵉîm*...[or] *yēṣᵉû* (1984a: 263-64). Meyers and Meyers explain the 'term *'šr-bh* should thus be understood distributively: "with it [the chariot] the black horses were going out; and the white ones, etc."' (1987: 324).

Zechariah 2.12 causes syntactical problems. Meyers and Meyers say, 'Hebrew *'aḥar*, normally a preposition or adverb, introduces a subordinate clause' (1987: 164; for a summary of the translation options see Kloos [1975: 729-31]).

Petersen says 'unclear words and syntax' make 4.12 'abysmally hard to translate' (1984a: 236, 215). This is, in Petersen's opinion, because, 'Some pious commentator took offence at the rather clear motif of divine–human interdependence and obfuscated that picture by the introduction of puzzling detail and cryptic syntax' (1984a: 237). The abundance of confusion in Zechariah appears more likely to be a compositional strategy (recognizing that the compositional strategy is a construct of my imagination), be it from the hand of an editor or an author, rather than a clumsy re-working of existing material.

Problems of Speaker

The difficulty of determining the narrator is just one part of a larger problem. Throughout Zechariah 1–8 there are many places where it is difficult to determine who is the sender (see Table 1) and who is the recipient of an utterance. This makes it difficult to determine exactly what is being said in Zechariah; it is difficult to discern who speaks, acts or is acted upon. While Zechariah narrates the entire episode, it is difficult to discern whose viewpoints he is representing. If the reader cannot determine who is acting or speaking it is very difficult to discern what is taking place in a story, to discern the plot in the narrative events, let alone the significance of the events in the story. Often in a prophetic book, statements are made which concern the future. If the reader cannot determine the speakers and actors, she cannot determine the significance of those statements. An attempt to closely read one of the more problematic of these sections will show the difficulties that attend this problem.

Problems of Identifying Speakers in Zechariah 2.5-17

To begin to interpret this passage, it is important to understand who speaks to whom. If one abstains from pursuing the symbolic implications of the proceedings in 2.5-8, and chasing the intertexts, the narrative is straightforward and relatively comprehensible until v. 7. Zechariah sees a man with a measuring line in his hand, questions him about it, and is told in reply by the man that he is going to measure Jerusalem to see how long and how wide it is (Sellin emends the text to read the explanation in 6b as provided by the conversing messenger; 1930: 438). While the reason why this individual wants to measure Jerusalem and the significance of this act are unclear, it is not difficult to understand the action that is occurring. After this act the conversing messenger goes to meet another messenger. This is all readily understood.

I will use the term 'the conversing messenger' to refer to the character designated as המלאך הדבר בי in Zechariah. Cohen argues the phrase דבר בי 'is a technical term for a distinct type of prophetic experience'

(1987: 220). She depicts the scene in Zechariah as one in which the מלאך ('messenger') speaks through the prophet (1987: 230). Perhaps she is correct, but this is not abundantly clear because: (1) the phrase דבר ב is very common and indicates speakers conversing in a normal manner (Gen. 23.16; Exod. 4.15; Deut. 5.1; 28.7, etc.); and (2) the character designated by this phrase converses in a normal manner with Zechariah throughout the visions. The term seems present to distinguish this messenger from the other messengers (מלאכים) in Zechariah 1–8 rather than to indicate a prophetic experience. After all, Yahweh speaks directly to the prophet (1.2-6; 7.5–8.23; perhaps in 2.4 and 6.9-15).

At v. 8 the textual boundaries between characters begin to blur. Several persons are unclearly specified. Who is the subject of ויאמר ('and he said') in v. 8? The speaking subject appears to be one of the two messengers identified in v. 7. I am inclined to view the speaker as the other messenger because of the third-person masculine suffix in v. 7 (the other messenger goes out to meet him, that is, to meet the conversing messenger [לקראתו]) and v. 8 (the speaker of v. 8 says 'to him' [אלו]; similarly Rignell 1950: 74-76). Obviously, this is not a conclusive argument. Furthermore, why do these two messengers need to go and meet each other to speak, and why does Zechariah overhear their conversation?

To whom is this subject speaking? Who is the young man to whom the individual addressed by the subject of this verse is supposed to run and deliver the speech dictated in vv. 9-17? Is the young man (הנער הלז) a new character, the man with the measuring line from vv. 5 and 6 (Sellin 1930: 439; Leupold 1971: 55) or Zechariah (so Rignell 1950: 75; Jerome identified this young man as the prophet, as pointed out by Ackroyd [1962: 647])? If it is the man with the measuring line, then v. 8 reprimands him for his desire to measure Jerusalem, and prevents him from doing this act. If the young man is Zechariah, it explains why Zechariah, as the narrator, knows this speech and passes it on to the readers of Zechariah. The problems with identifying the speaker of v. 8 are multiplied in the speech which follows (vv. 9-17).

From v. 9 onwards this passage constantly shifts between first- and third-person speech, making it extremely difficult to discern exactly who speaks to whom.[5] This problem is compounded by many levels of embedded speech, and further by the Semitic languages' 'lack of inter-

---

5. Many commentators divide 2.10-17 from 2.6-9.

est in providing a closure to quoted speech, or any device to indicate a return to a previous level of discourse' (Meier 1992: 320). The narrative situation is this: Zechariah is the narrator, narrating a story in which two messengers speak to each other. One messenger dictates a speech for the other messenger to relay to the young man. Within this speech are the quoted words of Yahweh and Yahweh Sebaoth.[6]

Because there are three levels of imbedded speech, it is very difficult to discern the speaker of a first-person statement. Who speaks the 'I' in this passage: Yahweh, the messenger (and which one?) or Zechariah? This is a problematic issue which surrounds first-person quotation. When first-person quotation is used within the speech of another individual, it is difficult to discern if the first-person speech is reporting speech or reported speech. Polzin distinguishes between reported speech and reporting speech: reported speeches are utterances that the narrator attributes to a character in the story—the words of a character that the narrator reports (Polzin 1981: 194-97); reported speech presents the reader with a character's point of view. Reporting speech is the words of the narrator as she or he relates the events in the narrative (Polzin 1980: 19). This issue is compounded in Zechariah as it is a book with a first-person narrator who frequently quotes first-person speech of the characters in the book.

Some commentators circumnavigate part of this problem by viewing vv. 10-17 as a narratorial intrusion by Zechariah.[7] This is indeed a valid possibility. This need not imply separate authorship for these sections. Rather, it is a move outwards from the messenger's level of embedded speech to Zechariah's level. But this solution does not resolve the problem concerning which words are spoken by Yahweh and which by Zechariah. This is easier to live with because it is always difficult to discern the words of Yahweh from those of his prophet. It is important, however, to bear in mind that there is no clear marker in the Hebrew

---

6.   Indicated by נאם־יהוה ('a saying of Yahweh'; 2.9, 10, 14) and כה אמר יהוה צבאות ('thus says Yahweh Sebaoth'; 2.12). That Yahweh and Yahweh Sebaoth are to be viewed as the same character in this narrative is seen in 1.4 where Yahweh quotes the words of Yahweh Sebaoth, and then claims that the people did not listen to 'me'. Why the text uses the two titles for the deity is difficult to discern. Needless to say, many excursions have been written on the use of 'Yahweh Sebaoth' and a footnote will not provide the solution to this enigmatic problem.

7.   See Baldwin (1972: 107); Mitchell (1980: 140); and Meyers and Meyers (1987: 163).

text of a change of speaker. Regardless of scholarly consensus, it is an interpretative decision to read vv. 10-17 as Zechariah's speech.

Layers of quoted speech are indicative of Zechariah's style. Meyers and Meyers have noted a similar structure of quoted speech in Zech. 1.1-6. About 1.1-6 they say:

> Not only is this section replete with quoted speech, but also the quotes are layered: there are quotes within quotes within quotes. It is not easy to keep track of where the layers terminate. This section is a nightmare for translators trying to signify the change in quoted material through the limited devices of English punctuation (1987: 100)

They examine this stylistic feature in 1.1-6 and conclude that it relates to Zechariah or his compilers (1) authorizing their material by the use of previous proclamations; (2) asserting the continued existence of Yahweh's word; and (3) performing inner biblical exegesis. They see it as indicative of 'the increasing tendency in the postexilic period for the word of Yahweh to be mediated to humanity through a growing array of supernatural, or angelic, beings' (1987: 102), which conforms to Persian literary convention where quoted speech is a stylistic trait that draws attention to the ultimate authority of a piece of work (Meyers and Meyers, 1987: 100-103).

Meier discusses how late biblical Hebrew literature's obsession with redundantly marking divine discourse (through phrases like היה דבר לאמר (x) -אל יהוה, כה אמר יהוה, נאם יהוה, and אמר יהוה ['It was the word of Yahweh to (x = proper noun) saying', 'Thus says Yahweh', 'A saying of Yahweh', 'Yahweh says']) 'results in the frequent placing of quotations within quotations and even these within further quotations' (1992: 222-30, 320). He adds further, 'The cumbersome multi-layering that actually subverts lucid discourse appears primarily in the prophetic material that ironically aims for precision in identifying speaking voices, e.g. Zech. 1.1-4' (1992: 321). Speaking specifically about Zechariah 1–8, he says 'when God's words are specifically marked as such, it is often already obvious that God is speaking and these markers are unnecessary' (Meier cites 1.3-4, 14-17a; 2.9-10, 14; 4.6; 7.13b-14; 8.2-3, 6-8, 10-17 as examples of this). He says further:

> perplexing is the frequent use of divine discourse markers to identify speech that on other grounds would be judged as originating from a voice other than God's [Meier here cites 1.1-2, 7-8; 4.8-9; 6.12-15; and 7.8-13a as examples]. It is as if an exuberant concern to identify God's words has abandoned any restraint, making all words in the text suscep-

tible to such marking. Unlike Haggai, a profusion of DD markers does
not mean that most voices are clearly demarcated (1992: 226).

On layers of quoted speech he says 'When such layering of citations
extends beyond two or three embedded levels, the resulting maze of
entangled voices may be more than irritating and become simply
incomprehensible' (1992: 320; see Meier's discussion of 'Multiple
Embedding of Direct Discourse' [1992: 320-21]). This certainly
appears to be the case in Zechariah.

A further problem in distinguishing who the speaker of a given utterance is is the ambiguous 'prophetic I'. Polk discusses Jeremiah's use of
the ambiguous 'prophetic I' to identify himself with both God and
people (1984: 125-26, 166). He concludes:

> neither the theory of the blending of voices, which everywhere sees
> Jeremiah's 'I' as a direct reflection of the community's 'we', nor the
> theory which at every point seeks a clean separation of voices, is ade-
> quate' (1984: 125).

Further,

> through his first-person speech Jeremiah enacts a prophetic identity of
> identification with both God and people... [so that the prophet] comes
> personally to embody the divine-human event such that his life becomes
> a vehicle for the event's interpretation (1984: 126).

> [Speaking of Jer. 8–10, 14]... a poetic blurring of distinctions between
> personae invited us to hear certain material as spoken by a composite
> voice... Ultimately, the literary ambiguities contributed to the book's
> depiction of the prophet as a theological paradigm (1984: 166).

Similarly, the voices of Yahweh, the prophet, the messenger of Yahweh
and perhaps a few other characters are merged in Zechariah (see my
section 'Problems of Speaker').

Ross discusses this topic:

> Thus the prophets, although they seldom called themselves 'messen-
> gers', used the form of the *Botenspruch* and claimed that their authority
> was that of one sent by Yahweh or from his council. They did not iden-
> tify themselves with the one who sent them; there is no 'mystic union'
> with the divine. Nevertheless, they did not 'prophesy the deceit of their
> own heart' (Jer. 23.26), for they had 'stood in the council' of Yahweh.
> The line is not easy to draw: does a messenger speak only the words of
> his lord, or are they in some sense his own? Perhaps we say more than
> we know when we refer to 'the message of the prophets' (1987: 118).

Likewise Meier, 'It is true that the fluctuation between the "I" of the prophet and the "I" of God is problematic for exegetes... Voices were not distinguished simply because poetry commonly did not do so' (1992: 209). But why did the prophets want to merge their words with the deities? (Delusions of grandeur?)

The use of the phrase כי כה אמר יהוה ('for thus says Yahweh') causes confusion in determining the speaker in vv. 12-13.[8] Meier has also discussed this phrase (1992: 273-91):

> The insertion of כה אמר יהוה does not serve to disambiguate speaking voices that are otherwise quite pellucid. On the contrary, it tends to complicate a reader's task by intensifying the multiple embedding of quoted speech...for it supplies redundant information as it emphasises what is already obvious from the words that are spoken (1992: 275).

He quotes Lighthouse's conclusion that 'Each of the prophets would seem to have had his own habit in connection with the phrase' (Meier 1992: 277). He concludes that the phrase 'does not by its very presence point to messenger activity in Hebrew... The formula is simply used to make citations of others' words' (1992: 284). On its proliferation in late prophetic texts, he argues it may 'represent a cultural phenomenon in which literary style underscored the source of authoritative words' (1992: 290).

The phrase כי כה אמר יהוה ('for thus says Yahweh') in v. 12 leads one to expect Yahweh's direct discourse to follow. Yet this would make Yahweh Sebaoth declare

> (after his glory sent me) regarding the nations that plundered you: Truly, one who touches you touches the apple[9] of my eye. See now, I am going

---

8. Meier says similarly about נאם יהוה ('a saying of Yahweh'), 'context is the only means of discriminating when נאם יהוה functions as a marker of the close of speech, the beginning of speech, or a medial marker in the midst of speech' (1992: 309). Rather, these phrases are 'oratorical devices' (he cites their use in Zech. 7.1–8.23 as an example of this; 1992: 297, 309-10). 'The prophetic use of these phrases shows little sign of stabilisation in the biblical material beyond the privileging of כה אמר יהוה to introduce divine speech and the privileging of נאם יהוה to mark its close (remembering that neither is obligatory and both may occur in other positions)' (Meier 1992: 313).

Meier argues that נאם and אמר could be used interchangeably and cites how they are translated similarly by the Targums and the LXX (1992: 311-12).

9. For a discussion of the possible derivation of בבת, see Robertson, who suggests it originally came from either a root meaning 'gate' or 'door' or a root mean-

> to raise my hand against them, and they shall become plunder for their
> own slaves. Then you will know that the LORD of hosts has sent me
> (NRSV),

as well as the material that follows in 2.14-17. But there are many contextual and conceptual difficulties which resist reading this way. Who
sends Yahweh Sebaoth? Yahweh? Is there thus a division between the
two deities Yahweh and Yahweh Sebaoth? When the speaker waves his
hand over the nations and they are plunder for their servants, the
addressee will know that Yahweh Sebaoth sent the speaker. The
speaker does not seem to be Yahweh Sebaoth, because it is Yahweh
Sebaoth who sent him. Obviously this is non-sensical [*sic*]: no one
sends himself or herself.

The reader must interpret the speaker of 12b to be either Zechariah,
the messenger, the messenger of Yahweh (Leupold 1971: 59), or the
conversing messenger: readers must decide how far out of the embedded speech to direct their attention. These difficulties lead many to suggest 12b is an editorial insertion (for example, Sellin 1930: 441; Sellin
believes Zechariah is the referent of all the speeches which reassure the
audience that Yahweh has sent Zechariah [2.12, 13, 15; 4.9; 6.15]
[1930: 421]). The difficulties of 12b lead Ackroyd to conclude, 'This
notoriously problematic passage cannot be satisfactorily explained'
(1968: 180 n. 31). The text has once again defied convention and de-

---

ing 'the tiny image reflected in the eye' (1937: 57-58).

In Zech. 4.10 Yahweh is also attributed with an eye, but this time he has seven
eyes. Are 'these seven' (שבעה־אלה) in Zech. 4.10 identifiable with the seven lamps
(שבעה נרת; 4.2), the seven wicks of the lamps (שבעה מוצקות; 4.2) or the seven eyes
on the stone (שבעה עיניב; 3.9)? If they are the wicks, or the lamps, then might the
one touching the apple of Yahweh's eye be touching the wick, putting the light out?
If the olive trees feed oil to the lamp, this makes their activity useless: what is the
point of feeding oil to an extinguished lamp? If the seven are indentifiable with the
stone, perhaps by touching the stone they are preventing the inscription from being
inscribed and thereby preventing the guilt of the land from being removed (3.9).

Not only is touching a pupil painful, but it also prevents vision. The ones touching the apple of Yahweh's eye may be preventing him from seeing. The מֹשׁוֹטְטִים
בכל־הארץ (4.10) of Yahweh's eyes makes them analogous (identical?) with the
horses and chariots which התהלך בארץ (1.10; 6.7). Does this suggest the horses are
the eyes of Yahweh? If so, perhaps they were being touched and were delayed in
accomplishing their 'spying' mission. Here is yet another example of the equivalen-
cies which are constantly being established in Zech. 1–8 between different elements
of the vocabulary stock.

mands the reader to understand a switch in speaker. But by this reading, what is the significance of preceding this speech with אמר יהוה צבאות כי כה? One might investigate other uses of this phrase in Zechariah to determine if Zechariah is using this phrase idiosyncratically and not as the more usual כה אמר יהוה צבאות. This does not appear to be the case, as the phrase כה אמר יהוה is used to introduce direct speech in 8.14, in accord with the norm. Is the reader to understand that Yahweh Sebaoth has informed the speaker that he (that is, Yahweh Sebaoth) has sent the speaker to the nations in 2.12? The speaker is then saying something akin to 'Yahweh told me he is sending me, after glory, to the nations plundering you'. Whoever the speaker is, he appears powerful—the waving of his hands over the nations which plunder Zion and the daughter of Babylon will result in the reversal of this plundering. Is this a symbolic or supernatural act of the prophet, the messenger or Yahweh?[10] Perhaps who performs this act is not terribly important, as the same results are achieved: plundering of the nations.

Flouting the convention of indicating direct discourse with the phrase כה אמר יהוה is deconstructive in this passage. The reader can no longer be certain that the convention indicates Yahweh's speech. This causes reason for doubt concerning speeches attributed to the deity throughout Zechariah 1–8. One cannot be certain that a first-person speech which contains a conventional marker of direct discourse is actually the discourse of the individual to whom the convention attributes the statement. When Yahweh appears to make a promise, is it actually the deity who is making a promise? When the text says in 8.3, 'Thus says the

---

10. Looking at intertextual referents, this activity seems more appropriate for Yahweh (see Isa. 11.15 and 19.16 where Yahweh destroys the tongue of the sea of Egypt by waving a hand) or Yahweh Sebaoth (see Isa. 19.16-17 where Yahweh Sebaoth makes Egyptians tremble with fear when he waves a hand over them and makes the land of Judah a shame to Egypt). Sellin, without evidence, suggests it is a 'Gestus bei Zauberriten und Dämonenabwehr' ('gesture in magic rites and warding off demons') (1930: 442). That this act could be performed by a prophet and possesses supernatural power is betrayed in 2 Kgs 5.11 (albeit that Naaman thinks a prophet would wave a hand to heal leprosy does not necessarily indicate an Israelite or Judaean conception that prophets work in the same manner). Though the verb is different in 2 Sam. 24.16 and 1 Chron. 21.16, the martial activity seems similar enough to the activity in Zech. 2.13 to suggest this type of activity is characteristic of the messenger of Yahweh (see also Num. 22). Tollington believes 'waving a hand' is 'the hand signal that begins military-style action by Yahweh on behalf of his people, or in the sense of a hostile brandishing of the arm' (1993: 229).

LORD: I will return to Zion, and will dwell in the midst of Jerusalem'
(כה אמר יהוה שבתי אל־ציון ושכנתי בתוך ירושלם), does it mean Yahweh
will himself dwell in the midst of Jerusalem, or does it mean Yahweh
has told the prophet (or a messenger) that he (that is the prophet, or the
messenger) will dwell in the midst of Jerusalem? Ultimately this invali-
dates perspectival narrative criticism: how can one employ this type of
criticism when it is impossible to discern whose perspective is depicted
in Zechariah?

Since the phrase כה אמר יהוה is used abnormally, one should investigate the other common phrase to indicate divine speech, נאם יהוה. Curiously, elsewhere in Zechariah, outside of Zech. 2.10-17, both phrases
function as one expects them to (נאם יהוה in 1.3, 4, 16; 3.9, 10; 5.4; 8.6,
11, 17; and כה אמר in 1.3, 4, 14, 16, 17; 3.7; 6.12; 7.9; 8.2, 3, 4, 6, 7, 9,
14, 19, 20, 23). Can one transfer this mistrust of the phrase כה אמר יהוה
to יהוה נאם? The evidence does not readily support such an act, but
since Yahweh's speech is already suspect by its use with the other
phrase, it is, at the very least, thrown in doubt throughout the text.

The overall effect, if Yahweh Sebaoth is not the speaker of v. 12,
changes my conception of how the introductory phrase כי כה אמר יהוה
צבאות ('Thus says/said Yahweh Sebaoth') works. It seems roughly
equivalent to claiming 'Yahweh Sebaoth told me'; that is, the speaker
says, 'Yahweh Sebaoth told me that he has sent me to the nations plundering you to bring about glory'. The instability of the conventional
ways of identifying speakers also causes the reader to reconsider the
use of the first person throughout this pericope: to re-read the 'oracle' to
see if individuals the reader initially thought were speaking in the first
person are indeed these individuals.

Zechariah 2.9 reads ואני אהיה־לה נאם־יהוה חומת אש סביב ולכבוד
אהיה בתוכה. Since the phrase נאם יהוה functions normally in Zechariah,
it seems appropriate to read the clause as the NRSV ('For I will be a
wall of fire all around it, says the LORD') and attribute this statement to
Yahweh. But 9b is problematic. Does the speech of Yahweh continue
or is it an interjection by whoever it is that is speaking? Who will be
within Jerusalem for 'glory'? This is usually taken to be Yahweh
(Petersen 1984a: 171; Jeremias 1977: 175-76; Rudolph 1976: 86).
Noteworthy is the similarity of content between this clause and the
indeterminate speaker of v. 12: both deal with כבוד ('glory'). In both
verses a directional marker precedes כבוד: ל in 2.9 and אחר in 2.12. If
one takes the glory to be the wealth of economic plunder then the

speaker of vv. 12-13 is sent to the nations which are plundering [you] to retrieve plunder, which is synonymous with glory. Clines discusses how the temple in Haggai functions as a treasure chest: the glory (כבוד) in Haggai 2 is the silver, the plunder and the treasure of Hag. 2.7-9 (1994: 63ff.). In Hag. 2.8 ל is used to indicate Yahweh's possession (for the use of ל as an indicator of possession see Joüon [1991: 487-89]). So, Hag. 2.7's לי הכסף ולי הזהב should be translated 'the money is mine' (Joüon 1991: 572) and 'the gold is mine'. That כבוד occurs in such a close context to appear synonymous with money and gold in Haggai suggests reading כבוד in Zechariah with similar connotations. Zechariah 2.9's ולכבוד אהיה בתוכה should then be translated 'possessing glory' (read 'wealth') 'I will be in its midst'.

This bears on the much debated אחר כבוד שלחני ('he sent me after glory') of Zech. 2.12. The primary debate concerns whether to read אחר as a preposition or conjunction. Scott takes אחר to mean 'with', or 'accompanied by' in Zech. 2.12 (1949: 178) and so the meaning here is Yahweh sent me with, or accompanied by, glory. This does not help clarify the confusion in this verse. Vriezen believes it can only be understood as a gloss (see his discussion of the whole passage in which he identifies the speaker of v. 12 as the 'angel' and, in his words, 'restores the right order of the text' [1948: 89-91]). C. Kloos suggests one read אחר in Zech. 2.12 so that '"kabod" is the purpose of the mission' (1975: 734; see 729-31 for a discussion of the issues that surround this preposition as well as the interpretative options; see 735 for a discussion of the possible speaker of this verse). Kloos identifies the speaker as the prophet and says the object of the prophet's mission is to restore Yahweh's honour among the nations (1975: 735-36; likewise Zanghi 1986: 181). Higginson believes 'the *glory* of Zechariah's time was the restoration of Jerusalem... *After* in this case means in search of the glory' (1970: 790). Meyers and Meyers translate this clause, 'Glory had sent me' indicating Yahweh sent the prophet (1987: 165; Sellin emends the text to arrive at a similar meaning [1930: 441]). I believe it here indicates the purpose of the mission, as Kloos, and the speaker's activity is to retrieve wealth from the nations (so Ehrlich, as quoted by Kloos, says the activity is 'nach Schätzen' ['after treasures'; 1975: 730]). The speaker is then following the wealth which has been plundered from Israel, Judah and Jerusalem and carried back as loot to the nations.

There is obviously a word-play occurring with the theological and monetary connotations of כבוד in this verse. One could read in a more theological vein and identify the glory with Yahweh's spirit. Yahweh's spirit is said to be at rest in the land of the north (6.8; the chronology of this phrase is debatable [see the section 'The Temporal Aspect'] but this reading will assume vision 6 is flashback and the events contained therein chronologically precede ch. 2). The speaker of 2.12 follows the glory to the nations (= the land of the north) to fetch the glory (= the spirit of Yahweh) back to Jerusalem. A word-play then occurs with 2.9, in which Yahweh returns to Jerusalem to receive glory/honour. Perhaps it is too ambiguous to capture the theological and the monetary nuances of כבוד. The passage as a whole signifies the retrieval of wealth, honour and Yahweh's presence from the nations (see also Koch 1983: 172).

To return to the discussion about the difficulty of determining speakers in Zechariah, if Yahweh is the speaker of 2.9, then it is after the speaker of v. 12 has retrieved the plunder that he (that is, Yahweh) returns *to* the glory (the plunder), which has now been brought back to Jerusalem. Alternatively, the speaker of v. 12 is the speaker of v. 9. He obtains accolades (glory) after waving his hand over the nations. Thus, Yahweh sent him with the goal of obtaining glory. When this individual returns to Jerusalem, he will be heralded and returns to Jerusalem to receive these accolades.

If we can trust נאם יהוה to identify Yahweh as the speaker, then Yahweh is the speaker of v. 10. Verse 11 is more problematic. Since the speaker of v. 12 is different from the speaker of v. 10, is v. 11 the speech of either of these characters, or a speech by the narrator?

Verses 15-17 appear to be the continuation of the speech of the unspecified speaker of vv. 12-14. Who will the many nations be joined to 'for a people'? Will they be joined to the prophet who was speaking in the first person, or has the prophet proceeded to speak in the first person for Yahweh? Interestingly, the prophet does not end this statement in v. 15 with נאם יהוה. These sentiments are similar to those found in Zech. 8.3 and 8.8 regarding Yahweh's return to Jerusalem and Zion.[11] Perhaps it signifies that both the prophet and Yahweh will dwell in the midst of Jerusalem. Alternatively, the prophet is the representative of Yahweh, and Yahweh's dwelling in the midst of the daughter of Zion is

---

11. Many aspects of this speech recall other passages: Yahweh's dwelling 'in your midst' recalls both the sanctuary in Exodus (Exod. 25.8; 29.45, 46), the camp and land in Numbers (Num. 5.3; 35.34), and the people of Israel in Ezekiel and Kings (1 Kgs 6.13; Ezek. 43.7).

symbolically fulfilled by the prophet dwelling in the midst of the daughter of Zion.[12] The prophet is merged with Yahweh in this passage and the line between them is blurred. The author melds the prophetic voice with Yahweh's by imprecisely demarcating changes of speaker.

Examining these verses may provide a clue betraying who this character is. Though the use of third-person speech is always dubious as an identifier of speaker, that both Yahweh and Yahweh Sebaoth are referred to in the third person *suggests* that the speaker is neither of those individuals (see the discussion above for the acknowledgment that Yahweh does speak about himself in the third person). This speaker asserts:

> Many nations shall join themselves to the LORD on that day, and shall be my people; and I will dwell in your midst. And you shall know that the LORD of hosts has sent me to you. The LORD will inherit Judah as his portion in the holy land, and will again choose Jerusalem. Be silent, all people, before the LORD; for he has roused himself from his holy dwelling (NRSV).

If we assume the speaker does not change, an assumption that is difficult to make in this unstable text, the speaker asserts that many nations will be a people for him; he will dwell in the midst of the implied audience and then the implied audience will know Yahweh Sebaoth sent him to them. Zechariah 2.14 causes confusion with these statements. There, the statement 'I will dwell in your midst' ends with the marker of direct discourse נאם יהוה. This suggests Yahweh is the one who will dwell (שׁכן) in the midst of the implied audience (likewise 8.3, 8). In 8.7-8 Yahweh says 'I am saving my people (עמי)...and they will dwell (שׁכנו) in the midst of Jerusalem and they will be my people

---

12. In 5.1 Zechariah turns or returns (שׁוב) and lifts up his eyes. With the predominance of the 'turn to me and I will turn to you' promise of 1.3, it is tempting to see this act as some kind of fulfilment of Yahweh's promises as enacted through his prophet. Does this act in 5.1 symbolize that Yahweh is again in the holy land? Immediately following this return the flying scroll appears. Is the scroll's cleansing of the land a fulfilment of the promise in 3.10 to cleanse the land in one day? Zechariah was aroused (4.1), as Yahweh was (2.17), and now he returns to the land which is being cleansed. As Yahweh is aroused from his holy place, so Zechariah seems pulled out of the heavenly council (a holy place?) of Zech. 3 when he is startled by the messenger in 4.1. In ch. 4 Zechariah appears to go on and see another holy place, though it is never specified as such, so perhaps the return in ch. 5 is a return from holy places (and perhaps the nations which Yahweh was sent to—a *double entendre*?) to Jerusalem.

and I will be their God'. The phrase 'they will be my people' is identical in 2.14 and 8.3 (והיו־לי לעם).[13] Verse 8.3 unequivocally identifies
the character who is dwelling in Jerusalem as Yahweh and 8.8 attributes
Yahweh with saying the people saved will be 'my people'. Does this
suggest one should read similar statements in 2.15 as Yahweh's discourse interpolated into the speech of the speaker of v. 15? Or should
one view the use of similar phraseology as a case of parallelism: both
Yahweh and this character of 2.15-17 are described in similar terms;
both of them will 'possess' the same group of people? The text does not
clearly indicate this and a haze surrounds this issue.

The determination of which character speaks depends on whether one
places more weight on the indicators of speaker in the text of ch. 2 or
on similar content being expressed elsewhere in Zechariah (and in other
biblical texts) as identifying the same actor. The aforementioned confusion concerning identifying the speaker of the 'I' in this section is
particularly acute here. It is difficult to ascertain whether many of the
first-person statements should be attributed to Yahweh or the speaker as
the text fluctuates between the two characters without marking a change
of speaker. A few options are open. Maybe the speaker of v. 13 is different from the speaker of v. 12, or the speaker refers to himself as
sending himself.[14] Alternatively, various individuals speak at different
moments in these verses, without being clearly introduced. This is dan-
gerous textual policy, to begin attributing verses and portions of verses
to different textual characters, but it is a necessity prompted by this text.

Another strange textual technique consistently employed throughout
Zechariah is the answering of questions by or to other characters than
those who originally asked or to whom the matter referred. There are
many examples of this phenomenon. In 1.10 Zechariah asks the conversing messenger a question and receives the response to his answer
from the man between the myrtles (1.10). In 2.4 Yahweh's discussion
of the horns only entails those that scattered Judah rather than the horns
that scattered Judah, Israel and Jerusalem (2.2). The conversing mes-

---

13.   Meier warns 'phrases such as "my people" must be used with caution in
discriminating God's voice. The words, "my people", come comfortably from the
mouth of God, but since they are found also on the lips of others, the phrase is not a
dependable gauge for confirming the presence of a divine voice' (1992: 208-209).

14.   Tollington believes the text is comprehensible once '2.13b, 15b (MT) are
recognised as editorial comments' (1993: 234). But is it the editor (the narrator?) or
the messenger of Yahweh who is speaking here?

senger appears to completely ignore Zechariah's question of 4.4 (beyond apparently ridiculing him for his ignorance in 4.5) and proceeds to deliver an oracle to Zerubbabel. Only when pushed to deliver an answer to the question in 4.11 and 12 does the conversing messenger finally answer Zechariah's question. Curiously, the messenger appears to answer an unsolicited question about the import of the eyes on the stone of 3.9 in this oracle to Zerubbabel (4.10). The question that the delegation from Bethel asks in 7.3 is responded to by an extensive speech directed to the people of the land and the priests. Eventually, after a lengthy digression, the subject matter of this question is again returned to in 8.19, but this response is directed to the house of Judah, rather than specifically to Judah (admittedly, Bethel could be a place in Judah [see BDB: 111] or Regemmelech; Hyatt proposes that the character from a Babylonian text, *Bīt-ili-shar-usur* may be identical with the *Bethel-sar-eṣer* of Zech. 7.2 [making it a proper noun] who may be a temple official [1937: 394]). This further compounds addressees and addressers and disrupts the logical flow of conversation.

It is hoped that this discussion has demonstrated the difficulties and confusion which surround determining speakers in portions of Zechariah. This type of analysis of changes of speaker can be applied to every example in Table 1. But the phrases discussed this far are not the only ones used in an aberrant way. Meier discusses the use of אמר+ענה as a marker of direct discourse (1992: 167-83) and notes that it is used both consistently and inconsistently in Zechariah (1992: 175). Of ch. 4 he says, 'The disruptive introduction of a divine revelation in v. 8 (ויהי דבר יהוה אלי לאמר), the double question of vv. 11 and 12, and the *Wiederaufnahme* [resumption] in the restating of the dialogue of vv. 2-5 in vv. 11-13 point to the fact that this interchange is not presently coherent' (1992: 175). The book of Zechariah is consistently inconsistent in its use of markers of direct discourse, whether it be היה דבר יהוה לאמר (proper noun) אל־, כה אמר יהוה or ענה + אמר. The net effect is confusion in identifying the speaker. Meier appears to share this confusion in discerning speakers in prophetic literature and Zechariah: 'how is one to evaluate a lack of resolution in prophetic literature when alongside such vague passages in the Hebrew text also occur other passages saturated with DD markers such as, "Thus said Yahweh" (יהוה כה אמר) or "oracle of Yahweh" (נאם יהוה)?' (1992: 207-208).

How is one to evaluate these techniques of producing indeterminate narrative? This is, from my perspective, a compositional technique employed by the author which the reader constructs for Zechariah. Why has this constructed author made it difficult to discern the actors? What is the significance of this merger of the narrator's voice with various characters' voices? One could view this as parodic: this refusal to demarcate the speaker highlights the relationship between the word of Yahweh and the words of the prophets. It exposes the major prophets as blurring the lines between their words and the words of Yahweh. Or, one could read this as yielding insight into Zechariah's character. That the personalities are blended might suggest the overwhelming nature of the situation Zechariah, the narrator, finds himself in. Because of the abundance of activities, and their bizarre nature, Zechariah has difficulties discerning who is speaking. The depiction is similar to a crisis situation in a hospital drama series, such as 'Casualty', shot from the patient's perspective while lying on a stretcher. Doctors' and nurses' faces appear in their vision and voices come from all around them. It is difficult, especially for a stranger to the hospital environment, to track who is speaking and acting. Perhaps a similar type of reporting is occurring in Zechariah. Zechariah is overwhelmed and struggling to take in as much of the scene as possible. The unclear specification of characters could be an attempt to pass this 'overwhelmedness' on to the reader. If so, it certainly succeeds.

Table 1. *Some Difficult Places to Determine the Speaker in Zechariah 1–8*

Zechariah	Possible Speakers
1.2	External Narrator,[i] Yahweh, Zechariah[ii]
1.6b	Yahweh reiterating the speech of the ancestors (אבותיכם), External Narrator's speech describing the response of the audience that Zechariah was commanded to address in 1.3
1.7	External Narrator, Zechariah
1.16a[iii]	Yahweh's speech as dictated by the conversing messenger, an interjectory comment interrupting Yahweh's speech inserted by the conversing messenger
2.4b	the conversing messenger, Yahweh
2.8	the conversing messenger, the other messenger from 2.7(מלאך אחר)
2.12b-13[iv]	the conversing messenger, the other messenger, Yahweh (Sebaoth),
(2.9-17)	Zechariah
3.4[v]	the messenger of Yahweh (Fleming 1989: 199), Yahweh
3.8-9	the messenger of Yahweh, Yahweh
4.2b-3	the conversing messenger, Zechariah
4.8-11	the conversing messenger, Zechariah[vi]
5.2a	the conversing messenger, Yahweh Sebaoth (as identified in 5.4)

Zechariah	Possible Speakers
5.3-4	the conversing messenger, Yahweh Sebaoth (as identified in 5.4)
6.6-7	the conversing messenger, Narrator, Zechariah
6.7b	the conversing messenger, the Lord of all the Earth (אדון כל־ארץ),[vii] Narrator, Zechariah
6.8	the conversing messenger, the Lord of all the earth
6.15	Yahweh dictating a speech for Zechariah to dictate to Joshua (and perhaps to the individuals with him), Zechariah making a narratorial intrusion at the end of the visions, the conversing messenger
7.7	appears to be a narratorial intrusion into Yahweh's speech
7.13	switches from third- to first-person narration in the middle of the verse; this switch to the first-person continues through v. 14.

i.   The individual 'External Narrator' is included for those who do not accept my argument that Zechariah is the implied narrator/implied author of Zech. 1–8.

ii.   Nogalski summarizes the problems of this section well: 'Zech 1:2-6 poses considerable problems because it frequently relies upon the interpretation of suffixes whose addressees must be extrapolated from the context, often without clear antecedents' (1993b: 241; see his discussion of the problem of identifying speakers and addressees in this section of Zechariah [1993b: 241-47]).

iii.   That is, the phrase לכן כה־אמר יהוה.

iv.   The confusion surrounding who speaks in the first person in verses 12 and 13 creates confusion surrounding who speaks in the first person for the entire pericope spanning from 2.9-15 (some may prefer to limit this confusion to 2.10-15 because of the *petuhah* at the end of v. 9).

McCarthy discusses how this confusion of speakers relates to the problem of the *tiqqune sopherim* in 12b (1981: 64-68). Regardless of the theological motives which may underlie the scribal adjustments (Craig suggests 'the scribes considered this anthropomorphic description too derogatory' [1990: 162]), the *tiqqune sopherim* in Zech. 2.12 demonstrates an early response to the difficulties which attend determining the speaker in this passage. Craig says, 'better to produce an ambiguous text than to reproduce an offensive reference to the Lord' is representative of 'the sopherim logic' (1990: 163).

v.   In addition, Fleming notes 'the identify of the speaker in 3.5aα is problematic' as the LXX, Vulgate and Peshitta omit translating ויאמר making the speaker of v. 5 'either a continuation of the previous speech (Yahweh as speaker) or the speech of another council member making a complementary suggestion' (1989: 199).

vi.   Van der Woude takes the speaker of all the 'you will know' texts (2.15; 4.9; 6.15) to be the conversing messenger (1988: 239).

vii.   Since the chariots present themselves before the Lord of the whole earth in 6.5, one may interpret האמצים as directing their request to walk the earth to this individual (6.7).

Since the conversing messenger was speaking until v. 5, and may narrate the entire section spanning from 6.5-8, it is also possible that he is the speaker who grants permission for these אמצים to walk the earth in 7b.

Haupt mentions that 'Darius is called *the lord of the whole earth*' (1918: 209). Might this suggest the individual the chariots report to is Darius? Neither Yahweh nor the messenger of Yahweh is mentioned in 6.1-8. This seems a bit far fetched though as the Lord of the whole earth is identified with the lampstand in 4.14. Are the chariots then presenting themselves to the lampstand? This would make the setting of the visions in chs. 4 and 6 the same (and maybe 1.7-17 the same as well). Does this then equate the chariots with the eyes of Yahweh which roam through the earth (4.10; see Tidwell 1975: 347)? Tidwell suggests such an identification by setting both in the temple (1975: 346) and places visions 1, 4, 5 and 8 in 'the heavenly council or court of Yahweh' (1975: 347; for more on the council see Kingsbury 1964; also see Robinson, who links prophetic inspiration and psychology with the concept of the council of Yahweh [1951: 156]). Once again, the perpetual sliding of signifiers pervades Zechariah.

Zechariah 1–8 as (Anti)Narrative

In order to determine the plot of Zechariah, it is first necessary to come to a working definition of plot. Chatman defines two types of plot:

> In the traditional narrative of resolution, there is a sense of problem-solving, of things being worked out in some way, of a kind of ratiocinative or emotional teleology... 'What will happen?' is the basic question. In the modern plot of revelation, however, the emphasis is elsewhere; the function of the discourse is not to answer that question nor even to pose it... It is not that events are resolved (happily or tragically), but rather that a state of affairs is revealed. Thus a strong sense of temporal order is more significant in resolved than in revealed plots. Development in the first instance is an unraveling; in the second, a displaying (1983: 48).[15]

Ska follows Chatman and elaborates:

> In a unified plot, all the episodes are relevant to the narrative and have a bearing on the outcome of the events recounted. Every episode supposes what precedes and prepares for what follows. In an 'episodic plot' the order of episodes can be changed, the reader can skip an episode without harm; every episode is a unit in itself and does not require the clear and complete knowledge of the former episodes to be understood. Most of the time, the presence of a central character gives unity to the episodes which are thematically connected by the consistency of this character,

---

15. Lodge shares a similar attitude to modern fiction: 'Plot has been described...as a completed process of change. A good deal of modern fiction has, however, avoided the kind of closure implied in the word "completed" and has focused on states of being in which change is minimal' (1992: 217).

his (her) normally patterned behaviour, and the similar situations which
this state of affairs generates (1990: 17).

So, if we adopt this classification, which type of plot is Zechariah: resolution or revelation?

Reading Zechariah 1–8 for plot is a very confusing undertaking. The
vision sequence is composed of a series of short cuts seen from Zechariah's viewpoint. Zechariah is the central character who holds the story
together. As with most episodic plots, the successive scenes in the
narrative are predominantly self-contained. Zechariah is the camera
lens which directs the reader's gaze on a vignette, lets the reader
glimpse the scene for a very short time, and then whisks the reader
away to another scene (the visions range from 4 verses [2.1-4] to a
maximum of 13 verses [if one reads 2.5-17 together, that would be the
longest vision comprising 13 verses]). The episodes do not obviously
'suppose what precedes' or 'prepare for what follows'; they do not
chronologically build on each other in a manner in which the previous
visions are necessary to understand the visions which follow. The episodes do not work like a connect-the-dots in which the reader sequen-
tially joins the episodes together to read a story which forms a clear
'picture' of the events which transpires once all the dots are joined.

There is a loose series of unravelling(s). The 'horses'' report appears
to trigger Yahweh's mercy in the first vision. This in turn leads to the
coming of the artisans who throw down the horns. The coming of the
artisans may provide the labourers for the construction of many of the
items in the visions including the measuring of Jerusalem and the frustrated attempt of the man with the measuring line (who may be an artisan). But how this measuring provides the means for the restored priesthood of Joshua is not clearly specified in the text. Perhaps it is the
building of the house promised in 1.16 that provides the basis for the
restoration of the priesthood.

In Ezekiel measuring refers to apportioning the land and providing
the Zadokites with the proper portion of their share in the land in order
that they might perform temple service (Ezek. 44.15–45.5). Perhaps this
type of thought underlies Zechariah. Having received his allotment,
Joshua is put in charge of it. One could then read the surreal lampstand
as one which is inside the temple, which is part of the compound of
which Joshua has been placed in charge. It is not stated that this is the
lamp of the temple: just that it is a lamp. The symbolic aspects of the
olive trees on each sides strongly suggest this is not an ordinary picture

of a real lamp but is more important in symbolic terms. This reader does not readily connect the flying scroll purging the land of thieves and those who swear falsely, the removal of the ephah, the multi-coloured horses with chariots, and the crowning of Joshua. They do not seem to build on each other. They may be related, but the text does no spell out *how* they are related. The reader must form constructs of associations between the textual elements to see them as related. Of course, surreal juxtaposition of objects is recognized as an artform and in that form the reader is challenged to ascertain why the juxtaposition is presented.

There are elements in the text which adhere to the plot of resolution. If one skipped reading the vision of the lampstand, one would not read 4.10b which interprets the eyes in the stone in the previous vision (3.9). If one skipped reading the vision in ch. 3, one would miss information about the branch (3.8) which may be important to the interpretation of the episode in 6.12-15 in which the branch also occurs. Another example of related subject matter is the horses in chs. 1 and 6. But these are fairly minor explanations of events and explain the significance of individual objects in the text, rather than the relationship between the objects. Furthermore, the plot which was constructed for the earlier portions of Zechariah 1–8 (the horse through to the lamp) is heavily dependent on intertextual readings of each of the elements rather than the definitions of the elements provided internally by the text. An individual reading Zechariah without any knowledge of the Tanakh would not construct this plot.[16] She may not even find a way of connecting the material together.

A further barrier to constructing a plot is the difficulty in determining the chronology of events in these visions: this task is principally a reader directed process in Zechariah 1–8. This does not imply that readers do not construct a chronology, only that the plot of the visions does not obviously contain a chronology. Rather, Zechariah is more like a music video, which quickly changes images in a pulsating manner that somehow manages to keep the reader viewing. The same intrigue which some have with Zechariah may underlie the popularity of the parade of short cut, sometimes bizarre, discontinuous images that pervades music videos in our culture. As with many music videos, the category of 'plot

16. Fleming finds other intertextual referents and posits that the plot of the divine council type scene underlies the plot of Zech. 1–8 (1989).

of resolution' is not the best description of the narrative in Zechariah 1–8.

While the plot of Zechariah is a loose parade of discontinuous narratives or pericopes, there are formal elements that unite this text: the formal structure is extremely tight. There are many devices which bind the episodes of Zechariah 1–8 together. Meyers and Meyers have listed these structures: the dating formulas which provide a chronological development from the second to the fourth year of Darius (1.1, 7; 7.1); the characters which recur throughout the work (1987: xliv; see my Table 2), the integral relationship between oracles and visions throughout the work (1987: xlv-xlvii, li); the structure of visions surrounded by a frame (1.1-6; chs. 7 and 8); phraseology and vocabulary links between the three sections of Zechariah;[17] the admixture of poetry and prose (1987: lii), the chiastic layout of the visions with correspondences of vocabulary, thematic, internal structure and topics between the corresponding chiastic portions (1987: liv-lvii; see also Baldwin 1972: 80-81, 85; Seybold 1974b: 107), and a progression from the universal to the temple and back again throughout this chiastic arrangement (1987: lv-lvi).[18] In addition to the Meyers' observations, some structures of unity which bind together the individual episodes of Zechariah 1–8, that they hint at but do not spell out, are the narration of the entire book of Zechariah 1–8 by the implied narrator/author Zechariah, characters which recur throughout the book that Meyers and Meyers have not listed,[19] locales which recur throughout the book (see Table 2), and the

---

17. See Meyers' and Meyers' charts 5, 6 and 7 for examples of the phrases and vocabulary that link sections 1.1-6 with chs. 7–8 and 1.7–6.15 with chs. 7–8. See their chart 9 for an example of formulaic language which recurs throughout the visions (1987).

18. Hanson believes this chiastic structure 'reflects the architecture of the temple and its surrounding precincts' (1987: 176). He proceeds to say this is a 'reflection of the heavenly temple within which Yahweh resides amidst his holy attendants' (1987: 176). This is unconvincing and is more in line with the theology of the book of Hebrews than Zechariah.

19. Meyers and Meyers mention, concerning Haggai and Zechariah, that 'the cast of characters in the two works is virtually the same: the high priest Joshua, the governor Zerubbabel, priests, the citizenry or representatives thereof' (1987: xliv). Here I am examining the internal coherence of the book of Zechariah and am noting the recurrence of characters such as Yahweh, Yahweh Sebaoth, the messenger who speaks with 'me', the messenger of Yahweh, the (former) prophets, the ancestors, the nations, Judah, Jerusalem, and so on. I strongly suspect that Meyers and Meyers

recurrence of a large proportion of the vocabulary in different episodes (see Table 3 [and Table 2]). The sheer abundance of repeated vocabulary links many of the episodes together and suggests it holds the key to understanding the confusing material: if the reader links the passages together with this vocabulary, the visions should mutually interpret one another. There are thus many structures which unite the visions. Overall, then, the visions have a dual character: they read as self-contained narratives, but contain much material that overlaps with material in other visions.

Table 2. *Recurring Characters and Locales in Zechariah 1–8*[i]

Word/Phrase	Zechariah
אבות, ancestors	1.2, 4, 5, 6 ~ 8.14
אדון כל־הארץ, Lord of all the earth	4.14 ~ 6.5
אדם, people	2.8(H) ~ 8.10
אלהים, god	6.15 ~ 8.8, 23
ארבע רוחות השמים, the four winds of heaven	2.10(H) ~ 6.5
ארץ צפון, land of the north	2.10(H) ~ 6.6, 8
בבל, Babylon	6.10
בת־בבל, daughter of Babylon	~ 2.11(H)
בהמה, animals	2.8(H) ~ 8.10
גוים[ii], nations	1.15 ~ 2.4(H) ~ 2.12(H), 15(H) ~ 7.14; 8.13, 22, 23
זכריה, Zechariah	1.1 ~ 1.7 ~ 7.1, 8
יהודה, Judah	2.2(H), 4(H) ~ 2.16
ערי יהודה, cities of Judah	~ 1.12
בית יהודה, house of Judah	~ 8.13, 15, 19
איש יהודי, a man of Judah	~ 8.23
יהוה[iii], Yahweh	1.2~ 1.10, 13, 17 ~ 2.3(H) ~ 2.15(H), 16(H), 17(H) ~ 3.2 ~ 6.15 ~ 7.2, 7; 8.21, 22
אמר יהוה, says Yahweh	1.3, 4 ~ 1.12, 14, 16, 17 ~ 2.12(H) ~ 3.2, 7 ~ 4.6 ~ 6.12 ~ 7.9, 13; 8.2, 3, 4, 6, 7, 9, 14, 19, 20, 23

are aware of these features, but do not spell them out because their task is to demonstrate the unity of Haggai–Zechariah 1–8 rather than Zechariah 1–8.

Word/Phrase	Zechariah
דבר־יהוה, word of Yahweh	~ 1.1 ~ 1.7 ~ 4.6, 8 ~ 6.9 ~ 7.1, 4, 8; 8.1, 18
נאם יהוה, a saying of Yahweh	~ 1.3, 4 ~ 1.16 ~ 2.9(H) ~ 2.10(H), 14(H) ~ 3.9, 10 ~ 5.4 ~ 8.6, 11, 17
היכל יהוה, temple of Yahweh	~ 6.12, 13, 14, 15
עיני יהוה, eyes of Yahweh	~ 4.10
יהוה צבאות, Yahweh Sebaoth	1.6 ~ 1.12 ~ 2.13(H), 15(H) ~ 4.9 ~ 6.15 ~ 7.12, 8.21, 22, 23
(כה) אמר יהוה צבאות, (thus) says Yahweh Sebaoth	~ 1.3, 4 ~ 1.14, 17 ~ 2.12(H) ~ 3.7 ~ 4.6 ~ 6.12 ~ 7.9, 13, 8.2, 4, 6, 7, 9, 14, 19, 20, 23
נאם יהוה צבאות, a saying of Yahweh Sebaoth	~ 1.3 ~ 1.16 ~ 3.9, 10 ~ 5.4 ~ 8.6, 11,
דבר יהוה צבאות, word of Yahweh Sebaoth	~ 7.4; 8.1, 18
בית יהוה צבאות, house of Yahweh Sebaoth	~ 7.3; 8.9
יהושע, Joshua	3.1, 3, 6, 8, 9 ~ 6.11
ירשלם, Jerusalem	1.12, 14, 16, 17 ~ 2.2(H) ~ 2.6(H), 8(H) ~ 2.16(H) ~ 3.2 ~ 7.7; 8.3, 4, 8, 15, 22
ישראל, Israel	2.2(H)
בית ישראל, house of Israel	~ 8.13
הנביאים (הראשנים), (the former) prophets	1.1, 4, 5, 6, 7 ~ 7.3, 7, 12; 8.9
המלאך הדבר בי, the conversing messenger	1.9, 13, 14 ~ 2.2(H) ~ 2.7(H) ~ 4.1, 4, 5 ~ 5.5, 10 ~ 6.4
מלאך יהוה, the messenger of Yahweh	1.11, 12 ~ 3.1, 3.5, 6
סוסים, horses	1.8 ~ 6.2, 3, 6
סוסים אדמים, red horses	~ 1.8 ~ 6.2
סוסים לבנים, white horses	~ 1.8 ~ 6.3, 6
ציון, Zion	1.14, 17 ~ 2.11(H) ~ 8.2, 3
בת ציון, house of Zion	~ 2.14(H)
צמח, branch	3.8 ~ 6.12
רעה, neighbour	3.8, 10 ~ 8.10, 16, 17

i   ~ indicates a section break (see the discussion above concerning the *petuhah* for more information about the section breaks).

There is some overlap between this Table and Table 3. This is because it is difficult to discern the difference between repeated words and characters at some stages. An example of this overlap is the word כהן ('priest'): does this represent an epithet or a character? Likewise, are the symbolic elements (for example, the horns) symbols, characters or both?

ii   It is debatable if the גוים ('nations') in these verses are necessarily the same character(s). These גוים are identified in the text as הגוים השאננים, 'nations at ease' (1.15); הגוים השללים קרן אל־ארץ יהודה, 'the nations who are lifting a horn to the land of Judah' (2.4); הגוים הנשאים אתכם, 'the nations plundering you' (2.12); הגוים רבים, 'many nations' (2.15); הגוים אשר לא־ידעום, 'the nations that they did not know' (7.14); קללה בגוים, 'a curse among the nations' (8.13); וגוים עצומים, 'strong nations' (8.22); לשנות הגוים, 'tongues of the nations' (8.23). One can read these nations as one character and construct a plot from this narrative in which Yahweh was angry with the implied audience (7.12) and thus stormed the implied audience to all the nations which the implied audience did not know (7.14). The nations are actively involved in this scattering of the implied audience initiated by Yahweh (or for which Yahweh takes the credit in 7.14): they help (1.15) Yahweh and lift up a horn to the land of Judah to accomplish this scattering (2.4). This makes the implied audience presumably Judaeans, or former Judaeans (that this text is in Hebrew might suggest that as well). The nations are the tools of Yahweh—they lift up a horn to fulfil Yahweh's scattering. Apparently these nations took their job too seriously, helping to the point of evil and thus (1.15) are plundering the implied readers (2.12) by lifting a horn to the land of Judah to scatter it (2.4).

iii   Craig, with Mettinger, does not see the name יהוה צבאות ('Yahweh Sebaoth') as implying martial connotations but as a reference to the deity who decrees the fate of the world (1991: 69). On this name in Zech. 1–8, 'the name of the God enthroned in the Jerusalem temple appears over and over again throughout the book of Zechariah. It disrupts the literary form and serves as an apparently liturgical invocation of the deity who is in control of the nations despite the imperial reign of the Persian king' (Craig 1991: 69). This name 'functions as the linguistic vehicle which mediates the "felt" cultic presence of YHWH in the temple' (Craig 1991: 69).

Tollington believes the title יהוה צבאות was used in the early monarchy and legitimizes the new temple and religious structure proposed in Zechariah 1–8 by 're-introducing the name applied to Yahweh in the cult of Solomon's temple' (1993: 70).

Another problem is the difficulty of discerning a meaning both for the individual episodes and for the narrative as a whole. The units, or vignettes, in Zechariah are basically self-contained. Beyond shared vocabulary and themes, there are no obvious story links between the visions.

The reader is not given a narrative description of Zechariah journeying between different locales where fantastic events befall him, such as is given in the *Odyssey*. In the *Odyssey* the journeying is part of the story; even though narrative description of a journey is absent from Zechariah. It is never stated in the visions where Zechariah is situated, even though many locales are referred to in the book (Jerusalem, the cities which surround Jerusalem, the mountain of Yahweh Sebaoth, Babylon, Shinar, Bethel, the myrtles, the cities of Judah, Zion, Israel, the land [5.3], the land of the north, the house of Yahweh Sebaoth, the Negev, the Shephelah, the holy place of Yahweh, the holy land, perhaps the temple complex [chs. 3 and 4], perhaps the divine council [chs. 1, 3 and 6; so Fleming 1989: 157], and, if one adheres to the mythological readings of chs. 1 and 6, the entrance to heaven).[20] Though scholars such as Galling (1964) attribute locales for most of the visions, this is ultimately a gap-filling enterprise as Zechariah's locale is not stated throughout the visions. This attribution of locales is a part of Galling's attributing various historical backgrounds for each vision, and the acceptance of the locales which he attributes for the visions is dependent on accepting the historical circumstance he suggests underlies each vision.[21] While chs. 1 and 6 may depict the entrance to heaven, this is by no means made clear and it may simply be a valley in ch. 6 and 'the deep' in ch. 1. The vision of the horns occurs in an unmarked locale. The messenger going out[22] to measure Jerusalem may proceed from this valley, but this is not specified.

Perhaps all the visions are seen in this valley, as there are no markers of a change of locale or miraculous transportation of the prophet to another locale as in Ezekiel. But perhaps they are visions of many different locales that Zechariah sees, but is not present in. Or maybe Zechariah does journey between different locales but the journey is not

20. Petersen discusses the locale of the first vision and concludes 'It is, however, best not to be too precise about assigning a location to this place. It is not the divine dwelling *per se*, nor is it the official entry into the divine abode' (1984a: 139-40).

21. Seybold, contra Galling, raises the issue of the difficulty of establishing the locale of the visions (1974a: 18). Yet, in another article Seybold links the imagery of the visions in chs. 1 and 6 with Babylonian and Sumerian mythology to represent a godly grove by the two metal mountains beside the primaeval sea where the seat of the gods and the entrance to heaven is located (1974b: 98; see Horst 1960: 198).

22. The verb used for this activity (יצא) occurs very often in Zech. 1–8. Wallis translates יצא as 'to appear (as someone), to enter' and proposes to read it this way throughout Zech. 1–8 (1978: 379).

indicated. The focus in the visions is certainly on the objects rather than the locale. The predominance of Jerusalem throughout the text suggests Zechariah might be there; he definitely seems there in chs. 7 and 8, yet his location throughout the visions is by no means certain. That he sees a figure setting out to measure Jerusalem in ch. 2, and that an oracle directed to those in the land of the north occurs in the same chapter, suggest Zechariah is not in Jerusalem but might even be in the land of the north. Some suggest he is in the environs surrounding Jerusalem. There is a 'neither here-nor-thereness' which characterizes the locales he inhabits. The transformation between visions, and possibly between locales, is marked by an indication of seeing or being caused to see (1.8; 2.1, 4; 3.1; 4.2; 5.1, 5; 6.1). It is as if a director has cut to another apparently irrelevant scene without providing a link between the two.

Regarding locales, is there a difference between the house of Yahweh Sebaoth and the temple of Yahweh? Yahweh Sebaoth is attributed with having a temple (היכל) and a house (בית) in Zechariah (1.16; 3.7). Yahweh is only attributed with having a temple (6.13, 15). As it is unclear whether Yahweh or Yahweh Sebaoth says 'my house will be built in it' in 1.16, this may be an indication of Yahweh possessing a house.

Further, Marinkovic calls for commentators on reading בית יהוה to 'not think automatically of a temple structure, but think as well of the [temple] community that it represents' (1994: 98). Marinkovic demonstrates how the verb בנה can be used figuratively to indicate 'the organization of a community, family, tribe or dynasty; especially when it is used in conjunction with the word בית' (1994: 98). After examining the uses of בית in Zechariah 1–8, he concludes 'the temple is of minor importance when compared with the main concern of the texts: the building of the community of YHWH and his people in Jerusalem' (1994: 101).

Marinkovic convincingly refutes the notion which many hold (for example, Barker [1978: 24], Halpern [1978: 169], Marks [1987: 225]; Meyers and Meyers [1992b: 1062-63]) that the temple is the central theme of Zechariah 1–8. Marinkovic says:

> First of all, the texts of Zechariah 1–8 contain hardly any statements about the temple. There are very few verses that deal with this matter, and those few that we have are basically marginal, or are part and parcel of pronouncements that express other concerns. Secondly, the greater part of the text of Zechariah 1–8 deals with other thematic matters. For example, not one of the eight visions is thematically connected with the temple as such or with its reconstruction (1994: 90).

The grounds on which many commentators claim to identify the theme of temple building as central to these visions is an identification of the objects in Zechariah 3 and 4 with temple apparatus. Meyers' and Meyers' comments can be seen as representative:

> although only the central two visions deal explicitly with the temple, the fact that the center is an integral part of a carefully constructed whole indicates that the entire sequence emerges from the prophet's acute awareness of the conceptual and political problems surrounding the reorganization of the postexilic community and the reconstruction of that community's institutional core... Zechariah addresses the meaning and symbolism of the temple as a legitimate and legitimizing expression of the new pattern of dyarchic leadership that accompanied the temple project (1992b: 1062-63).

As Marinkovic says above, this is by no means clear. Carroll has convincingly shown the problems which surround the vision of the lampstand. Neither can the renowned reclothing of Joshua scene be definitively proven to concern temple restoration. The significance of the apparel is unknown. The primary intertext with this passage suggests it is luxurious garments (Isa. 3) which were removed from the daughters of Zion. The similarity of the garments in Zechariah 3 with the high priestly regalia suggests that the comparison is somehow important. The Isaian intertext challenges the importance that should be attributed to the comparison. So the text hints that *perhaps* Joshua is being clothed for priestly duty, *perhaps* he is not. The image in either intertext implies restoration, but not necessarily for priestly duties. Does the difference in the garments suggest that (1) this high priest, that is, Joshua, is somehow different from the previous high priest; (2) Joshua is unworthy to wear the full regalia, and so the priesthood is not being completely restored; or (3) this passage does not deal with the restoration of the priesthood but rather with the restoration of the things Yahweh removed from the daughters of Zion. These intertexts tug at the reader, refusing to resolve my conundrum. The recognition of the intertext simultaneously congratulates and taunts the reader. The intertext speaks to the reader, 'You are clever to have discovered me. Well done! Now you must deal with the fact that *I am*, and *I am not* that which you seek'. To return to the case of Joshua, one cannot say Zechariah 3 necessarily deals with the temple. That the lamp was not disclosed to be in the temple further dismisses the notion that the restoration of the temple is the theme of the visions.

Precisely how the curse going out over the land is related to the temple is difficult to understand. So is the woman in the ephah, if one interprets her as representing something other than idolatry, such as a desired (sexual?) object. And what of the horses taking a spirit (Yahweh's?) to the north? If one takes this as the final event of the vision, it appears to represent Yahweh as dwelling in the land of the north and his return is far from imminent. This seems at odd with the assertions that Yahweh has returned to Jerusalem. One would expect Yahweh to be moving in the opposite direction if he was returning to his restored temple. So even Yahweh's return, though it is frequently alluded to and stated in Zechariah 1–8, is also dubious as the focus of the text, as elements of the text deny this return. To accept that the restoration of the temple is the focus or theme of Zechariah 1–8 is dependent on two hermeneutical moves. First, the reader must interpret the events of chs. 3 and 4 to concern the temple. Secondly, the reader must agree that the central item of a chiasmus (here, visions 3 and 4 in the cycle of visions) is to be read as *prominent* or the focus of the chiasmus. Poststructuralist thought has laboured to prove that every item of a narrative may be significant and narrative emphasis depends on which item(s) the reader elevates to prominent position.

The main uniting force in the visions is the surreal nature of the objects and events seen. With these transformations of scene, the relationship between the visions' symbolic elements is not readily apparent. It is not immediately, or even in the final analysis, obvious how the symbols are related. What do multicoloured horses, myrtles, the deep, the messenger of Yahweh, horns, artisans, a man with a measuring line, Joshua the priest, filthy and festal garments, a turban, a stone with seven eyes, a gold lampstand with two olive trees beside it, seven lamps, a flying scroll, an ephah, a woman, women with stork-like wings, Shinar, and four chariots with multicoloured horses have in common? There is no story built up that somehow links these objects. Nor are the relationships between them explained in the text. There is a surplus of words and structures uniting the visions, yet no obvious links specify how the principal objects and actors seen in one vision relate to the objects in the other visions. If one were to simply look at those objects one might guess they belong to a children's story by a very warped author (perhaps Tim Burton?). A further difficulty in ascertaining why and how these objects are linked together, is ascertaining what the objects mean in the vignette in which they occur. When one cannot understand the material on the microlevel of the individual *vignettes*, it is difficult to attempt to understand it on the macrolevel of the entire narrative. One cannot understand the part to understand the whole.

I imagine that the author of Zechariah would be sympathetic with the sentiments of the character of Jeff Torrington's *Swing Hammer Swing!*:

> Actual criticism of the novel by its rejectors was very thin on the ground, although the consensus of opinion seemed to indicate that its main weakness lay in its apparent 'lack of plot'. You can bet your granny's boots and braces it lacks plot. Plots are for graveyards. I'd rather drag my eyeballs along barbed wire than read a plotty novel. You can almost see the authors of such contrived claptrap winding up their childish prose toys, before sending them whirring across their fatuous pages in search of 'adventures'. See how perkily they strut and stride; observe the zany intermingling patterns they make with their inky bootees; listen, and you'll hear their valorous hearts grinding within their heroic breasts (1993: 162).

I am tempted to declare that Zechariah lacks a plot. Unfortunately, Chatman declares, 'a narrative without a plot is a logical impossibility' (1983: 47; had Chatman seen a music video yet when he wrote this?). Fortunately, Chatman provides a classification to which Zechariah neatly adheres: the antistory or antinarrative. Chatman discusses the antistory or antinarrative:

> If the classical narrative is a network (or 'enchainment') of kernels affording venues of choice only one of which is possible, the *antistory* may be defined as an attack on this convention which treats all choices as equally valid...what they call into question is, precisely, narrative logic, that one thing leads to one and only one other, the second to a third and so on to the finale. But it is incorrect to say that they are without plot, for clearly they depend for their effect on the presupposition of the traditional line of choice (1983: 56-57).

This definition provides both a classification for Zechariah, and a reason for its incoherency: it challenges narrative logic. This will be seen further in Zechariah 1–8's failure to provide a complex central character—which one would expect if this were a plot of revelation—use of extremely multivalent vocabulary, lack of temporality, and its provision of interpretations which do not adequately interpret the confusing aspects of the text.

Zechariah's Character

The difficulties which attend identifying speakers in Zechariah make it difficult to ascertain those speakers' characters: to which character should one attribute various thoughts and actions in the text? This ambiguity makes it difficult to determine the character of the narrator, Zechariah. (Does he have problems in differentiating individuals?) Also, the sheer lack of activity in which Zechariah engages denies much further material with which to construct a character for Zechariah.

To ascertain Zechariah's character it is nevertheless necessary to catalogue the few acts he does perform. Most of the narrative is occupied with Zechariah relating the speeches or actions of other entities. What are the clues to Zechariah's character and the actions Zechariah performs? To begin with, Zechariah is called a נביא. If Bar-Efrat's (1989: 90) and Sternberg's (1985: 329) observations on biblical epithets are applicable here, this identifies him but does not characterize him. It concerns not Zechariah's personality, but rather his role in society.[23] There is the possibility that prophets never existed and there were only storytellers who told tales of prophets. Prophets are then a literary type, like Fairies...but less pleasant...though preferable to Sirens.

What actions is Zechariah involved in? Zechariah sees (1.8; 2.1, 3); asks questions (1.9, 2.2, 4, 6; 4.4, 11, 12; 5.6, 10; 6.4); is commanded to declare 'oracles' (1.3, 14, 17; 4.6; 6.12; perhaps delivers a full oracle in 2.10-17, depending on whom the reader identifies with the quoted speech in 2.10-17); is awoken as if from sleep (4.1), 'lifts' his eyes (2.1, 5; 5.1, 9; 6.1); answers questions concerning what he sees (4.2,[24] 5, 13; 5.2); is commanded to collect[25] gold and silver, make crowns[26] and set

---

23. On the role of the נביא (prophet) in society, see Koch (1978: 15-28; 1983: 1-3, 11-12); Tucker (1987); Petersen (1981: 51-87); Barton (1992: 492-94 deals specifically with the postexilic role of the prophet); Kingsbury (1964: 285-86); Muilenburg (1965: 95-97); and Wilson for a summary of scholarship (1980: 1-19).

24. This depends on if the *qere* or *kethib* reading is followed.

25. The Hebrew for this is לקחה which, oddly, is 'an infinitive absolute functioning as an imperative' (Petersen, 1984a: 274; see Meyers and Meyers 1987: 337 for a discussion of this, as well as Lipiński, who takes it to be Tiberian Masoretic mistake in pointing for an earlier imperative form that is attested in texts from Qumran [1970: 33-34]).

26. See Lipiński (1970: 34-35); Meyers and Meyers (1987: 349-50, 362-63); and Redditt (1992: 252).

them on the head of Joshua; and receives an answer to the question of the delegation concerning fasts in a word of Yahweh. It is odd that Zechariah is commanded to make crowns: עטרות. This problem is further compounded by the use of the singular verb in reference to the crowns in v. 14, as well as the 'defective plural' of v. 14 (העטרת, 'crowns'). The passage is confusing. The use of two different forms for a plural 'crowns', one *plene* and one not, suggests once again the refusal of the text to adhere to stable referents (see above).

Curiously, Zechariah is never depicted actually carrying out the tasks assigned to him: he is commanded to make crowns but is never depicted doing so. In stark contrast to this are narrative depictions where a character is commanded by Yahweh to do something, and the narrative records that the individual did do so (see Nathan acting in accord with Yahweh's wishes and delivering the oracle in 2 Sam. 7.17 or Hosea fulfilling Yahweh's command in Hos. 1.3). Yet, it is common for a prophet to be commanded to proclaim something with no further record of the prophet fulfilling his or her mission (for example, Ezek. 11.14-21). The writing down of the message *is* the fulfilment. The prophetic works are blatantly literary and hint that the intended audience of the messages or oracles are really the reader, rather than the audience in the book to whom the prophet is commanded to proclaim.

Similarly, Zechariah is commanded to deliver speeches but is never depicted actually delivering them. Nor are the results of these prophecies presented.[27] The closest Zechariah comes to exercising individuality is when he orders a clean turban to be set on Joshua's head. With the ambiguity of the symbol of the turban, it is difficult to see what insight is given into Zechariah's character by this outburst: he likes clean hats? An examination of the symbolism surrounding the turban might provide an intertextual link with Isa. 3.23; 62.3 and/or Job 29.14. But little is added to the story by this outburst: the change in the garments executed by Yahweh in 3.4 carried enough symbolic force to demonstrate the symbolic aspect of the changing of the clothes and the removal of iniquity from Joshua. If he fulfils the command in 6.9-15 then he also makes and sets crowns on Joshua's head. The outburst in 3.5 anticipates Zechariah's crowning of Joshua in ch. 6. Zechariah's actions, outside of the role of narrator, are centred solely around headgear. Perhaps this lends more force to perceiving Zechariah as an artisan who specializes

27. With the possible exception of Zech. 1.6. This depends on whether one interprets it as the speech of the ancestors or of Zechariah's audience.

in making hats. Maybe these acts display insight into a character who
desires to see the completed picture unfold: maybe he is anxious to see
the festival which accompanies the headgear get underway. Alternatively, he is anxious to see justice restored to the land. That the garments with which Joshua is clothed appear to be luxury items might
also suggest Zechariah is anxious to see prosperity in the land again.

Overall, then, Zechariah does very little. He is a passive recipient of
many instructions, but rarely acts of his own accord. Zechariah is a *type*
or *flat* character. Berlin has described flat characters: 'Flat characters, or
types, are built around a single quality or trait. They do not stand out as
individuals' (1987: 23; see her full discussion of characterization [1987:
23-42]). Zechariah is initially described as a prophet. Unlike some
prophets who have strong personalities, Zechariah has no persona.

Furthermore, unlike some prophets, he does not have a typical prophetic calling. Habel discusses prophetic call narratives: '1. divine confrontation, 2. introductory word, 3. commission, 4. objection, 5. reassurance, 6. sign' (1965: 298). Habel lists a theophanic encounter with a
heavenly being, a מלאך יהוה (messenger of Yahweh; a character who
recurs throughout Zechariah) as fundamental to the divine confrontation
(1965: 317). Habel notes the verbs הלך ('walk') and שלח ('send') are
important to the commissioning of the person (1965: 318) and have 'a
technical connotation in this context' (1965: 299; see Tidwell's critique
[which is based on identifying elements of the genre of council scene to
Zech. 3] of Habel's call-*Gattung* ('genre') [1975: 347-52], as well as
his identification of the elements of a council genre [354-55]).

Press sees Zechariah 1 as the prophetic calling (*Berufung*) of Zechariah and correlates this to the call reports of Isaiah, Deutero-Isaiah,
Jeremiah and Amos (1936: 44-47). Fleming critiques Habel asserting,
'these episodes [of the divine council] should not be identified as prophetic inaugural calls. The divine council type-scenes and divine
council motif focuses on the message, not the office': it legitimizes the
prophet's message (1989: 155). Although Horst sees the visions as in
the council of Yahweh, he elaborates that none of the visions are a
Berufungsvision ('vision of a prophetic calling') (1960: 198).

Although Zechariah is never said to הלך and it is debatable if he is
שלח (this depends on which character is viewed as speaking in 2.12, 13,
15; 4.9 and 6.15), other characters are attributed with being sent (שלח)
by Yahweh (the horses [1.10, 11]; whoever is the speaker of 2.12, 13,
15; 4.9 and 6.15; the law and the words [7.12]) or commissioned to

'walk' by Yahweh (הלך; 1.10, 11; 6.7). The reassurance (that Yahweh
is with the individual) occurs on a much grander scale in Zechariah:
Yahweh says he is with the implied audience (1.16; 2.14; 8.3). The final
sign occurs on three levels in Zechariah: there are the men of omen
(3.8); the crowns as a זכרן in the temple (6.14; Blocher also correlates
the מופת of 3.8 with the זכרן 6.14 [1979: 264]); and the final statement
of 6.15 that the implied audience will know Yahweh sent the speaker of
6.15 when those who are far off will come to build the temple. While
obviously not all the features of the call narrative are present in
Zechariah, and they are certainly not contained in one stretch of narrative, the 'shotgun' effect of all of these connectives suggests the book
might be hinting at this aspect of the tradition, much as it hints at the
messages of other prophetic books but does not quote them verbatim.

Long believes that Zech. 1.8-17 is 'now oriented toward a commissioning of the prophet' (1976: 361). He says that while it 'does not
appear to legitimate in general the vocation of Zechariah...the report
does in fact carry a specific commission to proclaim' (1976: 361). Seybold also sees Zechariah 1 as a type of legitimating narrative, but wonders whether *Berufung* ('call') is the right technical term (1974b: 109).
That he feels compelled to address this issue betrays a sense on his part
of how the depiction of Zechariah is like a call narrative, but does not
quite adhere to modern notions of what comprises a call narrative (if
there really is such a genre). At any rate, he sees Zechariah as being
'commissioned' (*beauftragt*; 1974b: 109). This allusion to the call narrative form in Zechariah affirms the tradition while refusing to adhere
to its conventions. It appeals to the call narrative tradition while explicitly avoiding depicting its character precisely in these terms. The character has actually been displaced from the traditional view of the call
narrative as well. Whereas usually the call narrative concerns one
specific individual, in Zechariah 1–8 it concerns various characters in
the work. The central protagonist, Zechariah, does not solely receive all
of the call narrative's legitimizing power.

In addition, Zechariah's character does not develop (he appears static
throughout), and he exists only as a mouthpiece. Yet, he does not even
fulfil his role as a mouthpiece. Rather, all that exists is the written document in front of the reader. Is the reader to assume Zechariah did
indeed proclaim what he was commanded to proclaim? Or, is the reader
to assume that instead of proclaiming these matters, Zechariah wrote
them down? This opens up a whole range of reader-response options

for filling in the gap of why Zechariah did not proclaim the message: he lacked the courage to proclaim; he did not feel the events were comprehensible enough simply as proclamations and so wrote them down to make the visions available for public consumption as well as the oracles; or whatever other reason one may choose to interpret this gap.

Zechariah's character exists solely to pass on information. There is no Isaiah indignant with the house of David for wearying God (Isa. 7.13), Jeremiah displaying his wonder at Yahweh's deceit of Jerusalem (Jer. 4.10), or Jonah angry with the outcome of events (Jon. 4.4).[28] This is precedented for the character type 'prophet'. In House's analysis of characterization in the minor prophets he concludes 'Even the prophets are invisible as individuals at times, though they all work together to present the Twelve's message' (1990: 171). He explains this is the result of Yahweh acting as the principal character in the book of the Twelve, to the extent that 'every other figure in the book draws its personality from reacting to God' (1990: 171). The prophets, Israel, the nations and the remnant in the book of the Twelve function as composite characters and 'operate as one person': their characters are fused into composite personalities (House 1990: 171-72). House, who is the only commentator I know of who specifically addresses the issue of Zechariah's character (1990: 200-202), agrees with my assessment of Zechariah. Speaking of the characterization of the prophet Zechariah, he says, 'Zechariah 1–8 never deviates from this messenger pattern, which indicates that the book desires to set forth a concrete, clearly understood theme of Jerusalem's restoration that is viewed as coming directly from God' (1990: 200).[29] His conclusion, that this messenger pattern is to set out a clearly understood theme, is dubious: *perhaps* the theme of restoration can be understood in Zechariah, but, as this study aims to establish, the details of this restoration are contingent, far from clear and hardly concrete.

---

28. House lists Hosea, Gomer, Jonah and 'the messianic figures in Haggai–Malachi' as individuals in the book of the Twelve (although he limits the messianic figures as 'one could interpret them as different sides of a single image' [1990: 172]).

29. The assessment of Zechariah's character is different if one takes the whole of Zechariah (Zech. 1–14) as one's object of examination, as House does. Then, Zechariah is the 'complete prophet' who functions as messenger, symbol and co-revelator with Yahweh: 'he preaches all the major motifs of the prophetic genre' (1990: 202, 200).

That Zechariah is a type means one cannot read Zechariah 1–8 as a plot of revelation centred around Zechariah's personality. Zechariah is static and his character is not revealed. If it is a plot of revelation, Yahweh is the figure it reveals. This is odd for a modern reader of a first-person eponymous narrative: one expects the character who is revealed to be the narrator. If Yahweh is the character it reveals, what does it reveal about Yahweh? That he is open to making contracts? That he communicates ineffectively? That he is a source of confusion? That he cannot decide whether he is dwelling in Jerusalem or will dwell in Jerusalem? The book is established as a contract: if you obey Yahweh these things will happen. It is an expression of desire: these are the events the author wishes would happen. But it is a very confused expression of this desire.

If one analyses this story in psychoanalytic terms, in addition to literary terms, a different conception of character is obtained. In the visionary material, the symbols are interpreted and related to Zechariah via messengers, מלאךs who speak with him. Cohen believes 'in the exilic and post-exilic prophetic works the term *mal'ak* comes to be used as a synonym for the word *nabi*, eventually virtually replacing it completely' (1985: 16; likewise Blenkinsopp 1984: 239; Ross cites Isa. 42.19; 44.26; 61;1; Hag. 1.13; 2 Chron. 36.15-16; Mal. 3.1 and the title of the book of Malachi as evidence of this assertion [1987: 117-18]). If Cohen's and Ross's assertions are correct, and Isa. 44.26; Hag. 1.13; and 2 Chron. 36.15-16 certainly lend weight to their theory that the prophets can be spoken of synonymously as messengers, then Zechariah should be the מלאך. But Zechariah is refusing to act this way and accept responsibility for his message. Zechariah has split his prophetic persona by generating the alter-egos of the messengers: he has put the conversing messenger in the position of interceder and interpreter which he should occupy (Blenkinsopp 1984: 239; Ross 1987: 117-18).

Marks says of the conversing angel,

> it is he who now exercises the traditional prophetic prerogatives of intercession and proclamation (Zech. 1.12, 14-15). The change signals a shift in emphasis from the direction transmission of YHWH's word to greater reliance on revelations of the past, which, with the acceleration of scribal activity, are beginning to acquire authoritative status (1987: 228).

Higginson suggests the man in 2.5 may be Zechariah's 'own image projected into the night vision' (1970: 786). Here is yet another character who may represent Zechariah's fragmented personae. Zechariah is

even anxious to pass on the one prophetic prerogative he possesses—
access to the divine council—to Joshua in ch. 3.[30] Petersen notes similarities to the divine council scenes in 1 Kings 22, Isaiah 6, Jeremiah 23
and Zechariah 3 and concludes, 'If he [Joshua] so performs, he will
have prophet-like authority' (1984a: 208; likewise Fleming, 'this scene
allows the priest a level equal to a prophet' [1989: 206]). It is as if
Zechariah is attempting to distance himself as much as possible from
the character type of prophet to exist as a prophet in name alone.

The one place where Zechariah does show any character is his outburst concerning the clothing of Joshua. Blocher says here Zechariah
functions as the 'mouth of Yahweh' (1979: 267). Here is yet another
place Zechariah is seen as identical with Yahweh. Yet this is the only
outbreak of Zechariah's personality in Zechariah 1–8. Is this one slice
of personality to be taken away from his character too?

A very elaborate mechanism of projection exists in Zechariah: Yahweh dictates messages through the messenger(s) who dictate in turn to
Zechariah. Barker says, 'such a phenomenon of secondary personality
is often associated with visionary states, and the figure who appears as
the interpreting angel may well be the prophet transported outside himself' (1978: 26). The messengers and Zechariah speak in the same manner: all pepper their speech with formulas like כה אמר יהוה, 'thus says
Yahweh' (2.12; 3.7), נאם יהוה, 'declaration of Yahweh' (2.9, 10, 14;
3.9, 10; 5.4),[31] זה דבר־יהוה אל, 'this is the word of Yahweh to...' (4.6)
and presume to speak for Yahweh in the first person (1.14-17; 2.5-13;
3.6-10; 4.6-7; 5.4). The relationships between these personae is unclear.
Blocher says the relationship between Yahweh and the messenger of

---

30. For similarities between Zech. 3 and prophetic call narratives see Day
(1988: 118); and Jeremias (1977: 203-206). See Fleming for a discussion of how
the divine council motif structures and permeates the visions (1989: 184-207).

VanderKam says 'the conditional "keep my charge" would include supervision
of the cult and possibly care of the sanctuary' and may well also include judicial
activity (1991: 559) The מהלכים Joshua is promised is either direct access to Yahweh or indirect access through individuals who have direct access to Yahweh, of
whom Zechariah is one (VanderKam 1991: 560). Zechariah allows the high priest
access to what was once the prophet's domain. Zechariah appears to be preparing
the reader, at least in the final reading of the book, for the demise of prophecy en-
visioned in Zech. 13.

31. 2.12, 14 are ambiguous in this context as they may be the interjected
speech of Zechariah (see above).

Yahweh is 'enigmatic' and whether they are identical or distinct is not clarified (1979: 267).

These messengers pass on the meanings of the symbols to Zechariah, who simply records the events which take place and does not interject interpretations of his own. The meanings these messengers allocate to the symbols hardly explain them. But if there is a problem with the interpretation it is not Zechariah's fault; rather it is the messengers who told him what the visions mean. Zechariah has been shown secret, hidden things, but is ignorant of their full significance. In effect, Zechariah claims there is more going on than he can understand. Yet, in no instance does Zechariah know the import of the symbols (and must usually ask what the represented objects are), let alone try to discern their significance. The only chapter in which Zechariah does not ask a question is ch. 3, in which Zechariah seems cognizant of the ritual going on because he orders a turban to be put on Joshua's head. Zechariah even identifies all the players in the drama without prompting, lest the reader think he is 'thick'. With the exception of ch. 3, the import of which is still not clearly explained to the reader by Zechariah, Zechariah is the opposite of an omniscient narrator: he is the ignorant narrator.

Ultimately, even Yahweh is a projection of the author (echoes of Feuerbach?). Lacan says 'the signifier is a unit in its very uniqueness, being by nature symbol only of an absence' (1988: 39). Yahweh is the purest of signifieds, being perpetually absent, and represents a projection of Zechariah's desires onto the signifier 'Yahweh'; as Landy says, 'a metaphor or proposition concerning God is subject to infinite displacement' (1993: 230). This construction of projected personalities—Yahweh, the messenger(s) and Zechariah—begs one to psychoanalyse them as the projected character of Zechariah and its construction of desire. Of course, this is ultimately my projection, as reader, of a postulated desire onto the fictional character Zechariah, who is not truly conscious and cannot project. Unfortunately space, time, and a lack of expertise do not permit this analysis here.

Why is an ignorant narrator construed for this text? Does this suggest that if the narrator, who is a prophet does not understand the text, the reader should not feel silly for not understanding it either? Perhaps this is a critique of prophets and the deity. The message conferred is that these events are not understood by the prophet. So, why should the reader be able to understand them?

One is reminded of texts like Jer. 5.21 and Ezek. 12.2 in which people have eyes and do not see. Unfortunately, both of these passages negatively depict this state of being (it symbolizes rebelliousness in Ezekiel and foolishness in Jeremiah). Is Zechariah to be perceived as rebellious or foolish? It would be quite the departure from other examples of prophetic books to portray the protagonist as rebellious (bar Jonah) or foolish.

The above discussion has demonstrated that Zechariah narrates the story. Unlike some biblical narrators (for example, the narrator of the Deuteronomistic narrative[32]), Zechariah injects few narratorial comments which would provide the reader with insight into his character. Polzin discusses the need to establish the ultimate semantic authority of a work in order to understand the text in question; does it lie in the reporting speech of the narrator or the reported speech of the characters (1980: 21)? As Zechariah is the narrator, the lack of material attributed to him makes it difficult to use the narrator as a guide by which one can assess the actions in the story, as Polzin does with the narrator of the Deuteronomistic History (1980: 18). The rarity of reporting speech of the narrator which evaluates other character's comments in Zechariah makes it impossible to use reporting speech as the source of the ultimate semantic authority of the work and the guide to assessing characters' proclamations and actions. One must look elsewhere to find some ultimate semantic authority in the work.

(Con)Fused Leitmotifs

Zechariah confuses the reader by drawing on a small stock of words, and using this stock frequently (incidentally, Jonah also uses this tech-

---

32.   This term is borrowed from Eslinger in place of the term 'Deuteronomistic History' in order to avoid the connotations inherent in that term. Eslinger describes the narrator of the Deuteronomistic narrative as an external, unconditioned narrator (1989: 15; see Gunn's critique of the term 'omniscient' to describe a narrator or a character, including God [1990: 57-64]). This means that this narrator does not live in the story world of the Deuteronomistic narrative and is conventionally unlimited by the usual spatio-temporal restrictions of humans (see Eslinger 1989: 10-15; for a discussion of the narrator of the Deuteronomistic narrative and of narrators in general, see 4-7). When actions or speeches occur in narrative, the immediacy of the presentation is only illusory: the actions and speeches are always related through a narrator, whether the narrator's presence is overt, such as when he speaks, or covert, such as the narrator always is, because he is the one who relates the story (Cohn 1981: 170).

nique). Though a small basic vocabulary stock is characteristic of Classical Hebrew, an inordinate amount of words recur throughout the episodes of Zechariah. Words often occur in a different context (that is, in a different scene, or portion of the frame), in the manner of a leitmotif, yet with enough semantic overlap between the two occurrences to generate an uneasy feeling about the significance of this word in these two (or [often] more) places. As Henry's quote in the previous section has shown, simply repeating words has a certain effect.

Repetition affects interpretation in two principal ways. (1) It can explain a textual element. The repetition of the same word signals to the reader where the explanation is contained, or at least suggests to the reader that the repeated elements are related in some manner. This in turn suggests to the reader that the meaning of a confusing item may somehow be found in this relationship: it hints to the reader that maybe the other use of this word will solve the problem and allow an interpretation to arise which satisfies the reader. (2) Every word carries the connotations of its use in other contexts.[33] By manipulating these contexts, the writer adds new meanings to a word which can be triggered simply by the use of that word in the new context. This repetition thus affects interpretation. As discussed above, the repetition of a word links together the episodes in which the repeated words occur in the reader's mind.

But what happens when repetition appears as a structuring principle and is so prevalent it is difficult to discern which words are not repeated? Although this resonance is a common feature of literature, and is part of the pleasure of reading, the way this technique is used in Zechariah is baffling and suggests significance, but refuses to declare that significance. These words are interlaced throughout the narrative and occur in different visions and oracles so that an interpretative trail runs through the story with different branches coming off each word. This is the same process that creates connectives but on an intratextual level. Usually this is an intertextual tension but it is prevalent in Zechariah because of the episodic nature of its discourse. The symbols in this vision thereby interact with the symbols in other visions creating an

33. Bakhtin shows how this tendency results in the evolution of language(s). By constantly interacting with other words in new and different contexts, the semantic and syntactic fields of words are constantly changing in the individual and the collective spheres. If a change becomes widely used, it endures in the social sphere (see Bakhtin 1990: 288-300).

interplay in which the symbols mutually interpret one another. They swirl around each other as multicoloured mists threatening to merge and become indistinguishable, yet never quite achieving this yearning to lose their egos—they never return to the breast and encumber their unbearable lightness of being. The boundaries between the visions become indistinct, untraceable. The visions are thus intricately inter-related and constantly scraping meaning from the other visions.

When a reader is bombarded by as many recurring words as are found in Zechariah it is very difficult to know which episodes to use to mutually interpret one another. The sheer abundance of these repeated vocabulary items produces a text which is extremely intricately woven together in the mind of the reader: perhaps too tightly woven. The shared vocabulary connects every episode to other episodes. These links cause a tension in the reader/interpreter about deciding their significance. Of course, all textual and intertextual activity has this dimension. It just appears especially dense in Zechariah.

When the shared vocabulary links are perceived in Zechariah, interpretation is not simplified. Rather, it is made all the more perplexing, since the reason for the shared vocabulary is not readily apparent. Perhaps it is an indicator or example of artistic integrity. Unfortunately, I cannot shake the eerie awareness of the Uncanny which surrounds this lexical *déjà vu*. The Other uses of the word (as well as the Other uses of words within the same semantic field as the word) constantly threaten to merge with the focused occurrence of the word.

My first example will be Zech. 7.14's description of how Yahweh Sebaoth 'stormed them to the nations that "they had not known"' (NRSV). The 'them' of this passage is the ancestors. This connection is based on similar descriptions of Yahweh (Sebaoth; 1.2, 3, 4; 7.7, 12, 13; 8.14) being angry (קָצַף; 1.2; 7.12; 8.4) with the ancestors (אָבוֹת; 1.2, 4, 5, 6; 8.14), and sending the former prophets (הַנְּבִיאִים הָרִאשֹׁנִים; 1.4; 7.7, 12) to call (קָרָא; 1.4; 7.7, 13) words (דְּבָרִים; 1.6; 7.7, 12) to the ancestors, who refuse to listen (קָשַׁב; 1.4; 7.11‖שָׁמַע; 1.4; 7.11, 12, 13). Though there is no debate surrounding this identification, I have listed the lexical links between these texts (1.1-6; 7.7-14 and 8.11-14) to indicate how the text of Zechariah uses these linking processes in a straightforward, easily perceived fashion. This is an example of the processes being employed in a context where it is easy to discern their significance. That the process is employed there, hints that the process has significance when used elsewhere in the book.

A more complicated example of this phenomenon is the use of the word רוח ('spirit, wind'), in Zechariah 1–8. (Wherever a Hebrew word from these chapters is quoted in the following discussion, the purpose is to demonstrate the relationship between that word and another one from a different episode: to establish the resonance of that word in more than one vignette in Zech. 1–8.) It occurs in 2.6; 4.6; 5.9; 6.5, 8 and 7.12. Examining the use of this word throughout Zechariah should demonstrate the intricacy of the vocabulary links in Zechariah. But this examination will by no means limit itself to the word רוח. In the chase down the symbolic chain of רוח, many other vocabulary items become grafted onto its symbolic order. These new items become associated with the word under consideration and are in some ways inextricable from that word. So, the symbolic chain of רוח, which will be followed, will also lead the reader into other symbolic chains *ad infinitum*. The signifier is inexhaustible: only a small part of the symbolic chain can be examined here.

The point of entry into the symbolic order of Zechariah will begin at Zech. 6.5. There, the four chariots are identified as the four winds of heaven (ארבע רחות השמים). A metaphorical equivalence is created between the four winds of heaven and the chariots, as there are four of each, and they are identified as the four winds of heaven (see v. 1). This was chosen as a point of entry because of the metaphorical nature of the passage. What does this metaphor signify? The game is afoot.

In Zech. 2.10 Yahweh demands someone (presumably Zion, who is an inhabitant of the daughter of Babylon in the next verse), to flee from the land of the north, to which Yahweh has spread them as the four winds of heaven (כארבע רוחות השמים פרשתי). What is the significance of this simile? How is the spreading out of Zion like the spreading out of the four winds of heaven? Petersen says the four winds 'entail vast geographic extent, i.e., it is an appropriate way to depict the breadth of total destruction' and attributes this meaning to the simile in 2.10 (1984a: 270). But the metaphor could suggest Yahweh spreading Zion as far as the wind blows, or with the ease of the wind. The process of the winds of heaven going out from Yahweh is depicted in Zechariah 6, which might then be the key to the metaphor. The process depicted in Zechariah 6 is one in which the winds of heaven presented (מהתיצב) themselves to the Lord of all the earth and then the strong ones (האמצים; Petersen 1984a: 271), a designation which includes all four groups of horses (Meyers and Meyers 1987: 322),[34] seek (בקשׁ) to walk in the earth (התהלך בארץ). Though פרשׂ ('spread out') is absent from ch. 6, the scene is similar in depicting a spreading out of the chariots. How much of the context is exchangeable between this and ch. 2? Did Zion somehow seek to walk in the earth as the horses did?

The reader is encouraged to pursue the link between 2.10 and 6.8 by the presence of another connective in these two sections: ארץ צפון ('land of the north', 2.10/6.6, 8).[35] The ones going out[36] have caused the speaker of 6.8's spirit to rest (נוח) in the land of the north. This allows a metaphorical equivalence between Zion, which is commanded to flee from the land of the north, and the speaker's spirit, which is at rest in the land of the north; that is, Zion = the spirit of the speaker. Koch takes this 'wind of the spirit' as a negative destructive force:

> a gust blowing to destroy the foreign nations, so that Israel may be helped to achieve greater glory. According to 5.11, wickedness found its home in the north. It is here that it must be encountered, before the world can really be better (1983: 170).

Here is a plot Koch has constructed from the narrative of Zechariah: the evil is removed from the land in ch. 5 so that it may be destroyed in ch. 6. The exiles are told to flee from the land of the north in ch. 2 because this destruction is about to take place there (Koch 1983: 170). The wickedness of ch. 5 seems somewhat akin to a nuclear bomb, which one needs to remove from one's own territory before destroying it. This plot seems strange to me: why go to the trouble of having the winged women build a house for the woman in the ephah and place her on her pedestal (Zech. 5.11) if one is planning on imminently destroying this woman?

If the speaker of 6.8 is taken to be Yahweh (this is another verse where it is difficult to determine the speaker), then Yahweh's spirit may be taken to be Zion. Furthermore, it is the black horses that go out to the land of the north (הסוסים השחרים; 6.6). The black horses might then represent the spirit of the speaker. This is yet another place where the speaker is unclearly marked. Is it the conversing messenger or the Lord

---

34. Though 'strong' is attested in the Latin and Aquila, Baldwin believes 'a colour is much more likely, but no satisfactory meaning has so far been suggested. The Greek "dappled" or Aramaic "light coloured" are the nearest' (1972: 138).

35. Sellin has also noticed these connections (1930: 440).

36. Petersen sees these as 'the chariots, riders and horses' (1984a: 271).

of all the earth who cries out to Zechariah? If it is the Lord of all the earth, the scene depicts an angst ridden deity releasing its frustration. If it is the messenger, what does it mean for his spirit to be set at rest in the land of the north? This reading leaves us with a condensed metaphor: Zion = the black horses = the speaker's spirit = Yahweh's spirit.

The interpretation leads into other occurrences of the word רוח. Whatever the significance of the command in 4.6, and whatever it is Zerubbabel is to do (yet another confusing statement in Zechariah), he is to do it 'with my spirit' (ברוחי; that is, Yahweh's) rather than 'with strength' or 'might'. (Presumably this relates to Zerubbabel building the house and to the 'head stone'. Exactly what these objects signify is difficult to determine.) How does one do anything with a spirit? Is Zerubbabel to do it with: (1) the chariots; (2) Zion; (3) Yahweh's spirit; (4) the speaker's spirit; or (5) Zion? Another interpretational option creeps in: Yahweh Sebaoth's spirit is identified as the former prophets in Zech. 7.12: Yahweh's spirit = the former prophets. Since the former prophets are identified as the spirit of Yahweh, does that equivalence hold for present prophecy? If so, Zechariah, as a prophet, is claiming to be the spirit of Yahweh. He is, at the very least, suggesting an equivalence. Thus Zerubbabel is to accomplish his task with the spirit of Yahweh, that is, with prophecy. This prophecy in turn is the text before us which is the written word of prophecy: Zerubbabel is to follow the words of Zechariah to accomplish his task.

That the only beings who are attributed with having a spirit elsewhere in Zechariah 1–8 are Yahweh and Yahweh Sebaoth (4.6; 7.12) *might* suggest that the speaker of 6.8 is one of these two characters. If it is Yahweh Sebaoth, then setting Yahweh Sebaoth's spirit at rest in the north might mean the former prophets have been moved to the land of the north.[37] Perhaps this even suggests the present speaker, a prophet, is in the 'land of the north'. If one reads 2.12b as the speech of the prophet—'after glory he sent me to the nations plundering you'—the present prophet can be seen as one sent to the nations. This is one way to resolve the ambiguity of speaker in 2.12. But a more latent ambiguity surrounds the use of the metaphor 'four winds of heaven'. They may represent both Zion and the prophet. Perhaps the ambiguity indicates that they are both scattered in the land of the north.

Another passage connected with this associational chain is found in

37.   Blenkinsopp says this 'may refer to a prophetically inspired movement in the *gôlāh* that led a group of Jews to return' (1984: 239).

Zech. 8.20-22. There the inhabitants of many cities walk (הלך) to seek (בקש) Yahweh Sebaoth in Jerusalem. In Zechariah 6 the אמצים ('strong ones') sought the Lord of all the earth and then walked (התהלך) in the earth and set the speaker's spirit at rest in the land of the north. In ch. 8 strong or numerous nations (גוים עצומים; note the word-play and semantic overlap between אמצים ['strong', 6.7] and עצומים ['strong', 8.22]) walk (הלך) to Jerusalem to seek Yahweh Sebaoth. There is obviously a verbal connection between these passages. The significance of the link seems to be that it emphasizes a reversal of the picture in 6.1-8.

There is another case of semantic overlap which is hard to interpret when one compares 5.9 with 6.1-8. These two passages are associated by the similarity of the vocabulary surrounding the objects and events depicted in 5.9 and 6.1-8. This is a separate associational chain which briefly intersects with the associational chain surrounding רוח. In 5.9 two women come out (יוצאות; the same verb used for the chariots throughout ch. 6)[38] with wind (רוח; this is where the associational chains intersects) in their wings, and lift the ephah between the earth and the sky (שמים). They take (hiphil feminine part of הלך) this ephah to the land of Shinar, which is where Babylon is situated within the ארץ צפון ('and of the north', Gen. 11.1-9; see Jer. 46; Zech. 2.10-11; Zech. 6.8-10), and cause it to be set there (hophal third-person feminine singular of נוח) on its stand.[39]

The verb נוח ('set') only occurs twice in Zechariah 1–8 (5.11 and 6.8).[40] One is tempted to associate the two objects of נוח (that is, the 'my spirit' of 6.8 and the ephah of 5.9) which have both been taken northwards (one to the land of the north, the other to Shinar). It seems to be stretching the metaphor somewhat to associate the two, but the

---

38.   Petersen notes a few of the connections between 6.1-8 and the visions which precede it, such as the 'horses and their colors...the phrase *kol-hā'āreṣ* the mention of wind in the previous vision (5.9), and the explicit presence of metal in the last two visions serves to link this vision with those before it. The most pronounced link, however, is achieved through the use of the verb *yṣ'* ("proceed")' (1984a: 272). Furthermore, he says 'it is difficult to ignore the probable reason for the prominence of such language...surely this sort of action is designed to elicit another exit, that of the return of those in the north country to their homeland' (1984a: 272).

39.   1 Kings 7 provides a strange parallel to the stands in this passage. In 1 Kgs 7 the basins are set on the top of the stands; in Zech. 5 a dry measure is set on the top of the stand.

40.   Both occurrences are in a causative stem: hophal in 5.9 and hiphil in 6.8.

dense vocabulary links, as well as the locale to which both objects are taken, hint that there is some relationship between the two. Yet it is conceptually difficult to identify the spirit of the speaker, which is possibly the spirit of Yahweh, with the woman, who is a metaphor of wickedness (רִשְׁעָה; 5.8). Exactly what is the wickedness she is associated with? And is the wickedness of the woman symbolized by her action (she is sitting/ inhabiting [in] an ephah)? While one cannot unequivocally identify the two, an eerie awareness sets in over why the two are symbolically depicted with much of the same vocabulary. At the very least, these verbal links invite an associative reading. At the most, they imply the two subjects (the woman and Yahweh) are identical. Is the setting of Yahweh's spirit at rest in the land of the north a repetitive anachronism—that is, a 'return to a moment that has already been covered in the narrative' (Genette 1971: 97)—of carrying the ephah to Shinar? If so, it is a completive anachronism as well, as it supplies the missing information that the woman and the spirit of Yahweh are identical.[41]

Even if the ephah does contain idolatry, as many contend, a strange respect is being shown for it in depicting its voyage to the land of Shinar in similar terms and vocabulary to the spirit at rest (possibly Yahweh Sebaoth's?) in the land of the north, and in building (בנה) and establishing a house (בית) for it: an activity simultaneously being undertaken for Yahweh (Sebaoth?) in Zechariah (1.16; 4.9; 6.12, 13, 15; 7.3; 8.9). Simultaneously, some disrespect is portrayed for this woman in the violence perpetrated against her: the messenger casts (שׁלך) her down. שׁלך is a word-play on שׁלח (a common theme in Zechariah) which cunningly plays off the notion that the woman is cast down, and taken off to Shinar, whereas numerous things and people are sent, usually by Yahweh (but not always) throughout the visions (see 1.10; 2.12, 13, 15; 4.9; 6.15; 7.2, 12; 8.10). The horses of ch. 1 are among the most notable objects which are sent, as well as the spirit of Yahweh (note also the prophets; 7.12). Though a word-play does not unequivocally relate the two, it does juxtapose the woman with the spirit of Yahweh, or things sent by Yahweh, in an incomprehensible manner.

Another conceptual link is found with the near synonym ידד. The horns of the nations are thrown down (ידד) by the artisans in Zech. 2.4. Are the throwing down of the horns of the nations and the casting of the

---

41. See Genette (1971: 97ff.) for a discussion of the use of anachronisms in narratives.

woman into the ephah representing the same or a similar act? Is the woman somehow symbolically equivalent with the horns and perhaps representing the same thing? Maybe the idolatry reading is somewhat in mind here and the horns are thereby horns of altars to the idol (the woman?): in throwing the horns down, they throw her down as well. The horns of the nations were responsible for winnowing (זרה) Judah so that a man could not lift his head. What is winnowed is stored in an ephah.[42] Wind is an integral part of the winnowing activity: an object is thrown into the wind and scattered and winnowed by the wind (Jer. 4.11; 49.32, 36; Ezek. 5.2; 12.14). All of these images and objects relate to an agricultural theme.[43] If this theme is retained for Zechariah 2, when horns scatter or winnow they throw Judah up into the wind. Thus the woman may represent the good portion of the winnowed material which is kept in the ephah after the winnowing, and, after the winnowing, a man of Judah cannot lift his head because he is the chaff separated from the wheat, and the harvest, the plunder, is taken away to Shinar.

The semantic field of a word plays an important role in the interpretational process as well. The occurrence of זרה ('scatter') in the last example is one example of a word which attaches itself to the semantic field of רוח ('wind, spirit'). Another such word is סער ('storm') in the earlier example of Zech. 7.14. Yahweh Sebaoth describes how he stormed 'them' to the nations that 'they had not known' (NRSV). (Once more an ambiguity is present here in the phrase ואסערם על כל־הגוים אשר לא־ידעום. Who is the referent of each of the 'they' and the 'them' in ידעום; that is to say, is it the nations that do not know the ancestors, or the ancestors that do not know the nations, or both?)

Wind is an integral part of a storm (see Jon. 1.4; Ps. 55.9). Are the four winds of the heavens somehow to be understood as storm winds? They might be involved in the scattering process, so that the chariots of ch. 6 symbolically represent the winnowing and storming of Zion to the land of the north, which perhaps included nations that did not know Zion (or vice versa). In this case, the horns could represent some type of winnower who tosses Judah to the storming wind/chariots that carry the chaff (that is, Judah and Zion) to the nations, much as the women

---

42. In Ruth 3.2 barley (שׂערה) is winnowed (זרה). Barley is stored in an ephah (Num. 5.15; Ezek. 45.13; Ruth 2.17).

43. See Ruffin (1986: 107-12) for a treatment of the agriculture theme.

carried the ephah, and set Yahweh's spirit at rest, which is the prophet (or prophecy?) in the land of the north.[44]

The carrying of the ephah might import the connotation that some sort of economic transaction is involved in storming Zion among the nations. Furthermore, whereas women with wind in their wings (כנפים) carry the ephah to Shinar, men from all of the languages of the nations seize the hem (כנף) of a garment of a man of Judah when they come to entreat Yahweh.[45] This appears to be a lexical link to a symbolic reversal: if the woman in the ephah represented the carrying into exile of Zion, they were carried by כנפים and now come back with men from the nations seizing their כנף (Zech. 8.23). רוח and its semantic field create a network of meaning which is attached to many places in Zechariah 1–8.

It is hoped that this discussion has demonstrated by example both how interlaced the vocabulary is in Zechariah 1–8, and also the confusion that ensues when one attempts to hunt down the meanings and significance of these links. When one seeks to interpret the use of רוח in Zechariah 1–8, one is sent on a bizarre chase after the signifier. The symbolic order of רוח ('wind, spirit') is entangled with that of אמצים ('strong ones'), ארבע רוחות ('four winds, spirits'), ארץ צפון ('land of the north'), בית ('house'), בנה ('build'), בקש ('seek'), הלך, ('walk'), זרה ('scatter'), ידה ('strike [down]'), יצא ('go out'), יצב ('present one-self'), מרכבה ('chariot'), נוח ('set [down]'), סוס ('horse'), סער ('storm'), עין ('eye'), עצומים ('strong, mighty'), רשעה ('wickedness'), שלך ('throw [cast] down') and שמים ('heaven') (to list a small sample). On repetition, Brooks says:

> If repetition is mastery, movement from the passive to the active; and if mastery is an assertion of control over what man [*sic*] must in fact submit to—choice, we might say, of an imposed end—we have already a suggestive comment on the grammar of plot, where repetition, taking us back again over the same ground, could have to do with the choice of ends (1989: 286).

44. An intertextual construct can be seen with Ezekiel who is at the river of Chebar (in the land of the north).

45. To Meyers and Meyers this idiom 'depicts an act of submission or supplication; see, for example, 1 Sam. 15.27' (1992a: 131). That Saul loses his kingdom after he grabs the hem might suggest that the nations in Zech. 8 have lost their kingdom. As Meyers and Meyers say 'the picture of ten foreign men taking hold of the hem of a Yehudite conjures up a picture of submission and loyalty' (1992a: 131).

Readers choose how to relate the repetitions (ignore their significance, declare them significant, or declare them partially significant) and thereby choose the plot, the ending and the significance. The repeated words, in turn, carry and form their own symbolic orders and interlap in the same way with other words in Zechariah. This applies to all of the repeated words in Zechariah 1–8, as the text is fairly consistent in the manner in which it interprets symbols with other symbols. Zechariah is a dating agency for metaphors that endeavours to introduce as many symbols to other symbols as possible.

This discussion has discerned a symbolic macronarrative in Zechariah 1–8 which transcends the linear narrative: there is a second narrative or plot which is created by the symbols. In this symbolic discourse, the symbols and their semantic fields constantly intermingle and lend their symbolic energy to other symbol(s) with which they happen to collide. The symbols are constantly being metaphorically equated. This equation occurs because the symbols are not used in a straightforward analogical manner which would allow a reader to displace the energy of that symbol into a concrete analogue. Instead, the symbol is interpreted by another symbol, which in turn is interpreted by another symbol, in an ever continuing process.

One might ask how much of this interpretation illegitimately transfers the entire symbolic order of one symbol onto another when in fact only a portion of the other symbol's semantic field is transferable. Of course, this is to delve into the area of legitimacy in interpretation, which was dealt with in Chapter 1. I do believe, though, that the sheer interrelation of this material in Zechariah legitimates this transfer of metaphorical energy, and even begs one to make it. Because the text is so confusing on the narrative level, and due to the dominance of symbols in the text, the reader is demanded to think symbolically, to attempt to grasp the grammar of the symbols rather than just the grammar of the narrative. To do otherwise is to acknowledge interpretational defeat. The reader is encouraged to attach the attributes of one symbol to another. As Barker says of Zechariah 5, 'Thus, in one bizarre vision Zechariah juxtaposes a whole series of images, and we are left to draw our own conclusions, as his contemporaries doubtless did' (1978: 26). She also remarks, 'If we are to attempt to comprehend this, or indeed any, vision, we must allow all the elements to flow together, and settle where they will' (1978: 21). To decide how many of these elements flow together, and how far, is the major interpretative problem. Ultimately, these metaphors engender multiple interpretations, depending on which aspect of the symbolic order of a word the interpreter joins to another word. The net effect of all of this is an overdetermination of the symbols which denies the reader certainty in ascribing a significance to the symbol or metaphor: the reader is confused as to the significance of the symbol and can see the significance of the symbol assuming many valid realizations.

These metaphors in Zechariah are, then, both a unifying and disunifying force. In his study of symbolism in Zechariah, Ruffin recognizes that 'symbols travel with much baggage' and concludes that 'symbols tend to lend coherence to a work of literature' (1986: 214). He goes so far as to postulate that the symbols lend coherence to a reader's life (1986: 214-15). This seems a bit much to claim for the text of Zechariah 1–8; they certainly have not had this effect on me. On a more positive note, Ruffin's readings provide other examples of a similar process to the one I have described here. He has commented that the symbols 'contribute' to the plot of Zechariah (1986: 214). Obviously, I agree. The symbols weave the narrative together in a blatant abuse of artistic license while pulling the narrative apart by refusing to declare their significance. They force the reader to attempt to grasp the grammar of the symbols rather than just the grammar of the narrative: to seek out the symbolic syntax.

Table 3. *Some Recurring Words and Phrases in Zechariah 1–8*
(all verse references are to the Hebrew text)

Word/Phrase	Zechariah
אבן, stone	3.9 ~ 4.7, 10 ~ 5.4 ~ 5.8[i]
אדון, lord	1.9 ~ 4.4, 5, 13, 14 ~ 6.4, 5
אחר[ii], after	1.8 ~ 2.7 ~ 2.12 ~ 6.6 ~ 7.14
אחת, one	3.9 ~ 5.7 ~ 8.21
אלה, these	1.9, 10 ~ 2.2, 4 ~ 3.7 ~ 4.4, 5, 10, 11, 13, 14 ~ 6.4, 5 ~ 8.9, 12, 15, 16, 17
אן, where	2.6 ~ 5.10
(ה)ארבע, four(th)	1.7 ~ 2.1, 3 ~ 2.10 ~ 6.1, 5 ~ 7.1
ארך, length	2.6 ~ 5.2
ארץ, land	1.10, 11 ~ 2.4 ~2.10 ~ 3.9 ~ 4.10, 14 ~ 5.3 ~ 5.6, 9, 11 ~ 6.5, 6, 7, 8 ~ 7.5, 14; 8.7, 12
כל־הארץ, all of the land	1.11 ~ 4.10, 14 ~ 5.3 ~ 5.6 ~ 6.5
איש, man	2.9 ~ 3.2
בוא, to come	2.4 ~2.14 ~ 3.8 ~ 5.4 ~ 6.10, 15 ~ 8.7 (מבוא),8.8, 10, 20, 22
בחר, to choose	1.17 ~ 2.16 ~ 3.2

Word/Phrase	Zechariah
בֵּין, between	1.8, 10, 11 ~ 3.7 ~ 5.9 ~ 6.1 ~ 6.13
בַּיִת, house	1.16 ~ 3.7 ~ 4.9 ~ 5.4 ~ 5.11 ~ 6.10 ~ 7.2,[iii] 3; 8.9, 13, 15, 19
בֵּן, son	1.1 ~ 1.7 ~ 4.14 ~ 6.10, 11, 14
בנה, build	1.16 ~ 5.11 ~ 6.12, 13, 15 ~ 8.9
בקשׁ, seek	6.7 ~ 8.21, 22
גָּדוֹל, great	1.14, 15 ~ 3.1, 8 ~ 4.7 ~ 6.11 ~ 7.12; 8.2
גֶּפֶן, vine	3.10 ~ 8.12
דבר, speak	1.1, 6 ~ 1.7, 9, 13, 14 ~ 2.2 ~ 2.7, 8 ~ 4.1, 4, 5, 6, 8 ~ 5.5, 10 ~ 6.4, 8 ~ 6.9 ~ 7.1, 4, 7, 8, 12; 8.1, 9, 16, 18
דֶּרֶך, way	1.4, 6 ~ 3.7
הֵיכָל, temple	6.12, 13, 14, 15 ~ 8.9
הלך, walk	1.10, 11 ~ 2.6 ~ 3.7 ~ 5.10 ~ 6.7 ~ 8.21, 23
הֵם, they, these	1.5 ~ 1.9, 15 ~ 3.8 ~ 4.5, 10 ~ 5.10 ~ 8.6, 10, 23
הַר, mountain	4.7 ~ 6.1 ~ 8.3
זָהָב, gold	4.2 ~ 4.12 ~ 6.11
זָמַם, purpose	1.6 ~ 8.14, 15
חֵן, grace	4.7 ~ 6.14
טוֹב, good	1.13, 17 ~ 8.19
יָד, hand	2.13 ~ 4.9 ~ 8.9, 13
יָד(בְּ), by/with the hand	~ 2.5 ~4.10, 12 ~ 7.7, 12; 8.4
ידע, know	2.13, 15 ~ 4.5, 9, 13 ~ 6.15 ~ 7.14
יָמִין, right	3.1 ~ 4.3, 11
יסד, to found/establish	4.9 ~ 8.9
יצא, to go out	2.7 ~ 4.7 ~ 5.3, 4 ~ 5.5, 6, 9 ~ 6.1, 5, 6, 7, 8 ~ 8.10
ישׁב, to inhabit	1.11 ~ 2.8 ~ 2.11 ~ 3.8 ~ 5.7 ~ 6.13 ~ 7.7; 8.4, 20, 21
כֹּהֵן, priest	3.1, 8 ~ 6.11, 13 ~ 7.3, 5
כֹּל, all	1.11 ~ 2.17 ~ 4.2, 10, 14 ~ 5.3, 6 ~ 6.5 ~ 7.5, 14; 8.10, 12, 17, 23
כָּנָף, wind, skirt	5.9 ~ 8.23
מָה, what	1.9 ~ 2.2, 4 ~ 4.2, 4, 5, 11, 12, 13 ~ 5.2 ~ 5.5, 6 ~ 6.4
מָה(כְּ), as, what	~ 2.6; 7.3
נוח, rest	5.11 ~ 6.8
נחל, inherit	2.16 ~ 8.12
נחם, comfort, relent	1.17 ~ 8.14
נתן, to give	3.7, 9 ~ 7.11; 8.12
נשא, to lift up	2.1, 4 ~ 2.5 ~ 5.1 ~ 5.5, 7, 9 ~ 6.1 ~ 6.13
סָבִיב, surrounding	2.9 ~ 7.7
עֶבֶד, servant	1.6 ~ 2.13 ~ 3.8
עבר, to go out	3.4 ~ 7.14

Word/Phrase	Zechariah
עור, to wake up	2.17 ~ 4.1
עין, eye	2.1 ~ 2.5 ~ 2.12 ~ 3.9 ~ 4.10 ~ 5.1 ~ 5.5, 6, 9 ~ 6.1 ~ 8.6
על, with, on, upon	1.2 ~ 1.8, 15, 16 ~ 2.13, 16 ~ 3.1, 4, 5, 9 ~ 4.2, 3, 11, 12, 14 ~ 5.3 ~ 5.11 ~ 6.5 ~ 6.13 ~ 7.14
עמד, stand	1.8, 10, 11 ~ 3.1, 3, 4, 5, 7 ~ 4.14
עשה, to do	1.6 ~ 2.4 ~ 6.11 ~ 7.3, 9; 8.16
פה, mouth	2.4 ~ 5.8 ~ 8.9
פנה, in front of, before	2.17 ~ 3.1, 3, 4, 8, 9, 4.7 ~ 5.3 ~ 7.2; 8.21, 22
צפון, north	2.10 ~ 6.6, 8
קדש, holy	2.16, 17 ~ 8.3
קנא, to have zeal, be jealous	1.14 ~ 8.2
קצף, angry	1.2 ~ 1.15 ~ 7.12; 8.14
קרא, call	1.4 ~ 1.14, 17 ~ 7.7, 13; 8.3
קשב, to listen, heed	1.4 ~ 7.11
ראה, see	1.8, 9 ~ 2.1, 3 ~ 2.5, 6 ~ 3.1, 4 ~ 4.2, 10 ~ 5.1, 2 ~ 5.5, 9 ~ 6.1, 8
ראש, head	2.4 ~ 3.5 ~ 4.2 ~ 6.11
רב, many, multitude	2.8, 15 ~ 8.4, 20, 22
רוח, spirit, wind	2.10 ~ 4.6 ~ 5.9 ~ 6.5, 8 ~ 7.12
רחב, width	2.6 ~ 5.2
רחמים, compassion	1.16 ~ 7.9
רעה, evil	1.15 ~ 7.10; 8.17
שׁים, to set, place	3.5 ~ 6.11 ~ 7.12, 14
שׂמח, rejoice	2.14 ~ 4.10
שבעה, seven	3.9 ~ 4.2, 10
שבעים שנה, seventy years	1.12; 7.5
שוב, to turn, return	1.3, 4, 6 ~ 1.16 ~ 4.1 ~ 5.1 ~ 6.1 ~ 7.14; 8.3, 15
שכן, to dwell	2.14, 15 ~ 8.3, 8
שלח, to send	1.10 ~ 2.12, 13, 15 ~ 4.9 ~ 6.15 ~ 7.2, 12; 8.10
שלום, peace	6.13 ~ 8.10, 12, 16, 19
שם, name	5.4 ~ 6.12
שמים, heaven	2.10 ~ 5.9 ~ 6.5 ~ 8.12
שנה, year	1.1, 7 ~ 1.12 ~ 7.1, 3, 5
שני/שנים/שתים, two, second	1.1 ~1.7 ~ 4.3, 11, 12, 14 ~ 5.9 ~ 6.2, 13
שׁמע, near	1.4 ~ 3.8 ~ 6.15 ~ 7.11, 12, 13; 8.9, 23
שקר, to swear falsely	5.4 ~ 8.17
תוך(ב), (in) the midst	2.8, 9, 14, 15 ~ 5.4, 7, 8[iv] ~ 8.3, 8
תחת, under	3.10 ~ 6.12

i. ~ indicates a section break (the sections being 1.1-6 ~ 1.7-17 ~ 2.1-4 ~ 2.5-9 ~ 2.10-17 ~ 3.1-10 ~ 4.1-14 ~ 5.1-4 ~ 5.5-11 ~ 6.1-8 ~ 6.9-15 ~ 7–8.23. This roughly follow Meyers' and Meyers's division of the text but treats chs. 7 and 8 as one narrative viewing it as all part of one large scene (Meyers and Meyers do not extensively divide this section marking changes at 7.1-6~7.7-14~8.1-7~8.18-23). Meyers and Meyers view 4.6b-10a as an insert, but proceed to analyse it as part of the narrative section that spans ch. 4.

This is a somewhat arbitrary list composed of words which appear significant for interpretation. This does not even begin to be comprehensive in respect to all the words which are repeated throughout Zech. 1–8. Bergdall (1986: 208) as well as Meyers and Meyers (1987: liii) list verbal links between the visions and chs. 7 and 8. See the numerous charts in Butterworth (1992) for a listing of words that are repeated within the sections he discerns.

ii. Even-Shoshan (1989) cites all of these as derivatives of the verbal root אחר.

iii. The word occurs as part of the proper noun 'Beth-El' (בית־אל). With the frequency of this leitmotif, this occurrence is at least a word-play on בית ('house'). The prominence of the theme of building Yahweh's house in Zechariah makes reading בית־אל as a word-play even more attractive, especially in the context of the house of El inquiring from the priests and the prophets of the house of Yahweh Sebaoth (לבית־יהוה צבאות; 7.3). Even if historically there was no sanctuary at Bethel at the time, that there once was one provides an intertextual construct for a reader familiar with the Tanakh to notice this irony.

iv. This is the only occurrence of תוך in Zech. 1–8 which lacks the inseparable preposition ב.

Fluctuating Lists: Zechariah 1.1/1.7; 6.10/6.14; 1.8/6.1-7

The text of Zechariah 1–8 is even in flux with such simple things as lists of names.[46] In 1.1 the word of Yahweh is to זכריה בן־ברכיה בן־עדו ('Zechariah, son of Berechiah, son of Iddo'). Just six verses later, the word of Yahweh is to זכריה בן־ברכיהו בן־עדוא ('Zechariah, son of Berechyahu, son of Iddo'). Why has a suruq been added to Berechiah (ברכיה changes to ברכיהו) and an aleph been added to Iddo (עדו changes to עדוא)? Fowler suggests that shortened and full forms existed for some biblical names (1988: 150), but might this change in the spelling of Zechariah's ancestors signify something else?

Commentators often note Zechariah literally means 'Yah(weh) remembereth' (Mitchell 1980: 107) or 'Yahweh has remembered' (Fowler 1988: 90; Petersen 1984a: 128). Fowler suggests that theophoric

---

46. Interestingly, this same phenomenon occurs in Haggai, which is held by some (Pierce; Meyers and Meyers) to have the same author/redactor as Zech. 1–8 (compare בן־שאלתיאל in Hag. 1.1 with בן־שלתיאל in Hag. 1.12).

names formed from the roots זכר or ענה 'express that the deity remembered' 'the request of the parents for a child and has granted that request' (1988: 90). Similarly 'names denoting that the deity "has blessed" may well refer to the blessing of the parents by the gift of a child' (so ברכיה[ו]; Fowler 1988: 90). Tatford extends the etymologies to Berechiah, which means 'Yahweh has blessed' (Tatford 1971: 1; see BDB, 140), and Iddo, which means 'the appointed time' (Tatford 1971: 1; while Iddo is somewhat problematic, it may mean, more literally, 'his time', 'his count', 'until it', 'it again'). Reading the etymologies semantically, a story is presented in which Yahweh has remembered (something) and blessed it. Possibly, Yahweh remembered his count— an allusion to Daniel's observation that in the first year of Darius the 70 years which Yahweh revealed to Jeremiah for the completion of the desolation of Jerusalem was completed (Dan. 9.2)—and subsequently blessed the Israelites. How Yahweh blessed the Israelites is uncertain. If one extends the context to include Ezra, the remnant lives in the promised land again, and the etymologies suggest Yahweh remembered his count and blessed his people by returning them from exile (Ezra 1–2). Of course one cannot prove the author of Zechariah intended these etymologies to allude to Ezra when he wrote his work, but they are all valid, and somewhat encouraged in the mind of a modern reader familiar with biblical literature by v. 1's dating formula and genealogy.

Perhaps a way forward is to examine other changes in names in Zechariah. Another list of names in flux is that of the returned exiles.[47]

Zech. 6.10

לקוח מאת הגולה מחלדי ומאת טוביה ומאת ידעיה ובאת אתה ביום ההוא
ובאת בית יאשיה בן־צפניה אשר־באו מבבל

Zech. 6.14

והעטרת תהיה לחלם ולטוביה ולידעיה ולחן בן־צפניה לזכרון בהיכל יהוה

A focus on the words which have actually changed explores the significance of difference.[48] If one reads this text as history, then a change in names reflects a change in actual physical people who are acting or being acted upon. While a similar concept occurs in novels, novels also

47. See Petersen's (1984a: 278-79) as well as Meyers' and Meyers' (1987: 339-346, 364) discussion of the change of names in these verses.
48. Driver proposes these are corruptions of the names in v. 10 (1906: 214-15). Demsky, on the grounds of Aramaic, Old, Middle and Neo-Assyrian cognates, suggests לחן is a title and Josiah was 'in charge of the cultic apparel in the Temple of Jerusalem' (1981: 102).

have the added dimension of allowing the reader to inscribe significance into the names of characters. Lodge says, 'In a novel names are
never neutral. They always signify, if it is only ordinariness' (1992: 37;
see his discussion on 35-40; Sternberg [1985: 330ff.] discusses how
biblical names are essential to plot). Even if the characters in Zechariah
are historical figures, the work may still play on the names for stylistic
effect. This is seen in the common biblical device of changing the
names of its characters (for example, Abram to Abraham [Gen. 17.5],
Sarai to Sarah [Gen. 17.15], Jacob to Israel [Gen. 32.29]). Similarly, the
meaning of names sometimes plays a significant role in biblical narratives, even if only as a leitmotif, as is seen in the story of Isaac (note
Gen. 17.17; 18.12, 13, 15; 21.6, 9; 26.8).

Examining occurrences of proper names as stylistic features in the
minor prophets, Eybers discovers 8-13 places where the meaning of a
proper name is used as a pun, and 9-16 places where proper names were
used as paronomasia (1971–72: 92). Eybers believes Babylon is referred to as שׁנער ('Shinar') in 5.11 because he perceives paronomasia
between שׁנער and רשׁעה in 5.8. This identifies the רשׁעה ('wickedness')
as belonging to Babylon (see Eybers 1971–72: 91).

Moving to Zechariah, BDB lists חלד as meaning 'duration, world
(lifetime)' (317), חלם as the verb 'dream' (321), יאשׁ as 'despair'
(384),[49] and חן as 'favour, grace' (336). The חלדי of 6.10 becomes חלם
in 6.14. The occurrence of any word with a consonantal base of ח, ל
and מ in a book as surreal as Zechariah is instantly attention grabbing
because of its similarity to חלם ('dream'). If one reads חלד as the root
of חלדי then חלדי 'my world, my duration, my life' has become חלם, a
'dream'. Is the text somehow hinting at the dreamlike quality of the
book, which it cannot obviously write because of prophetic condemnations of other prophets' dreams (as Jeremiah's condemnations; see the
section 'Why Zechariah Uses Pastiche')?

Zechariah also changes יאשׁיה to חן. BDB lists יאשׁ as meaning 'despair' (384), and חן as meaning 'favour, grace' (336). BDB lists אשׁיה
'(support) buttress' as the root of יאשׁיה and lists יאשׁיה as meaning
'Yahweh supporteth' (78).[50] So יאשׁיה ('Yah's despair' or 'Yah supporteth') has become חן 'grace, favour'.

I sometimes wonder if 6.14 is the goal of the entire book, as is suggested by the establishment of a זכרון ('memorial/remembrance') in a

___

49. BDB reads the root of יאשׁתה as אשׁיה '(support) buttress' (78).
50. CHD lists 'tower' as the meaning for אשׁיה (412).

book entitled זכריה ('Yah remembers'). Furthermore, the visions end
once Zechariah is given the command to make a memorial. A sense of
completion is achieved—an inclusio between the word of Yahweh to
זכריה ('Zechariah', 1.1, 7) and the זכרון ('memorial') to be constructed
(6.14). Tollington believes Zechariah is identified with Moses in receiving silver and/or gold as offerings in relation to the temple/tabernacle
and these serve as a remembrance (1993: 124). A new Moses receiving
a memorial certainly seems to suggest a sense of climax.

As discussed above, Zechariah does the exact same thing with the
often noted changes in the lists of the colours of the horses. Many commentators have spoken on the blatant similarities between the two passages (1.8/6.1-7). The connectives between these passages are extra-
ordinarily conspicuous: red and white horses (1.8 סוסים אדמים...ולבנים/
6.2 סוסים אדמים/6.3 סוסים לבנים); 'the messenger who speaks with me'
(המלאך הדבר בי 1.9/6.4); Zechariah asks the question 'what are these
my lord' (מה־אלה אדני 1.9/6.4); and the concept of the horses going to
'roam in the earth' (להתהלך בארץ 1.10/6.7). Further, both passages
concern 'All the earth'—the horses report *all the earth* is quiet in 1.11,
whereas the horses present themselves before the Lord of *all the earth*
in 6.5 (see Petersen 1984a: 272).

A weaker link is that the events of ch. 1 take place 'between the
myrtles' (בין ההדסים; 1.8, 11) and the chariots of ch. 6 go out from
between two bronze mountains (מבין שני ההרים; 6.1). In addition to the
link of events occurring between places (another predominant link in
Zechariah 1–8 which this study has not taken up as extensively as it
could, and on which a similar interpretational matrix is produced as the
reading of רוח), there is the similarity of sound and appearance between
הרים and הדסים. The Septuagint's reading of 'mountains' (τῶν ὀρέων)
in 1.8 could be an attempt to reconcile these two scenes. Finally, the
same root is used in 1.8 and 6.1-2 (רכב ['ride', 1.8] and מרכבה ['chariot', 6.1, 2]). Incidentally, the same verb, רכב ('to ride'), is used to
describe the activity of riding, whether it be on horses or in chariots
(see Gen. 41.43; 2 Chron. 35.24). Though the verb is absent from ch. 6,
it is part of the semantic field of the noun מרכבה ('chariot').[51] These
two passages appear to form an inclusio for the visions that centre
around horses. That coloured horses are 'in the chariots' (במרכבה; 6.2,
3) suggests that the coloured horses of Zechariah 1 may be the same

---

51. See Meyers and Meyers for more examples of links between these two
scenes as well as vision 4 (1987: 332-34).

horses which pull the chariots in Zechariah 6. But more horses are involved in both visions. Why have the horses been described differently (שְׂרֻקִּים [1.8], שְׁחֹרִים [6.2], בְּרֻדִּים אֲמֻצִּים [6.3])?

Some may think this study has overinterpreted the variable spellings of names, on grounds such as Millard's: 'the use of vowel-letters and variability in spelling were optional in the alphabetic writing of ancient West Semitic languages' (1991: 114). It is difficult in a text such as Zechariah to recognize the limits of such word-play. I have difficulties in accepting that all of these changes in proper nouns are scribal errors, as Meyers and Meyers suggest for the change from Heldai to Helem (1987: 340). If these are scribal errors, then the scribe who copied Zechariah at this stage must have been nearly blind. This practice is so predominant in Zechariah that it is difficult to ignore. It does not appear haphazard. Rather, it appears to be, dare I say, a deliberate avoidance of writing the same list twice. The meaning of the changes in the lists of names is not as important as the fact that they are another element in flux. The implied author of Zechariah will not let a stable world exist. Nor will he let words be stable.

Petersen describes motion as a prominent feature in Zechariah's visions; 'Things are on the move. To be sure, not all the visions are filled with movement, but even the so-called static visions function to enable movement in the visions which follow' (1984b: 199). Zechariah uses this as a compositional practice all the way down to the lexical level: not even proper nouns are immune to Zechariah's desire to undermine stability. Zechariah keeps enough stability between the lists to make the changes noticeable and create confusion in the mind of the reader. The stable elements, such as בֶּן־צְפַנְיָה ('son of Zephaniah'), טוֹבִיָּה ('Tobiah') and יְדַעְיָה ('Jedaiah') in the example of the horses, allow the reader to recognize the similarity between the two lists, and then pause and cause for reflection on the differences between them. The lists provide a hermeneutical lesson to the reader. As the lists are constantly in flux, so are the rest of the words in Zechariah 1–8.

The Temporal Aspect

Another obstacle to determining the syntax or grammar of the symbolism is the related task of determining the chronology of the visions. A vision, by nature, can refer to the past, or the future (for example, Micaiah sees a vision of the past in 1 Kgs 22.19-23 and a vision of the future in 1 Kgs 22.17; Daniel sees visions of the future in Dan. 10.14–

12.7). Beyond the initial chronological indicator of 1.7 (the twenty-fourth day of the eleventh month of the second year of Darius), there are no temporal indicators of the material in the visions. The difficulty is determining the story. The text does not specify whether these events occurred before this date, are happening at this date, or will happen after this date.

On the historical legitimacy of these dates, Carroll says:

> the complexity of the visions suggests a considerable degree of reflective construction in their making and this factor in turn undermines the datings in the text. Unless the temple elements in the visions are purely literary or textual constructs (i.e. midrashic in the sense of being derived from text about the temple rather than elicited from experiences in an actual temple), then they presuppose a setting in a temple built in the past rather than in the process of being rebuilt or proposed for rebuilding. The visions are too convoluted to be as stated in the text (1994: 42).

While it seems certain that Zechariah, the (fictional) character *sees* the visions on this date, that is the temporality of the discourse, it does not specify when the events which are recorded in the visions will take place or have taken place. Leupold raises this issue in regards to the man who measures Jerusalem: 'Is the Jerusalem to be measured the actual or the future city?' (1971: 53). Leupold concludes it is the future city (1971: 54), but that he raised the question displays the chronological problems inherent in the visions. Seybold draws attention to this problem of the vision's chronology when he says, 'eine Nacht bildet den zeitlichen Rahmen der Erlebnisse, nicht der Gesichte' ('one night forms the temporal frame of the experience, not of the sights') (1974a: 109). Obviously, he sees the visions as operating in a chronology different from the narration. But this chronology is not indicated in the text: it is a readerly construct. Does Zechariah see visions of things that have taken place, are taking place, will take place, or a mix of some or all of these temporalities?

Furthermore, are the visions chronologically sequential? That is, do the events in the first vision take place after the events in the second vision, or are they just seen by Zechariah in this order and the events they depict occur at various times?[52] The answer to these questions

---

52. Koch sees an interrelated geographic and temporal progression over the course of the entire vision sequence: 'Geographically, events begin in the west and move over the centre of the earth to the east. This progression in space may perhaps correspond to a temporal sequence: evening (sunset, the west), midnight (the north),

affects the plot which the reader forms from the significance she has imputed to the symbols. This answer would also help limit whether one could interpret certain acts as poetic justice and a fitting reversal, or symbolically equivalent and representative of the same event.

While some of these difficulties have already been encountered (for example, in the similarity of the spreading of Zion and the spreading of the four winds of heaven), another example of the difficulties this engenders is provided by the often noted parallel scenes of the first and final visions. The similarities lead Richter to postulate, 'diese beiden Visionen ursprünglich eine Einheit bildeten und erst später von einem Redaktor in zwei verschiedene zerlegt wurden' ('originally, these two visions were one and were only later divided into two [visions] by a redactor') (1986: 96). He goes further and reconstructs an 'original' text which includes 1.8-15; 2.10-17; and 6.1-8. This reconstruction of an original text is highly conjectural. It is not the existence of an original text which is my concern. Rather, the process of a reader uniting these two texts in an attempt to join them betrays the same desire to discern a chronology for the events in the text.

It is predominantly the presence of multicoloured horses in each of the visions that encourages the reader to connect these two scenes (but see the list of connectives for this passage in the last section). If one connects the two scenes, the horses of ch. 1, when harnessed to chariots, may become the four winds of heaven in ch. 6.[53] But which scene takes place first? Many commentators attach martial connotations to the chariots of ch. 6 (Petersen 1984a: 265-67; Meyers and Meyers 1987: 317-19). The general gist of this interpretation is that Yahweh is exercising his martial might, somewhat similarly to the casting down of the horns in vision 2, to set aright the unacceptable world state which was reported by the horses in ch. 1. (The unacceptability of these world conditions is displayed by the outcry of the messenger in 1.12.) In this reading, the similar vocabulary serves as a second divine commissioning scene that initiates a fitting reversal of the situation depicted in ch. 1. In this reading, the initial commission of the horses, that sent

morning (sunrise, the east)' (1983: 171).

53.   Petersen says the chariots are the four heavenly winds (1984a: 269). He sets the scene as 'We have just missed a divine council scene and are now privy to the imminent enactment of its decisions' (1984a: 270). Galling, on the other hand, says the chariots are *not* the four winds (1964: 120 n. 2) but correspond to the four heavenly directions (1964: 120).

them on the mission they report on in ch. 1, is not depicted in the text. The horses have returned from completing this mission, delivered their report in Zechariah 1, and then are keen to correct the current injustice they have observed in ch. 6: they seek to roam the earth, but this time harnessed to chariots.

Fleming reads similarly:

> The reader meets Yahweh's roving patrol again. The first vision depicts the roving patrol returning with a message for [the divine] assembly. This vision [6.1-8] finds the roving patrol preparing to depart after the council had commissioned it in verse 5 (1989: 236).

Overall, 'an agenda initiated in the first vision finds its fulfilment in the last vision. That agenda is restoration and comfort' (Fleming 1989: 197). The horses are then spies in ch. 1, who have become martial figures once they are harnessed to chariots: the spies have become the avenging warriors of Yahweh. Yahweh's chariots do have martial connotations associated with them in intertexts (Isa. 66.15; Jer. 4.13). And yet perhaps chariots were seen as a suitable vehicle for Yahweh's spirit to be transported in. It is of interest that both of these passages depict hostile situations, lending more credibility to Petersen's as well as Meyers' and Meyers' military readings of 'chariot'. Jeremiah 4.13 also links chariots to speed. Perhaps it because they are speedy that chariots are mentioned in Zechariah. My point is not to deny that a military connotation may be present in this text, but to deny that it is the only interpretation, or even the interpretation that lends itself most readily to the situation.

The proleptic reading of ch. 6 is not the only temporal reading. In ch. 6 the horses seek to walk the earth and are granted their request. (Once again the speaker is equivocally indicated in 6.7. Who grants the horses the right to roam the earth: the messenger or the Lord of all the earth?) The text then states that they did indeed walk in the earth (6.7). The net result of their walking in the earth is that they cause the spirit of the speaker to rest in the land of the north. If one interprets the individual who grants the horses the right to roam the earth as the Lord of all the earth, and since they presented themselves before this individual it does seem the most likely interpretation, then, as the Lord of all the earth is identified with Yahweh in its occurrences,[54] it seems that it is Yahweh

---

54: אדון כל־הארץ ('Lord of all the earth') only occurs six times in the Tanakh: Josh. 3.11, 13; Mic. 4.13; Zech. 4.14; 6.5; Ps. 97.5. It is only in Zechariah that this

commissioning the horses in ch. 6. In 1.10 the horses are identified as those Yahweh sent to walk the earth. Both chapters seem to depict the same activity.[55] That the horses report on this activity in 1.11, and indicate they have walked the entire earth—'We have patrolled the earth, and lo, the whole earth remains at peace' (NRSV)—may be taken to indicate the activity commissioned in ch. 6 is being reported on in ch. 1. Chapter 6 is, by this reading, analeptic, and not an indication of Yahweh setting the world aright: the horses' report in ch. 1 depicts the results of their commissioning in ch. 6. Yahweh sets the world aright with the artisans; the chariots are not needed to accomplish this task.

That הלך ('walk') in the hithpael, as found in chs. 1 and 6, is never unequivocally used of military activities, and rarely occurs in a military context, further supports this non-martial interpretation of the activities of the chariots. It is related to travelling (Judg. 21.24; 1 Sam. 23.13; 30.31; Ps. 105.13),[56] ethics (Gen. 6.9; 17.1; Lev. 26.12; Isa. 38.3; Ps. 26.3; 101.2) and spying (Josh. 18.4, 8). The chariots and horses are said to התהלך ('walk to and fro, wander') rather than engage in martial activities. The results of their action appear to conform more to the transportational and reconnaissance aspects of הלך: they transport the spirit of the speaker, probably Yahweh, to the land of the north, and return with their report. The corral seen in ch. 1 would then be the horses reporting the results of their sojourn in the chariots.[57] This also would imply that Yahweh's spirit was at rest in the land of the north (6.8) in the past, and perhaps the present, rather than being set to rest during the narration of the vision in ch. 6, that is, on the twenty-fourth day of the eleventh month of the second year of Darius. Would the horses' presence by the מצלה ('deep') in ch. 1 thereby return Yahweh's spirit with it? Yahweh's statement 'I have returned to Jerusalem' (third-person masc. sing. of שוב) in 1.16 makes more sense then: Yahweh has been

---

individual is not clearly identified as Yahweh. Since the other occurrences unanimously identify this phrase as Yahweh's epithet, and Zechariah has no evidence to counter the claim, I will accept this entity as Yahweh.

55. So Meyers and Meyers (1987: 332).

56. A parallel to this passage is found in 1 Kgs 11.22. There Hadad asks Pharaoh to send (שלח) him to his own land. Pharaoh replies and asks why he is seeking to go to his own land (מבקש ללכת אל־ארצך).

57. Press similarly links the two passages to create a story in which 'Die Himmelswagen bringen dem Manne, den Sacharja zwischen den "Bergen" stehen sieht' (1936: 43).

brought back with the horses of vision 1 (this might also suggest a location for the vision: Jerusalem).

There are (at least) two options for the plot which the reader can construct surrounding the two commissioning scenes of the horses: one sees ch. 6 as analeptic, the other as proleptic. Depending on which chronology the reader applies to the plot, she will interpret the symbols and the narrative differently.

A central problem in discerning Zechariah 1–8's chronology of events is the final clause of 6.15: 'This will happen if you diligently obey the voice of the LORD your God' (והיה אם־שמוע תשמעון בקול יהוה אלהיכם). This verse has been debated as to whether it applies to the first half of this verse ('Those who are far off shall come and help to build the temple of the LORD; and you shall know that the LORD of hosts has sent me to you'), the final pericope (6.9-14), or the entirety of the visions (1.7–6.15). If one takes this verse to apply to the entire vision complex, then the visions are contingent upon this obedience. They are, thereby, contingent visions of the future. This plays havoc with the interpretation of perfect verbs throughout the visions. They are not completed actions, but contingent actions to be completed once the obedience has occurred. All of the visions are thereby proleptic. That Yahweh has zeal for Jerusalem and Zion (1.14), that he returns to Jerusalem,[58] that he is waving a hand over the plunderers over the nations, that he has come or is coming (2.13), and every other act in Zech. 1.7–6.14 is contingent on Yahweh being obeyed. Zechariah sees a *possible* world and restoration, rather than a world that has been, or is being, restored. Yet still the perfect verb tense troubles me.

If the clause in 6.15b only applies to 6.15a, then it is a self-fulfilling prophecy. Part of the implied audience[59] is in other lands (see 1.3[60] [that

58. The verb שבתי is problematic. While practically all agree it is a qal first-person singular perfect, whether or not it refers to the past (so Bič 1962: 26), present or is a prophetic future (Sellin 1930: 435) is a debated point (Mason 1977a: 38; Meyers and Meyers 1987: 123; Rudolph 1976: 79-80; Waltke and O'Connor 1990: 31.6.2b).

59. For discussions of the implied audience of Zechariah, see Ruffin (1986: 49-52, 221-23); and House (1990: 237-39; House identifies the implied audience of the book of the Twelve most closely with the remnant, but also with 'nations and sinful Israel' [203-17]).

60. Holladay views 1.3 as a covenantal use of שוב ('turn, return', 1958: 141). Petersen views this as ambiguous and entailing both a geographical and metaphorical aspects of Yahweh's demand for the remnant to שוב ('return') to him. Thus, this

the ancestors are abroad may be the gist of 1.5b]; 2.10-13, 15; [6.15?];
7.14; 8.7-8 [8.20-23?]). That the remnant is the implied audience is
indicated in Zech. 8.6, 11. This remnant appears to live in both Jerusalem (6.10) and abroad (8.7). Yahweh has demanded they physically
return to him (1.3; 2.6, 7) in Jerusalem (8.3). Obviously if they return,
then they have fulfilled what Yahweh promised will happen.

The demands Yahweh makes in Zechariah 1–8 are quite minimal.
Zechariah is commanded to declare some proclamations (1.3, 14, 17;
6.12) and to take silver and gold from the exiles, enter Josiah's house,
make crowns, and set one on Joshua's head (6.10-11). Joshua is
promised a conditional boon: if he will walk in Yahweh Sebaoth's ways
and keep his commandments he will rule Yahweh Sebaoth's courts and
have access to those standing at the scene (3.7). Yahweh commands
Zerubbabel to rely on his spirit (that is, Yahweh Sebaoth's spirit) rather
than strength or power (4.6). The ancestors of the implied audience, or
the implied audience (this is another place where the audience is ambiguous) are commanded to practice lovingkindness (חסד) and compassion (רחם) to one another and not to oppress widows, orphans, resident
aliens, or the poor nor plan evil in their hearts against one another (7.9-
10). Yahweh demands that the implied audience turn to him so as not to
be like their ancestors (1.3-4), flee from the northland (2.10), and let
their hands be strong (8.9; presumably to build, but perhaps to engage
in all kinds of crafts?). Zion, a part of the implied audience, is commanded to escape from Babylon (2.11). Yahweh commands the daughter of Zion, a portion of the implied audience, to sing and rejoice (2.14;
the daughter of Zion may be the implied audience of the previous verse
as well, since Babylon is in the north). Yahweh demands all flesh to be
silent (2.17; are animals thereby part of the implied audience?).

Yahweh specifically delineates what is demanded of the implied
audience in 8.16 with the words 'These are the things you will do' (אלה
הדברים אשר תשו). They are not commanded to return to the former
covenant (in fact the word ברית ['covenant'] is curiously absent from
Zechariah) but to 'Speak the truth to one another, render in your gates
judgments that are true and make for peace, do not devise evil in your
hearts against one another, and love no false oath' (8.16-17). Finally the
house of Judah, another part of the implied audience, is commanded to
celebrate four feasts (8.19). The entirety of Zechariah is a very elabo-

is a demand for the remnant to physically return to Jerusalem and to ethically return
to Yahweh (1984a: 131-33).

rate structure to say, basically, speak the truth, judge justly, do not think evil, and PARTY! Even the building of the temple can be considered a part of this overarching goal: the temple is to be built so that the festival can be held. If the implied audience does all of these things, then the festivals will occur.

Some of the temporal difficulties are embroiled in the symbolic nature of Zechariah 1–8. Henry says 'in the ideation process temporal "properties" such as past and present have little meaning...[and] work against...a linear time line. The accumulation of images and thus of new meaning is time independent' (1990: 97). Craig says similarly of Zech. 1.7–6.15:

> readers are directed above the historical landscape of transgression and retribution to a series of eight extraordinary vision reports where mundane space and time are in refrain... In contrast to specific chronological reminders of the time of subjugation (to the Persian King Darius), here readers are launched into the ahistorical space and time of YHWH (unpublished: 9-10).

The symbolic nature of Zechariah 1–8, the difficulty of identifying the temporality of a vision, and the contingent nature of the visions all contribute to make it very difficult to determine the chronology of the visions in Zechariah. One cannot determine if the events follow a continuous chronology (the events occur in the order in which they are narrated by the discourse, for example, the chronology of the visions is 1-2-3-4-5-6-7-8), or are anachronistic (the discourse narrates the events in a chronological sequence different from that in which they occurred, or will occur).[61] The visions in Zechariah conform to Genette's category of achronisms: 'episodes entirely cut loose from any chronological situation whatsoever' (1971: 98). They follow the temporal dimension of Zechariah's seeing them (the discourse), but the temporal situations to which they refer are indeterminate.

The oracles in Zechariah also contribute to the difficulty of determining the chronology. Marks says:

> in the oracle, as opposed to the Romantic lyric, the temporal, narrative and allegorical dimensions are all omitted (or better, to use the language of the epitaph poem itself, 'bypassed', transgressed—though they still continue to operate at the level of expectation (1990: 77).

---

61. See Genette (1971: 96ff.) for a discussion of these two types of narrative temporalities.

Marks goes so far as to postulate that prophecy 'represents the abroga-
tion of temporality' (1990: 70). If so, then the nature of Zechariah's
genre resists temporal mapping. Prophecy is the expression of a desire
for change, for a utopia, but like all desires, especially those for utopia,
this desire will never rest; not even in the land of the north.

One final problem with establishing the temporality of Zechariah is
the reader's relationship to the sheer quantity of repeated vocabulary.
Brooks says that repetition 'appears to suspend temporal process, or
rather, to subject it to an indeterminate shuttling or oscillation which
binds different moments together as a middle which might turn forward
or back' (1989: 288). Repetition is a textual energy which 'can become
usable by plot only when it has been bound or formalised... Repetition
can take us both backwards and forwards because these terms have
become reversible: the end is a time before the beginning' (Brooks
1989: 290-91). Brooks has hit on the central notion which underlies
repetition when he declares 'repetition works as a process of *binding*
toward the creation of an energetic constant-state situation which will
permit the emergence of mastery' (1989: 289; his italics). How does
one begin to bind the incredible abundance of repetition in Zechariah
1–8? The flow of time is constantly subverted in the reader's mind with
every repeated word and phrase and lexeme, and so on, in the book. It
becomes very difficult to bind textual elements to times to use those
bound elements to construct a plot. The text is antilinear. This antil-
inearity creates a situation in which the reader cannot *master* the text,
but is mastered by it: the reader is defeated by a text which refuses to be
imprisoned in the reader's plot.

Zechariah and the Reader: Dumb and Dumber

Throughout the vignettes symbolism predominates. I later discuss how
the author which I have constructed for Zechariah 1–8 is self-conscious
of his belatedness to the prophets (see the section 'Zechariah's Remembrance of Things Past'). The text is also conscious of the difficulty of
understanding its symbolism. This is manifest in various ways.

Eleven times in the booklet Zechariah asks a question about the
object he sees (1.9; 2.2, 4, 6; 4.4, 5, 11, 12, 13; 5.6, 10; 6.4). Zechariah
remains ignorant throughout the visions, and it is only in the visions of
the clothing of Joshua and the flying scroll that Zechariah does not ask
a question about the meaning of the vision. Even though Zechariah
could identify the object in the vision and does not question the con-

versing messenger on the vision's import, the conversing messenger proceeds to supply an interpretation of the vision (5.3-4). Similarly, there are explanations provided in the vision of ch. 3 as well. The 're-clothing' ordeal is explained as the removal of iniquity (3.4). The significance of the 're-clothing' is indicated by the admonishment to Joshua in 3.7. A further possible significance for the 're-clothing' is Yahweh promising to remove the iniquity of the land in one day (3.9), which may also be taken as an hermeneutic example. Joshua may be taken to stand as synecdoche for the land, as both have iniquity removed from them (though different words for removed are used to describe what is done to Joshua [hiphil of עבר] and the land [מוש]). This might suggest reading the other symbols as synecdoche. As mentioned above, 4.10b provides an interpretation of the stone of 3.9. That interpretations are supplied in these chapters that lack questions from Zechariah suggests that these visions are not self-explanatory.

In 1.9 the messenger who speaks with Zechariah tells Zechariah he will show him what a vision means (אני אראך מה־המה אלה; 1.9). The messenger's choice of words is interesting here. Zechariah had already seen the sight and described it (1.7), yet the messenger still says he will show (ראה) Zechariah what it means. There is no problem with Zechariah's sense of sight, rather, it is with his comprehension. Even so, it is the man between the myrtles and the horses themselves, not the conversing messenger, who tell Zechariah their importance ('These are those whom Yahweh sent to patrol the earth' and 'We have walked in the earth and behold all the earth is sitting [or inhabited] and quiet'; 1.10-11). Even then the full significance of these horses is not revealed until the entire scene plays out, and the reader realizes this is a lamentable state of affairs because it appears that Yahweh was not acting on behalf of Jerusalem and Zion. Perhaps this is how the messenger 'shows' Zechariah what they mean. That is, the messenger shows Zechariah the full significance of this scene by letting the entire scene play out before Zechariah's eyes. This would imply the messenger is causally responsible for the rest of the scene playing. This makes the messenger who speaks with Zechariah into a kind of projectionist, who lets the film roll before Zechariah. Yet the film is more akin to a David Lynch production than a 'straightforward' run-of-the-mill Hollywood production.

Zechariah usually asks the messenger who speaks with him 'what are these [my lord]' [אדני] מה־אלה (1.9; 2.4; 4.4; 6.4) or 'what is this'

מַה־הִיא (in the vision of the ephah). In some visions he asks more than one question: in the second vision he asks first of all 'what are these?' (מַה־אֵלֶּה) and on seeing the horns he asks 'what are these coming to do?' (מַה־אֵלֶּה בָּאִים לַעֲשׂוֹת; 2.4). In ch. 4 Zechariah asks three questions after seeing the lampstand and olive trees: 'what are these my lord?' (מַה־אֵלֶּה אֲדֹנִי; 4.4), 'what are these two olive trees on the right and the left of the lampstand?' (מַה־שְּׁנֵי הַזֵּיתִים הָאֵלֶּה; 4.11) and 'what are the two streams of olive oil which empty out through the gold spouts upon them?'[62] (מַה־שְׁתֵּי שִׁבֲּלֵי הַזֵּיתִים אֲשֶׁר בְּיַד שְׁנֵי צַנְתְּרוֹת הַזָּהָב הַמְרִיקִים מֵעֲלֵיהֶם הַזָּהָב; 4.12). In the fifth vision he asks not only 'what is this?' (מַה־הִיא; 5.6) but also 'where are they taking the ephah?' (אָנָה הֵמָּה מוֹלִכוֹת אֶת־הָאֵיפָה; 5.10).

From the first vision until the last, Zechariah, the prophet and narrator, is ignorant about the importance of the sights he sees and sometimes even about what he is seeing. Obviously seeing the object does not provide enough information about its significance. This lack is displayed by his questions. Petersen, speaking about Zechariah's questioning the conversing messenger in 1.9, says this question shows that 'the vision is not at this point self-interpreting' (1984a: 144). These are not symbols which an ancient reader would quickly understand, and which we do not understand because we are modern readers: this symbolism is equally confusing to all readers. Zechariah, in seeking explanations for the visions, stands in the text for the reader and shares the reader's confusion. Amsler says of Zechariah's confusion, 'Cet aveu fonctionne d'ailleurs dans le récit comme un facteur retardateur qui renforce l'attente du déchiffrement' ('Moreover, this functions in the account as a retarding factor that reinforces one's expectations of decipherment') (1981: 362). He describes this focus on deciphering the enigma of Zechariah as 'défi à la curiosité' ('defying curiosity') (1981: 362). Zechariah is a foil to the conversing messenger: Dr Watson to Sherlock Holmes. His confusion parallels the reader's confusion (see Amsler 1981: 362) as does Watson's confusion. His questions draw attention to how confusing these symbols truly are. In the fashion of Holmes, the conversing messenger explains to Zechariah the import of these atypical nocturnal occurrences. The analogy ends here because Holmes does explain the minute details and the series of events miraculously 'makes

62. As translated by Petersen who adds, 'Verse 12 is abysmally hard to translate' (1984a: 215 n. e).

sense' after Holmes describes what has occurred. This does not happen in Zechariah.

Pyper's comments on David's conversations with Nathan and the woman of Tekoa are pertinent here. He says they 'represent acts of interpretation by a character, reflecting to the reader her or his own acts of interpretation' (1993: 163). He examines the use of these as hermeneutical guidelines and concludes:

> We seem to be presented with a model of interpretation which is inconclusive, and which is complicated by being caught in the infinite interplay of reflection between two stories which have a parodic relation, like an image multiplied endlessly between two mirrors (1993: 164).

Zechariah similarly presents an inconclusive interpretational model but guises itself as an equivocal interpretation. Anticipating the discussion of the next chapter, when other intertextual forces are brought into this metaphor, there are often many, many stories which mutually reflect each other: a house of mirrors. The result is the same—infinite interplay—but the trajectories of light bounce from text, to text, to text, back to the first text, and off again to another text, endlessly.

Another item which demonstrates the text is conscious of the difficulty of its symbolism is the conversing messenger's use of interrogative statements. The messenger interrogates Zechariah in 5.2. In 5.3-4 Zechariah receives an explanation without asking for one. Perhaps the messenger felt Zechariah's answer to his question in 5.2 was inadequate and filled in the details missing from Zechariah's response. Zechariah's continued ignorance eventually results in the messenger asking Zechariah what he sees as if to ascertain whether Zechariah can indeed see or not and suggests the import of the vision is not known to Zechariah (4.2; 5.2). If one accepts the *kethib* (ויאמר, 'and he said') rather than the *qere* (ואמר, 'and I said') in 4.2, then the messenger asks what Zechariah sees, and then describes what he himself (that is, the messenger) sees (the *qere* and *kethib* are ancient attempts to sort out the problems of identifying the speaker in this verse). It is as if the messenger is giving Zechariah a lesson in seeing visions. He first asks him what he sees, and then, without waiting for a reply, tells Zechariah what he himself sees (a lesson for the reader in the hermeneutics of visions?). This reading is based on the *kethib*. If one reads with the *qere*, then Zechariah dictates the vision. Either way, my reading is not that different. If one accepts the *qere*, then the messenger has all the more reason for amazement. Zechariah has told him what he saw, and still does not understand.

The messenger asks again in 5.2 what Zechariah sees, but in ch. 5 he allows Zechariah to answer the question himself. While the messenger who speaks with Zechariah amicably shows him the importance of the sights he sees in the early visions, by the fifth vision he seems bewildered, and perhaps exasperated, that Zechariah does not know what the lampstand, bowls, lamps and olive trees mean (4.5, 13). After all, he has already dictated what he himself (that is, the messenger) saw.

The messenger not only seems bewildered, but even evasive. When first asked what they mean, he asks 'Do you not know what these are' (Zech. 4.5; NRSV),[63] and then proceeds to dictate a word of Yahweh to Zerubbabel, and a word of Yahweh to Zechariah, which are scarcely related to the vision of the lampstand, if at all. The only lexical connection is ראש ('head'). Furthermore, 4.10 relates more to the vision in ch. 3 (3.9) than ch. 4. How should the reader fill in this gap? The conversing messenger was absent from ch. 3. He left in 2.10 (he went out [יצא]) to meet the other messenger in 2.7) and returned (שוב) in 4.1. This might provide an explanation for 4.10, which is often viewed as an interjection. Perhaps it is added to the messenger to explain information that was not provided in ch. 3 and which Zechariah could not ask the conversing messenger because the conversing messenger was not present in ch. 3. When Zechariah asks the messenger specifically what the two olive trees are, he receives no reply and must ask a third question: 'What are these two branches of the olive trees which pour out the oil through the two golden pipes?' (4.12, NRSV). That the messenger waits so long to answer Zechariah could be interpreted as his waiting for the right question. It is the focus of the question which is important: it is when Zechariah asks what the שבלי ('branches') of the olive trees are, rather than just the olive trees, that he receives his answer (Zech. 4.12). Even then he receives a second chastisement—'Do you not know what these are?' (NRSV)—before he receives an answer. The situation is somewhat akin to a child in school being chastised by a teacher: 'Don't you know what that means?' Zechariah is even depicted responding in a downcast fashion, 'No, my lord' (לא אדני; 4.5, 13).

---

63. A somewhat parallel passage to this is Jesus' bewilderment at the disciples' ignorance in Mk 4.13.

The significance of these temple objects has been discussed.[64] Carroll's cautions concerning the lampstand are pertinent to this matter:

> whether the details of the menōrâ and the things associated with it in Zechariah 4 should be accepted as technical information about the physical contents of the second temple or whether we (i.e. modern readers of the text) should read the text as symbolic reflection on the temple literature is a matter for much debate (1994: 42).

He stresses, 'the force of these visions is a symbolic one rather than a literal description of the temple furniture' (1994: 42). Zechariah's lampstand may be pure fiction. To return to the lampstand, that gold is flowing from one of the 'funnels' certainly suggests this. This brings the reader to one of the difficult issues in interpreting Zechariah: when does the symbol become the literal and vice versa? Some verisimilitude is necessary in texts to orient the reader. But when does Zechariah stop relating to 'real' ancient Near Eastern life and objects and enter the world of its symbols? The lampstand is a perfect example of its hazy boundaries. One can interpret the object flowing out as gold in 4.12, or one can see it as representing golden olive oil. Which is right?

This ignorant state of the prophet is somewhat parallel to the depiction of Daniel's ignorance after a vision (8.27; 12.8; see Freer for a discussion of the 'motif of seeking understanding' in Daniel [1975: 82-86]). Freer compares this motif to Zechariah's quest for understanding and finds:

> the pattern of questioning in Zechariah is much less developed than 'seeking understanding' is in Daniel... Although this pattern exhibits a superficial similarity to Daniel's seeking an interpretation by asking an intermediary (7.15-16), the questions to the interpreter in Zechariah are direct and do not use words like 'truth' or 'understanding', in a technical sense (1975: 84).

Curiously, truth (אמת) is also a recurring motif throughout Zechariah 7 and 8 (7.9; 8.3, 8, 16, 19), though the context in Zechariah 7 and 8 is not concerned with the interpretation of visions. It is strange for a text that is so opaque to stress truth: What is the truth this text is so concerned about and how is the reader to identify it?

The net effect of all this ignorance, at least on this reader, is to suggest that these things are incomprehensible to the narrator/protagonist, who is the implied author of the work. Two questions present them-

---

64. See Smith (1964: 5); van der Woude (1974: 266); North (1972a: 186).

selves. (1) Is this an incompetent prophet? (2) Are these things supposed to be comprehensible to the implied reader, who does not possess
authorial omniscience or prophetic cognizance? The answer to these
questions depends on which character the reader identifies with. Psychoanalytical film theory has convincingly undermined assertions that
viewers necessarily identify 'with the protagonist when viewing a film.
Rather, viewers constantly switch the characters they identify with in
accord with their desires, lacks and repressions' (Donald 1989: 137-38
[see the whole article]; likewise Greig 1989: 186; and Lyon 1989: 151).
It is not a great leap to suggest this shifting of identities occurs in reading literature as well as in viewing films.

Readers oscillate in their identifications with different characters
depending on a multitude of personal psychological reasons (really for
the same reasons one individual likes another whom they have only
seen or heard, but never spoken to). The conversing messenger implies
that Zechariah is a little slow-witted and should understand these
visions. If the reader understands the symbolism she might agree with
the conversing messenger's implication that Zechariah is dull-witted
and imperceptive (but good luck finding a reader who will understand
the symbolism). If the reader shares Zechariah's bewilderment in the
face of these visions (as I do) and thereby identifies with Zechariah,
then she is chastised by the conversing messenger's questions along
with Zechariah. Does the reader not know what these are? Or, she
might see these statements as a veiled critique of the divine camp and
of prophetic texts. The divine camp produces texts which are difficult to
understand and expects the reader to understand them. This is indicated
in the frame of Zechariah's understanding of prophecy. Yet the material
contained in those divine revelations is confusing. The divine camp
expects the reader to understand and is bewildered when a reader does
not. Does this imply the divine camp does not understand humanity?

The answers Zechariah receives to his questions, the so-called explanations of the visions, do not clarify the symbols they interpret: they do
not make the text easier to understand. Enlightenment is not suddenly
attained with these interpretations. The example of the four horns will
be used here to illustrate the difficulties present in interpreting all the
visions.

The Second Vignette: 2.1-4

ואשא את־עיני וארא והנה ארבע קרנות 2 ואמר אל־המלאך הדבר בי
מה־אלה ויאמר אלי אלה הקרנות אשר זרו את־יהודה את־ישראל וירושלם ס

3 ויראני יהוה ארבעה חרשים 4 ואמר מה אלה באים לעשות ויאמר לאמר אלה
הקרנות אשר־זרו את־יהודה כפי־איש לא־נשא ראשו ויבאו אלה להחריד אתם
לידות את־קרנות הגוים הנשאים קרן אל־ארץ יהודה לזרותה ס

Zechariah's second vision is extremely enigmatic. He lifts up his eyes
and sees four horns. He asks the conversing messenger 'what are (of)
these?' The conversing messenger replies that these horns scattered
(winnowed)[65] Judah, Jerusalem and Israel. How does a horn scatter or
winnow a land, people or a city? The initial explanation does not make
sense. Thankfully, the vision continues, and Zechariah sees four artisans. But how is an artisan related to a horn? Zechariah also has difficulty with the relationship between these images and must ask 'what
are these coming to do?' Before delivering this information to Zechariah, Yahweh[66] first expounds on the role of the horns: these are the
horns of the nations that winnowed Judah so that a man could not lift
his head.

Yahweh is reticent on what the horns did to Israel and Jerusalem. He
may be politely contradicting his messenger, hinting that the horns only
scattered Judah, but did not scatter Israel and Jerusalem, as the messenger stated in 2.2. Or he may be elaborating on the role of the artisans
and how they have come to terrify and cast down the horns which scattered Judah but not necessarily the horns which scattered Israel and
Jerusalem. The direct answer to Zechariah's question is that the artisans
come to act upon the horns: to throw them down and to terrify them (or
to make them tremble; BDB, 353). While Yahweh technically answers
Zechariah's question, does this answer make the vision much more
comprehensible, if at all? Yahweh's answer does provide more information to use in interpreting the horns: the horns belong to nations.
Nonetheless, it is a very confusing answer. Knowing that artisans come
to terrify and throw down the horns of the nations that are lifting a horn
to the land of Judah to scatter it (to the extent that a man could not lift
his head) does not enlighten the reader as to what the horns *signify*. This

65: זרה can mean either scatter or winnow (BDB, 279).
66.   Some want to read this character as the messenger of Yahweh, but the text
clearly states it is Yahweh who shows Zechariah the artisans.

supplies more questions than answers. It brings into play other lines of
thought that start the reader on other lines of inquiry.

The reader previously wondered what the horns signified. Now,
knowing that these horns belong to the nations, she is confronted by
new questions. How does a nation have a horn? How does a horn winnow the land of Judah? Winnowing is a cultural activity undertaken by
men and god in the Tanakh and only here in Zechariah does a natural
object perform this act. Does the fact that an object performs this act
point to a symbolic rather than literal reading? What does it mean for
Judah to be winnowed so that a man cannot raise his head? How do
artisans make a horn tremble? Is there any significance to the number
four? Needless to say, the interpretation of the vision which Yahweh
and the messenger provide raises many questions, rather than ending
them. In fact, it increases the ambiguity: there are even more possibilities of what the horns might mean. The reader only had to interpret the
symbolism of horns on nations in vv. 1 and 2. Now she is faced with
further metaphors. The vision remains cryptic. It is surreal. As with
Dali's art, it is not obvious why the objects in Zechariah are pictured
together. Part of the artistry of Zechariah 1–8 is the challenge it poses to
the reader: why have these incongruous images been painted together
on the narrative canvas? Another aspect of the artistry is the beauty of
the extraordinary.

This section will analyse how one can make sense of this pericope on
intratextual grounds, in order to control the interpretation. The goal is to
examine how one can make sense of these symbols while, basically,
staying within the boundaries of the text under consideration. This is
not as simple a task as it might seem to be, for I am not a native speaker
of classical Hebrew. Some intertexts will be consulted in this task, but
these are principally to analyse the linguistic aspects, that is, the semantic fields of words, rather than to import an entire intertextual context.
That is to say, the intertexts are consulted for linguistic purposes, and to
demonstrate linguistic similarities, rather than to intertextually link the
two texts. This is a working distinction adopted for heuristic reasons as
it is ultimately a false dichotomy between inter- and intratexts: the act
of reading the intertext places it in some capacity in the reader's mind
(as the discussion above established), and the linguistic similarities do
indeed link the texts in some capacity. The issue is one of context: in
the so-called 'intertextual' interpretations offered later on in this work,
the goal is to incorporate visual contexts which readers imagine and

which may inform Zechariah. An example of an intertextual context would be Ezekiel 40–48's temple building and division of Jerusalem. A linguistic link would be noting that a precious stone is part of a crown in 2 Sam. 12.30.

A secondary goal will be to demonstrate how within the confines of Zechariah 1–8 these symbols are not unequivocally explained. This may seem like a defeatist gesture, but it arose out of the attempt to make the text mean. With this failure, I decided to pass on the negative results as this monograph. No matter what the outcome of its production, I have failed in my task before I described it. An appropriate title for this monograph, other than the one given, might be '(Anti)thesis' or 'A Diary of Failure'.

Horns (קרן) do not occur elsewhere in Zechariah 1–8. One could view the use as synecdoche for the object to which it is attached (for example, as an altar[67] or cow). Unfortunately, the only object in Zechariah to which a horn might be attached is a beast (בהמה; 2.8; 8.10). These two passages do not help interpret the horns of Zechariah 2. Thus to interpret the function of 'horns' in Zechariah 1–8 intratextually one must look to what function it performs, rather than the noun itself.

Since the horns belong to the nations, the other uses of nations (גוים) in Zechariah 1–8 might help in understanding the activity of the horns. In 1.15 Yahweh is angry with the nations at ease (הגוים השאננים) who helped Yahweh for evil. (Note the sound similarity with the הגוים הנשאים of Zech. 2.4.) The secure nations are depicted as the nations lifting a horn to the land of Judah. In 2.12 the nations are plundering (participle of שלל) and touching (participle of נגע) the implied audience (presumably Zion, as it was identified as the audience in 2.11). The close context of 2.12-13 (2.10-17 is often viewed as the oracle which brings together the first three visions), and the use of participles for both נשא and שלל, suggest that the activity the horns are engaged in when they lift a horn is plundering Judah. This is concomitant with the activity of winnowing: the goal of winnowing is to extract the good from the chaff. How a horn is used in this activity will be investigated in my next chapter. The nations at ease are the ones raising a horn to the land of Judah to winnow it and thereby plunder it.

---

67. Amsler takes the horns to belong to an altar (1972: 228).

How do horns winnow, or scatter, (זרה) so that a man cannot lift his mouth or head? In winnowing, grain is thrown up and the good is separated from the bad by the wind. In the qal this can be done with a winnowing fork (Jer. 15.7; Isa. 30.24; מזרה) or winnowing shovel (רחת; Isa. 30.24; BDB, 935).[68] In both the qal and piel this scattering or winnowing is often done to (ל) the wind (in the qal, Isa. 41.16; Ezek. 5.2; in the piel, Jer. 49.32, 36; Ezek. 5.10, 12; 12.14. Jer. 4.11 also associates wind with winnowing/scattering.), so it seems somewhat merited to believe that the wind is often an agent in winnowing or scattering when זרה is used. If this sense is kept for Zechariah 2, then horns scatter or winnow, that is, they throw Judah up into the wind so that a man cannot lift his head. This visual construction, when imagined, is violent and grotesque—the horns of the nations (be they bull, ram, goat, other beasts, or disembodied) are plunged into a man, who, presumably, is a synecdoche for all of Judah (though this is an interpretative decision), and throw him up into the wind. In 2.10 Yahweh spreads the implied audience like the four winds of heaven. If the similar term 'to spread' (פרש) in 2.10 is conceived as analogous to the horns winnowing of 2.4, the horns work in conjunction with Yahweh.

This theme is again picked up in 7.14, where Yahweh storms them (the implied audience) to all the nations (גוים) they did not know. Since storms (סער) occur with wind (Jon. 1.4; Ps. 55.9) another element falls into place in the interpretation of this vision. The horns winnow, that is, they throw a man of Judah to the wind. Yahweh then storms them, that is, he figuratively carries them away on the wind to the nations. Both Yahweh and the nations are involved in this act: they work together. This is indeed implied by 1.15 where the nations help Yahweh for evil.[69] All of these verses are mutually interpreting. The nations are Yahweh's 'instruments' (Ackroyd 1962: 647). It is ironic that Yahweh is angry with his partner in this crime. Brueggemann's comment about Babylon in Isaiah is also applicable in the book of Zechariah: 'God's very tool of exile has become the object of God's indignation' because Babylon is expected to know Yahweh demanded them to show mercy (רחם) for Jerusalem, even though they were not specifically told as such

---

68.   Seybold discusses the 'winnowing' aspects of זרה (1974b: 104).

69.   This creates an intertextual construct between Isa. 47.5-7 and the messenger of Yahweh's demand for Yahweh to show mercy to Jerusalem and the cities of Judah in Zech. 1.12.

(1991: 10). But is the role of the nations evil because of the extent of the scattering or because they are still raising a horn to the land of Judah?

A part of this difficult symbolism has been interpreted. But how does one make sense of the mixed metaphor—Judah is winnowed so that a man cannot lift up his head? In the act of winnowing the man's head should be thrown into the air. Is this man an individual, a specific individual, or does he stand as a synecdoche for the nation? Meyers and Meyers view the idiom as focused on the individual (1987: 141). Yet, they admit its collective sense as they say it focuses on 'the individual autonomy of *deported Judeans*' (1987: 141). Should I infer some sort of narrative lacunae so that the man is unable to lift up his head after he has landed hard on the ground, that is, he cannot lift his head because he is 'punch drunk' from the hard fall? Or, should I follow many commentators and simply view this as symbolic of the degradation of Judah and its subservience to the nations (which, incidentally, fits into the previous vision). I accept that it appears to be a symbol of degradation, but am still curious about what other connotations it holds. That the book of Zechariah does not allegorically interpret the symbol allows the reader the freedom to draw out further implications of the symbol. One might even say the use of a symbol demands such teasing out of its implications.

There are three avenues of approach in understanding this idiom. One can look up the occurrences of man (אִישׁ), lift (נָשָׂא) and head (רֹאשׁ) in Zechariah 1–8. The connotations of these words elsewhere in Zechariah 1–8 can then be brought back to Zechariah 2 to see if they aid interpretation.

The word 'head' (רֹאשׁ) occurs in three other places in Zechariah (3.5; 4.2; 6.11). In 3.5 a clean turban is set (שִׂים) on Joshua's head (עַל־רֹאשׁוֹ), along with garments. With this act Yahweh, in a prelude to cleansing the land of iniquity (3.9), removes Joshua's iniquity. In 6.11 crowns are set (שִׂים) on Joshua's head (רֹאשׁ). The word with pronominal suffix רֹאשׁוֹ is present in 2.4; 3.5 and 4.2. Does this suggest a cunning wordplay or hint to the reader that these passages should be viewed as related? In 6.12 and 13, if one equates Joshua with the man of v. 12, two other word-plays are present: אִישׁ ('man', 6.12) and נָשָׂא ('lift up', 6.13). The man in 6.13 bears (נָשָׂא) majesty. Is this a reversal of the scene of 2.4? In 2.4 a man cannot even bear/lift his head, whereas in 6.13 the man bears majesty. Is Joshua the man whose head cannot be lifted, in order that a crown could be set on it? ירד ('to go down') is an appropriate verb to describe the removal of a crown from a head (Jer. 13.18). Perhaps that the horns are lifted somehow prevents Joshua's head from being raised to be crowned. That a crown is set on Joshua's head might explain why the artisans are involved in throwing down the horns of the nations: they fashion a crown and thereby symbolically displace the ascendancy of the horns. Even though artisans (חרשים) are not specifically attributed with making a crown in the Tanakh, that the materials found in crowns (כסף ['silver'] and זהב ['gold']; Zech. 6.11) are worked on by artisans (Hos. 13.2; 1 Chron. 29.5) suggests they are the profession responsible for making crowns. Perhaps these artisans fashion the crown that Zechariah has made in 6.11. Perhaps Zechariah is the artisan (more below).

The other occurrence of ראש ('head') is the head-stone (האבן הראשה) of Zech. 4.7. Zerubbabel causes this to go out (hiphil of יצא; 4.7). The hiphil of יצא is used in Isa. 54.16 to describe the product of an artisan. This provides further evidence to view Zerubbabel as an artisan. That he הוציא the head-stone suggests he works it: he fashions it.[70] The precise definition of this head-stone is a matter of much debate. The outburst of הן הן לה ('grace, grace to it') in 4.7b[71] may be the encouragement of other artisans for the work which Zerubbabel has constructed when this text is read in the light of the continued commands to חזק in Zechariah (8.9, 13 read in the light of the use of חזק with a sense of 'encourage' in Isa. 41.7. In Isa. 41.7 artisans encourage [חזק] one another). Needless to say, not knowing exactly what a head-stone is makes it difficult to discern how this relates to the throwing down or

---

70.   E. Lipiński believes this verb is used to indicate the transfer of the stone to a repository (1970: 32).

71.   Le Bas sees this cry as elicited by the consummate magnificence of the object: he translates it to be a cry of '"beautiful, beautiful", the duplicated term expressing superlative loveliness. The corner-stone, as an architectural feature, would be a sculptured and polished work of art' (1950: 105; see 1951: 143). Further, Le Bas believes the seven eyes of Yahweh are the rejoicers and *not* the builders (= artisans?; 1951: 145). For interpretations of the eyes see Blenkinsopp ('seven planets'; 1984: 238), and Lipiński ('springs' [also עין]; 1970: 26-30). Oppenheim believes this is a theological take-over of the 'eyes and ears of the king' (1968: 175). They are analogous to the secret service of the King. Oppenheim believes Zechariah relates the riders, the chariots, and the Satan to this agency (see 1968).

terrifying of the horns in 2.4.[72] In this verse (4.7) a tall object (the great mountain) is made smaller (into a plain) as the uplifted horns are thrown down in 2.4.[73] A reversal of height is occurring and a crafted object is taking place at its top.[74] It is being 'raised' (though the root נשא ['to lift up'] is not used in Zech. 4.7) as the work of an artisan. There are at least symbolic similarities between the two incidents so one could speak of a theme of 'height' or 'altitude' changes. If the top stone is indeed the pyramidion, or something of the like (perhaps the top of a building), that the horns have scattered so that a man cannot raise his head may be taken to mean a man could not erect this headstone because of the horns. How horns have prevented this task is difficult to discern, but how an artisan can fulfil it is easy to imagine.

Another way to interpret this passage is to search out possible activities of חרשים ('artisans') in Zechariah. Rudolph defines a חרש as an 'Arbeiter in Holz oder Metall (Eisen) oder Stein...aber auch allgemeiner "Handwerker"' ('workers in wood, metal [iron] or stone... generally, "craftsmen/artisans"') (1976: 81 n. 3; likewise Sellin 1930: 437). Yahweh says he will engrave an inscription on the stone of 3.9.[75] חרשים (the artisans) engrave in stone (see Exod. 28.11; 2 Sam. 5.11). Perhaps Yahweh makes this engraving in Zech. 3.9 through the agency of the artisans. חרשים are responsible for making many of the objects found in Zechariah: they make lampstands (מנרה; Zech. 4.2, 11, 12; see Exod. 37.17 in accord with Exod. 35.35), lamps (נר; Zech. 4.2, 11, 12; see Exod. 37.23 in accord with Exod. 35.35), pedestals (מכונה; Zech. 5.1; see 1 Kgs 7.27-43 in accord with 1 Kgs 7.14); they stretch a line (נטה קו[ה]; Zech. 1.16/Isa. 44.13) and build (בנה) houses (בית; Zech.

---

72. There have been many interpretations of this stone; see Petersen ('former stone'; 1974: 368-70); Lipiński ('la première pierre' [which is lead]; 1970: 32-33); Petitjean ('an engraved foundation stone'; 1966: 53); van der Woude ('Mt. Zion'; 'Zion'; 1988: 241-42); and Le Bas (a 'pyramidion'; 1950: 105; see 107 for a listing of the options commentators have offered for the stone).

73. Petersen suggests that the adversary of Zerubbabel in 4.6b-7 may be Joshua as a word-play is occurring between the high priest (3.1; הכהן הגדול) and the great mountain (4.7; הר־הגדול; 1974: 367; contra VanderKam 1991: 566).

74. Isa. 40.4 similarly depicts mountains being levelled. Dan. 2.35 depicts a large object being cast down.

75. Harrelson suggests that either 'Holy to Yahweh' (as in Exod. 28.36-38; 39.30-31) or 'My Servant, Branch' is the inscription the stone of 3.9 will receive (1982: 120). Petersen suggests one reads (קדש ליהו; 1984a: 212). Henshaw says it is the name of the servant which will be engraved on the stone (1958: 250).

1.16; 5.11; 8.9/2 Sam. 5.11). 1 Kings 7.33 implies that artisans fashion chariot wheels (מרכבה; Zech. 6.1-8). While the exact role that the חרשים play in the manufacture of the priestly garments is difficult to discern in Exodus 28 and 35, they are involved in the production of these garments in some capacity (see Exod. 28; 35.30–36.7; 39.1-31). This is not to say that Joshua is necessarily clothed in priestly garments (though perhaps he is). Rather, Joshua is clothed in very fine garments of a standard which requires artisans to work on them. That Zechariah sees four artisans in the second vision is perhaps a prerequisite to the rest of the visions: these artisans are responsible for the manufacturing of the majority of objects seen in the latter visions.

Though some may find this highly conjectural, as it is, one may even attempt an identification of these artisans. The first artisan is Zechariah who is told to fashion (qal of עשׂה ['do']—*not* a causative hiphil or piel) a crown out of silver and gold (Zech. 6.11). Torrey claims 'one of the features of Zerubbabel's temple was a foundry' (1936: 247). Though this is extremely conjectural, perhaps Zechariah, who many commentators have noted may have priestly connections (based on Neh. 3.1 and 12.4; for example, Baldwin, who notes this with caution [1972: 60-61]), is a priest who works in the foundry of the temple. The obsession with metal and metal working throughout the book of Zechariah 1–8 may subtly betray this fact (artisans in 2.4; gold in 4.2, 12; 6.11; tin in 4.10; gold in 4.12; lead in 5.7, 8; bronze in 6.1; silver in 6.11; chariot in 6.1, 2, 3; and crowns in 6.11, 14). His obsession with headgear may label him as a worker who adds metal trim or features to hats. Zerubbabel is the second: he has founded the house (4.9; חרשים are part of the foundation laying process in Ezra 3.6-7). Exodus 35.31-35 also provides an interesting intertext for viewing Zerubbabel as an artisan. In Exod. 35.30-35. Bezalel is filled with the spirit of God (רוח אלהים) which provides him with many artistic skills including engraving (חרשׁת) in stone (אבן) and wood (עץ). This fullness of God's spirit provides Bezalel with the skill to fashion the paraphernalia for the temple and to teach others to fashion these items. Perhaps a similar infilling of spirit for Zerubbabel is implied by Yahweh Sebaoth's injunction 'Not by might, nor by power, but by my spirit' in Zech. 4.6. Zerubbabel is filled with Yahweh Sebaoth's spirit in order to be skilled to carry out his work.

After identifying these two individuals as artisans it becomes a bit forced to identify other artisans in the text. Perhaps the man with a measuring line is an artisan (2.5).[76] But this is based on an equivalence of stretching a line ([ה]וק נטה; Isa. 44.13) with carrying the measuring cord (חבל מדה). One may still see this as an individual trying to perform the measuring out by cord imagined in Ezekiel 47–48. Perhaps this is an artisan, but this is not a task necessarily performed by an artisan. This cord is usually employed in partitioning land (Deut. 32.9; Ezek. 47).[77] Ultimately though, this individual is foiled in his task and does not accomplish it. If one does not identify Joshua as the branch, then perhaps the branch is one of these חרשים as he builds the temple (בנה את־היכל; Zech. 6.12, 13). So, tentatively, but not conclusively, there are four artisans. At the very least, there is a theme of artistic activity running throughout the book.

Perhaps one could see the activities of the artisans as indicating how many there are. The objects which may be fashioned by artisans in Zechariah are stone (3.9), garments (3.4), a lampstand with lamps and a bowl (4.2), chariots and houses. These might relate to four different types of artisans Zechariah sees coming: a mason, a fashion designer, a metalworker and a builder. Together they provide the necessary skills to form the objects seen in the visions. Unfortunately the activity of the artisans seems unrelated to ch. 5: there is no basket weaver present to weave the ephah. Fortunately, there is an object with which artisans work: the ככר. A ככר is a measurement of metal. Metal is a medium artisans work with (see 1 Chron. 29.4-5). It is notable that ככר occurs with other precious metals numerous times in the Tanakh (silver, Exod.

---

76. P. Marinkovic holds on contextual evidence (Yahweh will be a surrounding fire, Jerusalem will be an unwalled city) that the man with the measuring line is involved in 'the construction of a city wall' (1994: 91-92 n. 13). Carstensen argues contrarily that 'the measuring line which the man (some think Zerubbabel) intends to use is not for building but for limitation, to mark the city's boundaries so that walls can be built' (1972: 505). Though he does not argue extensively for this, that Yahweh receives Judah as his portion in 2.16, and that a line is used for this kind of activity elsewhere (Deut. 32.9; Ezek. 47) is contextual evidence that suggests this reading is correct. The activity sustains an ambiguity as contextual evidence argues for both readings.

77. There are good reasons to see the text of Zechariah as a rebuttal of Ezekiel's picture of the restored Jerusalem. 'when a young man goes out with line to measure Jerusalem he is rebuked for setting his sights too low' (MacKay 1968: 199). There are many of what Riffaterre calls connectives between the two texts. For a full discussion of links between Zechariah (1–14) and Ezek. 40–48 (as well as other texts) see MacKay (1968).

38.27; gold, Exod. 37.24), but only occurs with lead (עפרת) in Zechariah 5. This suggests there is an abnormality with the lead stone of
Zechariah. That it is also called an אבן, a stone or a weight, suggests it
might be a heavy weight. It is either an abnormality, a designation
which is usually applied to a precious metal being applied to an ordinary metal, or an unjust weight. Either option implies corruption. Perhaps the artisans come to refashion it, to melt it down and end the
corruption.

We now move to other elements in the vision. Who might the man
be? Should one view this as a general expression meaning 'one' or look
to specifically identify the man? איש ('a man') occurs in Zech. 1.8, 10;
2.4, 5; 3.8, 10; 4.1; 6.12; 7.2, 9, 10; 8.4, 10, 16, 17, and 23. Do any of
these occurrences of איש correspond to the man in Zech. 2.4? If one
interprets Joshua in 6.11 to be the same character as the branch of
6.12,[78] then perhaps he is the man, the איש, of 2.4. By conflating the two
stories, Joshua becomes the man who could not raise his head (2.4;
6.11) in order to be crowned. The leitmotif of lifting up or bearing (נשׂא)
in Zech. 2.1-4 suggests an interpretation for the man. Zechariah frequently lifts his eyes throughout Zechariah (Zech. 2.1, 5; 5.1, 5, 9; 6.1).
If Zechariah is a man now lifting his head, do we encounter irony, or do
we understand that the horns' winnowing was preventing the seeing of
visions from occurring?

This interpretative maze stretches throughout the entire vision. After
pursuing the analysis, the reader does not understand what these metaphors (horns, artisans) represent. She is left 'high and dry' in a state of
bewilderment. Some meaning is attributed for the symbols, but they are
by no means allegorically explained. The fact that there is a multitude
of metaphors interpreting each other makes it difficult to understand

---

78.   The identity of 'the branch' is debated. Koch notes the term 'seems to have
been intentionally chosen as a word-play on the name Zerubbabel, "branch of
Babylon". But is it intended to indicate the *identity* of the two, or their antithesis?'
(1983: 164). Characteristically, the interpretational options are multitudinous and
most commentators say it is Joshua, Zerubbabel or 'someone else'; many claim that
editorial activity has been undertaken on these passages. For a discussion see
Amsler (1972: 227); Baldwin (1964: 95; see 95-97); Carroll (1979: 166-67); Harrelson (1982: 120-21); Haupt (1918: 211); Mason (1982: 147-48); Petitjean (1966:
63-71); Tollington (1993: 161, 172); and VanderKam (1991: 561). Suffice it to say,
it is uncertain who 'branch' is. Here is another portion of the text where Zechariah
refuses to identify a symbol and lets it drift around unattached to a concrete
signified.

when the import of the text focuses on the symbol and when on the referent: the reader is overwhelmed by metaphors and the options to interpret them. If a few of the metaphors had stable referents, it might be easier to interpret the passage. That *all* of the metaphors are somewhat loose produces 'metaphor stew'. This reader is left desiring to understand the text more: the text remains 'almost interpreted'.

Zechariah's Remembrance of Things Past: The Conception of Prophecy in Zechariah 1–8

Zechariah is a text which frequently reminds the reader of other texts. This awareness of other texts is betrayed in Zechariah in several ways:

1. In the dating formulas, which are the latest dates in the prophetic corpus with the exception of Haggai (Zech. 1.1, 7; 7.1). Only the material in Zech. 1.1-6 (eighth month of Darius's second year; Zech. 1.1) pre-dates the dates in Haggai (twenty-fourth day of the ninth month in Darius's second year; Hag. 2.10). The vision sequence (twenty-fourth day of the eleventh month in Darius's second year) occurs later than the events in Haggai.

2. In the narration of the results of past prophecies (1.3-6; 7.7-14; 8.14).

3. In the use of ביד ('by the hand'). One way the author betrays his self-conscious awareness of the literary role of his predecessors is in his description of Yahweh's words as proclaimed or sent ביד, by the hand, of the former prophets (Zech. 7.7, 12; see Mason [1977b: 414-15] for a discussion of the use of this phrase). Verhoef describes the difference between ביד and אל ('to') as that of between reception and communication (1988: 267 n. 25). While ביד is a well-known messenger formula, it seems to also hint at literacy, especially in postexilic works. At Belshazzar's feast in Dan. 5.5 it is a finger of a *hand* (יד) that writes (כתב) the message. Couple this with Neh. 8.14's discovery that was written (כתב) in the Law which Yahweh had commanded (צוה), by the hand (ביד), of Moses. Deuteronomy and Exodus exemplify this too, as they frequently make self-conscious statements that they are written works of Moses (Exod. 34.27; Deut. 28.58, 61; 30.10). Daniel appears to read 'the word of Yahweh to Jeremiah the prophet' from a scroll in Dan. 9.2. In the same chapter, Daniel relates how Yahweh gave his Law ביד ('by the hand of') his servants the prophets. Prophecy delivered by the hand is clearly being linked with literary creations. Though ביד is

missing from Zech. 1.6, there, as with Moses, Yahweh commands (צוה), his words and statutes by his servants the prophets. So ביד might mean, in the context of a messenger, the carrying of a written message. But clearly it also means the *writing* of a message. The formula sustains an ambiguity. The prophet's activity is even the same as the orator, that is, they קרא, they read or call their messages. In addition to being a messenger idiom, ביד could be seen, in modern terms, as handwriting. If this reading of ביד is adopted, the implied author displays his awareness of his *literary* precursors, the prophets.

4. In the threefold mention of the former prophets (Zech. 1.4; 7.7, 12; see 1.5-6).

5. In Zechariah's genealogy. Zechariah's genealogy betrays his indebtedness to his literary prophetic ancestors. He is identified as the son of Berechiah, the son of Iddo, the prophet בן־ברכיה בן־עדו הנביא (Zech. 1.7 uses *plene* spellings for Berechiah and Iddo [ברכיהו and עדוא]). There is debate over who the epithet 'the prophet' applies to, but it is usually attributed to Zechariah. Rather than reading it as solely applicable to Zechariah, however, in its present position it may indicate all three of the aforementioned individuals are worthy of the epithet 'prophet'. נביא ('prophet') is thereby an inherited title like 'Duke of Westminster'. At any rate, it displays the depiction of the implied author Zechariah as a prophet. Even if one applies the epithet to Iddo, this makes Zechariah a son or a grandson of the prophets, as opposed to Amos who denies all relationship to a prophetic office (using the term בן נביא, 'son of a prophet'). Zechariah is depicted as a descendant of the prophets but whether he is a prophet himself remains unclear.

6. In relating Zechariah to the prophets (נביא; 1.1, 7). This is usually interpreted as his claim to the office of the role of the prophet, that is, to imply he is fulfilling a social role. If he views the prophets as literary though, then he is claiming an authorial role. Prophets are then 'secretaries' or 'scribes' of Yahweh rather than spokespersons. This is still a social role, but it might even be pseudonymous authorship. The real author of Zechariah could be the local butcher. The ancient publishing industry would then only claim to have received this manuscript from a third party and to be circulating the document for the good of the community, rather than for an individual's prestige.

7. In the frequent referral to the implied audience's ancestors (אבות; Zech. 1.2, 4-6; 8.14).

Zechariah constantly refers to previous literary works.[79] As David Petersen, Janet Tollington and many others have demonstrated, Zechariah 1–8's frame, its prologue found in 1.1-6 and epilogue found in chs. 7 and 8, mirrors many Deuteronomic and prophetic themes, especially those of Jeremiah.

Petersen calls 1.1-6 'a pastiche of typical prophetic materials as those were known to the author of this part of the book of Zechariah: typical prophetic formulae, typical prophetic rhetoric, typical prophetic vocabulary' and concludes this is so to demonstrate 'Zechariah's place within this prophetic tradition' (1984a: 135). Beuken says 'Diese Einleitung besteht praktisch ganz aus stereotypen Ausdrucksweisen' ('This introduction consists practically entirely of stereotypical expressions') and proceeds to display his opinions on which traditions disparate elements of this pastiche come from (Levitical, Deuteronomistic-Chronistic, Deuteronomistic, Chronistic, Jeremianic-Deuteronomistic and Jeremianic [1967: 111]). Tollington calls 7.9-10 a 'pastiche of teaching typical of the pre-exilic prophets' (1993: 26; for a comprehensive analysis of Zechariah's use of previous traditions in composing his corpus see Tollington's work).

Almost every word, phrase and concept in this frame recalls earlier texts. Collocations like 'turn to me and I will turn to you', 'turn from your evil ways and deeds', 'my words overtook your ancestors', as well as a host of other phrases, echo Isaiah, Jeremiah, Ezekiel, Hosea, Joel, Obadiah, Zephaniah, Deuteronomy and other texts. Zechariah is a work self-consciously written in the style of a prophet and seems to (consciously?) allude to this body of literature. The assumption that these bodies of literature existed makes these comments in Zechariah references to past *literary* precursors rather than oral precursors (such is betrayed by Jer. 36 or Ezek. 3).

One could use Bloom's theories to explain psychologically Zechariah's dependence on his prophetic precursors. Bloom focuses on intrapoetic relationships and believes that poets strive to influence others while wrestling with the anxiety of having been influenced by their precursors. In order to gain a forum from which to influence, poets must

79. Fishbane similarly speaks of a canonical consciousness which is displayed in works like Zechariah that draw from previous traditions (his example is Zechariah's literal interpretation of Jeremiah's 70 years). He asks if these texts might be drawing on a textual canon, but contents himself with labelling these works a 'cultural (textual?) canon' (1980: 359-60).

deal with their dead literary precursors: they must wrestle with the anxiety of their predecessors' poetic influence, that is, the knowledge that the poet did not create him- or herself but is indebted to his or her precursors. Poems are thus responses to other poems: the meaning of a poem is another poem. Poets misread other poets to correct the original poem and clear space in society for themselves to occupy. Not even in the poetic world is there creation *ex nihilo*. More shockingly, in the case of Zechariah creation *ex nihilo* does not even exist in the revealed prophetic world.

But how is this genre that Zechariah is reacting to portrayed in Zechariah? The examination of one prophetic book's depiction of prophecy will yield an ancient conception of prophecy, rather than a modern extrapolation, as well as provide insight into what function the concept of 'prophecy' plays in the book of Zechariah.

In the frame of the visions (Zech. 1.1-6; chs. 7 and 8), Zechariah interprets prophecy as focused on predictions and their subsequent fulfilment. This is shown in the picture of prophecy which is produced by combining Zech. 1.1-6 with chs. 7 and 8. This composite picture is subconsciously produced in the minds of some readers (at least this one) while linearly reading the text. On account of his (great) anger (1.2; 7.12; 8.14) Yahweh sent his Law and words by his spirit (7.12). The spirit of Yahweh, which is the former prophets (7.12), demanded the ancestors to turn to him (7.13). These ancestors refused to listen to the prophets (1.4; 7.11-13) and were subsequently overtaken by the words and statutes which Yahweh commanded his servants the prophets (1.6). The implication is that Yahweh's word is sentient and continues to exert itself: past prophecies are still pending and still 'pursuing' their object. The result of the ancestor's refusal to listen to the prophets was, ultimately, that Yahweh scattered the ancestors among all the nations they did not know (7.14). The land was left desolate with no one passing through it (7.14). The ancestors accept this punishment and proclaim that Yahweh has dealt with them as he planned, and as their deeds deserved (1.6).

The efficacy of the prophetic word is stressed, one might even say laboured. As Yahweh planned, and presumably threatened to do, he did. While this is an issue of interpretation, presumably the rhetorical questions, 'your ancestors, where are they?... But my words and my statutes...did they not overtake your ancestors?' (1.5-6, NRSV) refer to the prophesied deportations of the implied audience's ancestors.

Nowhere in Zechariah 1–8 does Yahweh threaten to scatter or deport the people. It recounts that Yahweh scattered people (2.10; 6.10, 15; 7.11-14; 8.7-8, 13, 23), but to accept this establishment of the efficacy of the prophetic word, that is, to accept that Yahweh did indeed prophesy such things, the reader must form an intertextual construct with other prophetic works that predict Judah, Israel and Jerusalem being scattered among the nations. Such texts as 1 Kgs 14.15; Jer. 13.24; and Ezek. 6.8 are examples of prophetic texts which would fulfil this function for the reader. The implied reader must also accept, in Carroll's terms, the myth of the empty land and the myth of the impurely occupied land.[80]

The text assumes the reader is familiar with the prophetic corpus and that the reader interprets the prophetic corpus the same way it does; that is, it assumes the reader will also acknowledge that Yahweh's words overtook the ancestors, that the words of the prophets rang true. It further assumes that the reader accepts the prophets' ideologies. It does not allow the implied reader, nor the implied audience depicted in the book to question specific prophecies as unfulfilled—the reader is not allowed to reflect on the cognitive dissonance present. Carroll proposes that Haggai and Zechariah respond to the dissonance caused by the lack of fulfilment of earlier prophecies, notably the lack of the appearance of the new age (1979: 158-65). It is important to bear in mind that this document may be an example of Douglas Coupland's 'Legislated Nostalgia: To force a body of people to have memories they do not actually possess' (1991: 41).

Furthermore, this writing strategy is confessed in 8.9 when the implied audience, who are listening to these words from the mouth of the prophets, is addressed. While some postulate the prophets speaking would be Haggai and Zechariah, I view this as a self-conscious reference to the text's rhetorical style of incorporating previous prophetic concepts in its narration: a baring of the device.

However, the former prophets are not quoted verbatim. The prophets

80. See Carroll, 'A land empty over a lengthy period of time is simply a construct derived from the ideology of pollution-purity values in the Second Temple community. It ignores the social reality of the people working the land and living there because they do not belong to the sacred enclave. They are invisible in ideological terms...they have been marginalized because they do not belong to the deportation group which returned from Babylonia at a certain point in the past' (1992: 90).

are, in a sense, heard in Zechariah through the re-use of prophetic collocations, themes and formulae. When the character Zechariah speaks,
he constantly re-uses prophetic motifs so that one hears the echoes of
the prophets in his voice, but never unambiguously hears any one particular prophet (see Table 4). The prophets' voices are filtered through
the narrator Zechariah. The work contains many allusions to other
prophetic works found within the visions and recollections of the past.
Despite this constant appeal to prophetic authority, and near quotes of
their work, the final product is the voice of Zechariah. Only one prophet, namely Zechariah, is speaking. Only his voice is heard throughout
the book. So the former prophets are only permitted to speak through
the voice of Zechariah. He is the mouth of the prophets. And how are
the mouths of the prophets heard? Through narration, that is reading,
calling—קרא ing—the scroll(s) of the prophets, or recalling them in
one's own writing. But the only voice to hear is the voice of Zechariah.
And, of course, there is not even a voice, only the words on the page to
read, to קרא.

The entire prophetic corpus is blended into one entity and their individual differences are elided. The individuality of each prophet is
replaced with a corporate entity. Their differences are ignored, or at
least downplayed as they are blended together. Where many individual
voices once proclaimed their varying messages, now only one voice
speaks. The voices of Isaiah, Jeremiah and Ezekiel are now the monologic voice of the former prophets: they speak with the one voice of
הנביאים הראשנים ('the former prophets'). In this way the messages of
the individual prophets are merged together. Their distinctive attitudes
towards issues are presented as the composite attitude of the former
prophets, and ultimately, as Zechariah's message. Zechariah has over-
come his anxiety of influence by amalgamating his strong poets into
one identity and then into his work to make them serve his purposes.

Zechariah 1.5's rhetorical questions 'Your ancestors, where are they?
And the prophets, do they live forever?' are another indicator of the
work's sentience. The work is conscious that it stands in the shadow of
its strong poets, the prophets. It is overtly aware of the cultural force
inherent in the prophets' words. As Coupland says, 'Nostalgia is a
weapon' (1991: 151). The resonance and wonder that surrounds the
prophetic texts is understood all too well. The work suffers from the
anxiety of the prophets' influence and is in a belated struggle to replace
or displace the prophetic poets it wishes to succeed. It clearly marks its

character's place as their successor by calling him a prophet (1.1, 7). Not only does the work struggle to replace the prophets, but it silences them by implying they are all long dead—'and the prophets, do they live forever?' No one can voice dissent against the views of prophecy offered in Zechariah. This is a self-effacing question though, as it implies Zechariah himself will one day be dead and someone will be free to appropriate this work (John of the apocalypse comes to mind, as well as the present writer). At the same time, it asserts the eternality of its words: its purposes will be accomplished.

To write after the prophets, the book of Zechariah must re-negotiate their cultural influence.[81] To provide a literary space to work in, Zechariah enters into dialogue with the prophetic world by representing their words and image structures; it thereby undermines the prophetic world from within. By not copying the works verbatim the precursors are modified in the act of copying: they are given new connotations and a new significance. Zechariah's dialogue takes the form of an overt intertextual rivalry which self-consciously adopts the prophetic and primary historian's styles, the primary historian being the author or editor of Genesis–2 Kings. In (f)using them in this way, Zechariah ultimately modified and critiqued them. After reading Zechariah, one cannot read the preceding prophets in quite the same way again.

Zechariah 1–8 implicitly views prophecy as comprehensible. If not, how could the ancestors be condemned for disobeying previous prophetic proclamations? They must understand the text in order to obey it. No quarter is given for the notion that perhaps the messages of the prophets are intentionally incomprehensible, as Isaiah's message is depicted in Isa. 6.10, or as the sealed visions of Jer. 29.11 which are incomprehensible even to those who can read. Not only are the messages of the prophets comprehensible, they are totalitarian—they must be obeyed. This totalitarian viewpoint is characteristic of prophetic speech—the prophets claim to speak for God and demand to be heeded (this is not usually a winning personality trait). Zechariah does this by beginning the book היה דבר־יהוה אל־זכריה בן־ברכיה בן־עדו הנביא לאמר (1.1). This can be interpreted to imply the entire book is the word of Yahweh—not the humblest of ways to begin a book. The condemnation of past generations for failing to comply with previous prophetic proclamations implies that Yahweh will be angry with the implied readers of

---

81. See the work of Stephen Greenblatt (1988, 1989) for extensive examples of how cultural 'energy' is constantly undergoing negotiations for controls of its force.

the text if they fail to obey its dictates, as he was with the ancestors who refused to obey the former prophets who demanded them to act. By writing in the prophetic style, Zechariah is claiming this same totalitarian right to be heeded—it claims its protagonist is a servant of Yahweh, who possesses the spirit of Yahweh (7.12) and who speaks not only the words of Yahweh, but his Torah. It claims a privilege tantamount to Moses for this protagonist.

The frame makes one expect the book of Zechariah to proclaim a comprehensible message which can be obeyed. Yet, the message delivered in 1.7–6.15 is far from this. The reader is assaulted with a barrage of polyvalent symbols which disharmoniously echo the cacophonous voices of the prophetic precursors. Zechariah begins and ends with a totalitarian prophetic frame. In this frame prophecy is characterized by injunctions which must be obeyed in order for future threats to be avoided. The efficacy of the prophetic word is uppermost. Surprisingly, this frame is filled with an ambiguous message in which the symbols and syntax are unruly, indefinite and dreamlike. How is the reader supposed to understand and heed it? The text is being extremely unfair! The symbols refuse to be amalgamated into a neat, tidy allegorical scheme and defy the explanations given for them. The *mysterium* surrounding them is never dissipated.

Table 4. *A Very Small Sample of Zechariah's Intertexts*

Zecharian Theme	Zech.	Intertexts[i]
Yahweh was angry (קצף) with some ancestors	1.2	Isa. 47.6; 54.9; 57.16-17; 64.4, 8 (64.5,9e); Lam. 5.22
Yahweh issues an order to turn (שוב) to him and he will return (שוב) to them	1.3	Deut. 30.2-4; 1 Kgs 8.33-36
Admonishment to turn (שוב) from (evil [רעה]) ways (דרך) or (evil [רעה]) deeds (מעלל)	1.4	2 Kgs 17.13; Jer. 18.11; 23.22; 25.5; 26.3, 13; 35.15; 36.3, 7; Ezek. 33.11
The implied audience will not hear (שמע) or heed (קשב)	1.4	Deut. 30.17; Jer. 6.17, 19; 11.3; 17.23; 22.5; 26.5; 29.19; 36.31; Ezek. 2.7; 12.2
My servants the prophets (עבדי הנביאים)	1.6	2 Kgs 17.13; Jer. 7.25; 26.5; 35.15; 44.4; Ezek. 38.17 (to be precise, it reads here ישראל עבדי נביאי)
My commandments (משפתי) and my statutes (חק[ו]תי)	1.6	Lev. 18.4; 25.18; 26.43; 1 Kgs 6.12; Ezek. 5.6-7; 20.16-24
Overtake (נשג)	1.6	Deut. 28.2, 15, 45; Jer. 42.16

Zecharian Theme	*Zech.*	*Intertexts*[i]
Seventy years (שבעים שנה)	7.5	Jer. 25.11-12; 29.10; Dan. 9.2
I (Yahweh) would not listen to them (ולא אשמע)	7.13	Jer. 11.11; Ezek. 8.18
The land becomes a desolation (לשמה)	7.14	Isa. 13.9; Jer. 2.15; 4.7; 25.9, 11, 38; 44.22; 50.3; 51.43
Curse (קללה) among the nations (גוי)	8.13	Jer. 26.6; 44.8
Holy Mountain (הר קדש)	8.3	Isa. 11.9; 27.13; 56.7; 57.13; 65.11; 66.20; Jer. 31.23; Ezek. 20.40; 28.14; 43.12

i. Many commentators discuss how Zechariah has re-used previous themes and how the conception of prophecy changes in the Second Temple period to a focus on reinterpretation of previous prophecy; see Blenkinsopp (1984: 239, 256-67); MacKay (1968); Sinclair (1975: 42-45); and Tollington (1993).

Summary and Solution?

In the first vision Zechariah, in the night, sees a man riding on a red horse standing between myrtles in a glen. Behind him are red, white and sorrel horses. When Zechariah asks, 'What of these, my Lord?', he is told ' I will show you what these are' (1.9). A scene then unfolds and the man in the scene answers Zechariah's question by saying, 'These are those whom Yahweh sent to roam the earth' (1.10). This is the direct answer to Zechariah's question. But many threads of the vision remain unravelled and unexplained. Why is the reader never given an explanation of what the myrtles, colours or glen represent? Why the horses are multicoloured is never answered. That so many commentators have been drawn to comment on possible interpretations for the colours displays the search for significance these symbols elicit from readers. What is the significance of the מצלה ('the deep')? Why does Zechariah see these visions at night (is he asleep?)?

Only a small part of the symbolism is explained, and even that is not explained very adequately. The vision which follows expresses lament over a quiet and peaceful world (1.11-12). What type of warmonger laments peace? Why is a peaceful world a lamentable affair? The text goes on to explain that this lament arises because it signals a lack of compassion on Yahweh's part. Yet, I am still left in the lurch wondering why peaceful and quiet conditions (ישבת ושקחת) indicate a lamentable state of affairs. Does the text elsewhere (in another vision) interpret this, or must one seek an intertextual referent to clarify this issue?

More questions arise from the so-called interpreting oracle (1.14-17). How did the nations help for evil? What does the promise that a measuring line will be stretched over Jerusalem signify? Why does Yahweh promise that his cities will again be scattered from good (עוד תפוצינה ערי מטוב)? What does it mean for Yahweh to choose Jerusalem?

In 2.5-9 Zechariah sees a man with a measuring cord. How does this cord relate, if at all, to the measuring line of 1.16? Zechariah is told this individual's task is to measure Jerusalem to determine its width and length. He is halted from this task. Why? What does it mean for Yahweh to be in the midst of Jerusalem for glory (לכבוד)? How are the four winds scattered, and how does this relate to the scattering of the implied audience? What does 'after glory' (אחר כבוד) mean and why does Yahweh send the speaker of v. 12 in search of it? What is the significance of Yahweh being awoken from his holy place? Why does all flesh need to be silent now that he is awake?

Curiously, all the earth is to be silent (הס) before Yahweh when he is in his holy temple (בהיכל קדשו; Hab. 2.20). Is the holy temple in Hab. 2.20 the same locale as Yahweh's holy place in Zech. 2.17? If so, the situation is the opposite: in Habakkuk 2 all the earth is to be silent because Yahweh is in his holy temple, but in Zechariah 2 all flesh is to be silent because Yahweh is awoken from his holy place. The previous context discusses how an idol cannot be awoken (עור; Hab. 2.19). Is Yahweh 'awoken' in Zech. 2.17 to prove he is alive? Apparently so. In Zeph. 1.7 the audience is told to be silent before Yahweh (actually, אדני יהוה) because the day of Yahweh is drawing near. One could see the two intertexts as combined to show the day of Yahweh is near, which is symbolically depicted by Yahweh being awoken from his holy place.

The vision in ch. 3 is similar. What does it mean for Yahweh to rebuke an individual? What or who is the satan/adversary and why is he accusing Joshua?[82] What does it mean for Yahweh to rebuke Joshua's accuser. What does the metaphor of a brand plucked from the fire signify when applied to Joshua (3.2)? What is the significance of this re-clothing of Joshua? What is the significance of Joshua being clothed in מחלצות ('festal clothes') and a צניף ('turban')? What does it mean for Joshua to have 'walking privileges' or visiting rights (מהלכים) among those standing there (3.7)? What are men of a sign (אנשי מופת)[83] and

---

82. For a list of interpretative options see Day (1988: 117).

83. NRSV translates 'they are an omen of things to come'. Petitjean sees these individuals as priests (1966: 42). For a discussion of how these are men of מופת

how are these individuals this? What is the significance of men of a
sign or symbol in a text in which almost every entity is a symbol? Further, the sentence this occurs in is difficult to understand—these men
are a symbol, for behold I am bringing my servant, branch. The most
obvious character who is a symbol is (the) branch. Does this hint at a
self-consciousness in the text? One has a feeling that the author is playing with the reader; not in the deft overtly self-conscious style of
Calvino (1993), but through subtle implications which break the surface
of the text in various locations like this. Further, what kind of stone is
this which has seven eyes and contains an inscription, and what does
this stone have to do with the removal of the iniquity of the land?
Finally, what is the significance of closing this pericope on a statement
that people will call their neighbours to visit them under a vine and a fig
tree (3.10)?

When Zechariah asks about the import of the lampstand, bowl, seven
lamps and olive trees he is ignored at first. The answer he receives—the
oracle in 4.6-10b—is too complicated to consider here how it relates to
the question Zechariah asks. Most commentators treat the oracle as an
insertion into the text. At least a portion of this insertion answers a portion of Zechariah's question—'These seven are the eyes of the LORD,
which range through the whole earth' (4.10b, NRSV). How this answer
relates to the oracle is, as many have noted, problematic. But in a text
that is so problematic, is it fair to make consistency the guiding line by
which to make sense of the text? One of the few consistencies I see, is
incomprehensibility. Zechariah does receive one direct answer in the
oracle ('These seven are the eyes of the Lord, which range through the
whole earth' [v. 10b, NRSV]), but to a hypothetical question he never
asked: what is the stone before Joshua? Or does the response in 4.10b
describe the seven lamps or the seven wicks of 4.2?

After receiving this answer Zechariah again inquires, but this time
specifies precisely what he is curious about and asks the import of the
two olive trees. Not having received a reply to this second question,
Zechariah finally asks the import of the two branches of the olive trees
which pour out gold (or oil: Rost declares that זהב [gold] should be read
זוב [to flow] and might be related to the first pressing [of olives, pre-
sumably] [1952: 219 n. 1]). This is a fascinating choice of word. שִׁבֲּלֵי
may come from the root שִׁבֹּלֶת (flowing stream) or שִׁבֹּלֶת (ear of grain).

('signs') and how this relates to the crowning episode in 6.9-15, the references to
צמח ('branch'), and the diarchy, see Eichrodt (1957: 510-15).

This ambivalence results in multiplicity of translations. NRSV 'What are these two branches of the olive trees, which pour out the oil through the two golden pipes?'; JPS 'What are the two tops of the olive trees that feed their gold through those two golden tubes?'; NASB 'What are the two olive branches which are beside the two golden pipes, which empty the golden *oil* from themselves?'; KJV 'What *are* these two olive trees upon the right *side* of the candlestick and upon the left *side* thereof?'

The intertext of Judg. 12.6, in which שִׁבֹּלֶת is used to discern linguistic variance, is tough to repress in a text like Zechariah which plays with language so much, and which makes so many covert suggestions about its toying with language and difficult symbolism. In a vision which is so difficult to understand, one wonders if the text is once again teasing the reader on linguistic grounds: the reader may look to Judges 12 as a way to solve this dilemma, but ultimately fails in her search to distinguish the significance of this word here. It is ironic that in a text like Zechariah 1–8—where so many words relate to other words to an extent that it is difficult to determine their significance—there exists a reference to a text in which the mispronunciation of a single letter would result in death.

The answer Zechariah finally receives, after asking three times, is 'These are the two sons of oil who stand by the Lord of all the earth'.[84] Again, myriad questions arise. What exactly is being depicted here? Van Zijl says this, 'symbol is complex: Joshua and Serubbabel are the providers of oil for the candelabrum and its lamps; the lamps again are the eyes of Jahweh looking down upon Serubbabel with benevolence' (1971: 64). He parallels the eyes of Yahweh in Zechariah with the eyes of Yahweh in 2 Chron. 16.9 to see them as a symbol of spying, justice, comfort and protection (1971: 63). Van der Woude interprets this vision when speaking of 4.6aß-10a:

> first of all the lamp-stand is explained as the temple mountain (verse 7), then the 'bowl' on top of it as the temple building (verses 8-9), then the lamps as the eyes of the Lord (verse 10), and finally the olives as the two 'sons of the fresh oil' (verse 14), who should not, as is usually thought, be identified with Joshua and Zerubbabel, but with the expected messianic king and high priest of 6.13 (1988: 239-40).

What does it mean to be a son of oil? Redditt argues it cannot mean 'anointed ones', as many scholars and the NRSV read, because יצהר

---

84.   So Meyers and Meyers translate (1987: 228).

('oil') is not used for anointing (1992: 250-51; likewise van der Woude 1974: 264-65; and Tollington 1993: 177). Van der Woude believes it designates Joshua and Zerubbabel' (1974: 267-68). Redditt reads it intertextually and relates it to Isa. 5.1's בְּקֶרֶן בֶּן־שֶׁמֶן and says this designates 'a hill as "a son of oil"...i.e. very fertile' (1992: 251). He thus reads the phrase בְּנֵי־הַיִּצְהָר as meaning 'the olive trees are sated with oil' (1992: 251). Isaiah 5.1 is a very difficult passage to use as an intertext. The productivity of the vineyard planted on this hillside is uncontrollable (Isa. 5.2). Because of the occurrence of horns in Zechariah 2 and Isaiah 5, and this odd construction of two somewhat parallel terms which are both odd constructions (בְּנֵי־הַיִּצְהָר ['the sons of oil'] and בֶּן־שֶׁמֶן ['a son of oil']) a strange resonance surrounds both passages. Are they related in some way?

Meyers and Meyers say יִצְהָר 'designates the fresh new oil of olives' and Zechariah's use of this term 'generalizes the fertility implied by the new oil, and it also designates, more specifically, two individuals who accompany God's restored presence among his people' (1987: 258). They relate it to the tithe system and as an indication of official responsibility in the new temple (1987: 258-59). Strand believes they are called '"sons of oil" because they *furnish* oil, for that is the function of the olive trees with which they are identified' (1982: 258). Tollington believes בְּנֵי־הַיִּצְהָר ('the sons of oil') here indicates 'the two figures are worthy of divine blessing or indeed have been so blessed' (1993: 178).

The term יִצְהָר is definitely linked to tithes and prosperity (see Num. 18.12; Deut. 7.13; 12.17; 14.23; 18.4), and is used to denote Yahweh's blessing (Deut. 7.13) as it is part of the blessings (Deut. 11.14) and curses (Deut. 28.51) of Deuteronomy. This theme is taken up in later texts (assuming the Bible's internal plot rather than the 'actual' history of the biblical texts) to denote the enemy from the north (Jer. 31.8; Joel 2.20) or distant nations coming (Deut. 28.49), at which time the יִצְהָר is removed from the land (Deut. 28.51; Joel 1.10; Hag. 1.11). When the people are returned to the land, the יִצְהָר is returned and is a symbol of the restoration (Jer. 31.12; Hos. 2.24; Joel 2.19, 24). The lack of יִצְהָר is linked to Yahweh withholding rain from the land (Hos. 2.23-24; Joel 2.23; Hag. 1.11). The presence of יִצְהָר in Zechariah 4 may signify Yahweh's return of rain on the land and the agricultural blessing that ensues—יִצְהָר activates these texts in the mind of the reader.

While many commentators identify these two sons of oil with leadership in the postexilic community, and specifically two leaders, it is by no means ambiguously stated that leadership is the 'root' of the metaphor. Rost takes a different approach and investigates the task of the בני־היצהר who עמד על ('stand beside') the Lord of the whole earth. He shows how עמד על depicts a servile relationship, and thus the two sons of oil serve the Lord of the whole earth as king and priest of the *Heilzeit* ('salvation time') (1952: 218-19). Their service is in the running of the cult (1952: 220).

Strand opposes interpreting the two sons of oil as Zerubbabel and Joshua as he sees ch. 4 as dealing solely with the leadership of Zerubbabel, and ch. 3 as dealing solely with the leadership of Joshua (1982: 257). He understands the two olive trees as somehow symbolic of 'the Spirit or his work' based on the admonition in the oracle to Joshua 'not by might, nor by power, but by my Spirit' (1982: 258). He equates the lampstand with Joshua, who is fed by the trees (1982: 258-59). The equation between these two sons of oil and leadership is focused around the number 'two' and the equation of these two sons of oil with the counsel of peace which will exist between the two 'of them' (Zech. 6.13). It is not unequivocally clear that the 'two' in 6.13 must be leaders or even individuals; they could be the crowns, which are dual; or the acts of bearing honour on the throne *and* being a priest on the throne; *or* the occurrence of two metals in the crowns (silver and gold; 6.11) or just about any other thing in the text which one can find two of. Furthermore, the two olive trees could be identified with just about any other objects in the text of which there are two, such as the two mountains (6.1), or the two women (5.9), or maybe even the two מלאכים (the messenger of Yahweh and the conversing messenger).

Furthermore, is the lampstand symbolically equivalent with the Lord of the whole earth? This equivalence can be made in a roundabout fashion. Two objects are identified as the sons of oil in v. 14. Is it the two שבלי branches of the olive tree which are identified as such or the two olive trees themselves? The two olive trees themselves are the object of Zechariah's question in v. 11 to which he did not receive an answer. Did he not receive an answer because it was the significance of the שבלי rather than the olive trees which was under consideration? Whether it is the שבלי or the זיתים which are the two sons of oil, they both flank one object: the lampstand. That the lampstand is flanked by these two objects on the right and left (vv. 3, 11) suggests the lampstand is the Lord of the whole earth. Is the entire lampstand with the bowl the Lord of all the earth? What does it mean to depict the Lord of all the earth as a lampstand with 49 lights and a bowl on its head? What kind of theology is this? What is a son of oil? What does this entire picture (lampstand, bowl, lights and olive trees), when imagined, look like?

This identification of problems in the text could proceed throughout the entire vision sequence. I think by now you will have grasped the point, and I will refrain from pursuing this activity further. I am sure the reader can identify her own confusion when reading Zechariah. The point of all this is twofold. First, these visions are extremely enigmatic and confusing. This is agreed by most commentators. Secondly, the explanations the conversing messenger provides for these symbols do *not* interpret the text adequately. These embellishments do not explain the text: these are not answers. He provides more confusing lines of thought to follow. Why some commentators persist in labelling this figure 'the interpreting angel' (Bergdall; Meyers and Meyers; Tollington) is beyond the realm of this commentator's comprehension.

Intratextually, Zechariah 1–8 refuses to explain its symbols. I would go so far as to suggest the author intentionally muddles and multiplies the interpretational possibilities of the words in the text. I use the word 'author' here in a postmodern sense, recognizing intentions are impossible to perceive, but pragmatically feel it ridiculous to attribute characteristics of the words on the page to a 'text', as if the text were a living entity. The author is, of course, my construct, but I feel it is a helpful term still and avoids talking too much about myself (my reading, my implied author, etc.), which is sure to bore any reader.

Besides, I do not know how a text intentionally does anything. The book, anthropomorphically, is conscious that it cannot be understood, but still suggests it is comprehensible by offering interpretations. It is, in essence, teasing the reader, as well as the character Zechariah. The text presents a bizarre vision, and then depicts the divine camp as assuming that the human camp should understand what it means. When the reader does not understand the meaning of these texts, she is intimidated into accepting the interpretation: no fourth and fifth questions about the significance of these matters come from Zechariah. This questioning of what they mean for almost all the visionary objects points to seeing them as symbols. The text presents bizarre symbols, questions their import, delivers interpretations, and then acts as if the explanations it provides are sufficient to understand the symbols. In reality, these explanations do not even begin to dissipate the tension of incomprehensibility that surrounds them. It gives Zechariah no chance to ask for explanations of the interpretations. The text is at odds with itself. It is formally tight and semantically loose. It is a collection of bizarre, enigmatic *vignettes* which are impossible to understand as self-contained narratives. These narratives are united by various devices:

1. one continuous narrator, whose character is undefined.
2. heavily symbolic narratives.
3. symbols which are formally interpreted, but this interpretation does not solve their enigma and often makes them more confusing. So Niditch on the interpretation of the seven lamps as the eyes of Yahweh: 'yet what are "the eyes of the Lord"? Does not the reply contain another riddle? Clearly the interpretation of the symbol remains on a mysterious and mythic level. To some extent the same applies to the symbolic objects themselves' (1983: 102).
4. recurring characters and locales.
5. a predominant narrative style of unclearly marking the speaker.
6. abnormal (problematic) grammar. While many commentators may call this 'errant' grammar, that no one to date, to my knowledge, has found an ancient classical Hebrew grammar demands caution in determining precisely what is 'errant' grammar. It seems incredibly arrogant for a non-classical Hebrew speaker to determine what is 'errant' about that language. The most one can determine is that an element does not conform to expectations.
7. the impossibility of determining a chronology for these events beyond the event of Zechariah seeing.
8. the absence of a plot.

Furthermore, there are many links within the text which are not satisfactorily resolved within the narrative: it is difficult to discern the importance of these intratextual connectives. The symbols in Zechariah are overdetermined and the narrative refuses to determine them. This is not a conventional narrative grammar. Despite the structures of unification, the narrative remains impenetrable. The narrator of this text almost appears to be 'deliberately' confusing the reader.

What is one to make of this narrator? He accepts interpretations which bewilder this reader. Should one postulate he understands these matters, or is too diffident, or intimidated, to ask further? He does not seem to know what he is speaking about: confusion dominates his discourse. This, in turn, demands a very active reader. Because the narrator does not clearly define speakers, the reader is required to, and thereby to inscribe meanings for those equivocal utterances. Zechariah's repeated solicitations for meanings of the visions display the text's awareness of how difficult it is to understand its symbols. That the text does not permit Zechariah, Yahweh, or a messenger to allegorically explain the visions' symbols leaves this responsibility to the reader. The overall effect is the transfer of responsibility for the prophetic message onto the reader. Zechariah has not only generated the alter-egos of the messenger of Yahweh and the conversing messenger, but has ultimately passed the responsibility for the prophetic message onto the reader who is cognizant of other Hebrew texts.

Zechariah has displaced the prophets and replaced them, not with himself, but with the reader. The reader seeks a level beyond the surface level, and beyond the narrator and his projected personalities, to understand this narrative: the syntagmatic level is incoherent (similarly, Craig 1991: 79). The references to the prophets, as well as the recognition of prophetic intertextual material in the visions by any reader with the slightest knowledge of other prophetic texts (for example, the צמח is quickly recognized), suggest to the reader that the prophetic texts may be the route out of this aporia. That is, rather than searching solely for a syntagmatic meaning, perhaps importing paradigmatic meanings, as found in the intertexts, into the surface level may create acceptable 'meanings' for Zechariah 1–8. That Zechariah refers to the Law (תורה) and the words of the prophets,[85] and the frequent echoes of prophetic and Deuteronomic material suggests those texts may hold the key to cracking Zechariah's code. The text of Zechariah is extremely confusing and begs for deciphering while refusing to provide enough evidence to do so. Simultaneously, it contains a map to where the key to decipherment is hidden: the Law and the words of the prophets. It demands the reader to intertextually generate explanations for the symbols and oracles: to enter the symbolic order of the text. The text is incomplete and can only be completed by a competent, active reader cognizant of the intertextual materials.

85.   Does this reference to the Law and the words of the prophets imply an early canonical consciousness such as is found in Mt. 5.17 (see Meyers and Meyers 1987: 402)?

Excursus: Reading in the Frame of the Minor Prophets:
Zechariah 1.7-17

House and others have recently proposed interpreting minor prophetic books in light of their canonical context (House 1990; Coggins 1987: 84-86; Conrad 1999; Nogalski; *inter alia*). A pre-fabricated frame exists for Zechariah. What interpretation results if one heuristically assumes the book of the Twelve is a unified narrative structure, even if this is only an editorial structure, and reads the book of Zechariah in that context? In some ways, this is an intertextual experiment to see how the concept of the minor prophets as a complete work influences exegesis of one of its books. Narrative criticism is also incorporated because, as demonstrated above, it is not simply the symbolism in Zechariah which causes difficulty in reading this text. Many narrative disjunctions occur, and these will also be investigated. In general, this section will examine the impositions on each other of the text's symbolic and narrative structures.

Zechariah sees his phantasmagoria on the *twenty-fourth* day of the eleventh month of Darius's second year (Zech. 1.7). This date recalls the events which occurred in Haggai on the *twenty-fourth* day of the sixth and ninth months of Darius's second year (Hag. 1.15; 2.10, 18, 20; Unger 1963: 26). Yahweh made some promises via Haggai on the twenty-fourth day of the ninth (month) in Darius's second year, in the interim between Zechariah's first reception of Yahweh's word, in the eighth month of Darius' second year (Zech. 1.1-6), and this reception in the eleventh month (Zech. 1.7-17). He promised to send blessings, presumably on both the land and the people (Hag. 2.16-19; Petersen 1984a: 95); by implication, to stop smiting the people's agricultural work (see Hag. 2.17); to shake the heavens and the earth; to overturn kingdoms' thrones; to destroy the strength of the nations' kingdoms; and to make Zerubbabel like a signet ring (2.22-23). That these visions are dated by a foreign king using his calendar system—the Babylonian month name Shebat is used (שְׁבָט; Petersen 1984a: 138; Smith 1984: 188)—suggests Haggai's promises are unfulfilled (Hag. 2.22). Zechariah sees these visions in the context of a subservient culture living under the control of a foreign king.

Zechariah begins his first-person narration with the declaration, 'I saw this night,[86] and beheld a man riding on a red horse and he stood between the myrtles which (were) in the deep and behind him were red, sorrel and white horses' (RSV: 1.8). Berlin points out that the term 'behold' (הנה) 'is known to sometimes mark the perception of a character...it functions in much the same way as interior monologue...to internalize the viewpoint; it provides a kind of "interior vision"' (1987: 62).[87] When Zechariah uses the phrase throughout the book it shows what he himself perceives.[88] Zechariah thus starts to speak in the first person and relates the tale from his internal perspective beginning with the word הנה ('behold'). The narrative pans away from the present narrating situation of Zechariah to the scene which he narrates. Simultaneously, narration is shifted away from the narrator's objective third-person narration to Zechariah's subjective first-person perspective.

The word הלילה (the night; that night) links v. 8 with the previous verse and specifies that it is on the evening of the twenty-fourth day of the eleventh month of Darius's second year that Zechariah sees the appearances. He sees them beside the מצלה, 'the deep'. The term מצלה (the deep)[89] is enigmatic, but does occur thrice in the minor prophets: Yahweh cast Jonah deep in (the) heart of seas (Jon. 2.4), Yahweh will dry up all of the depths of the Nile (Zech. 10.11), and Micah hopes Yahweh will cast all of the remnant's sins into the depths of the sea (Mic. 7.19). מצלה in the minor prophets describes either seas, the sea or the Nile.[90] Zechariah sees one of three possible locales with three dif-

---

86.   While there is debate over the meaning of הלילה it seems best translated as 'this night' and thus refers to the evening of the twenty-fourth day of the eleventh month of the second year of Darius (whether the day begins in the evening or not is irrelevant as far as its importance in the dating scheme is concerned). The evening is the evening of the twenty-fourth, even if the reader conceives this evening as preceding the daylight of the twenty-fourth (see Petersen 1984a: 136, 138; Keil and Delitzsch 1989: 228; Mitchell 1980: 116; Perowne 1890: 69; see also Waltke and O'Connor 1990: 13.5.2b).

87.   See her discussion of the term (Berlin 1987: 62-63; 91-95). For a discussion of the use of the term in prophecy, specifically Amos, see Wolff (1977:142-43). For a general discussion see Lambdin (1973:168-70).

88.   Long describes its use in Zech. 1.8 as 'opening in a general way a complex description' (1976: 356). He further notes that it may indicate 'a shift in scenes in the midst of a longer vision-sequence' (1976: 356).

89.   Reading מְצֻלָה (Zech. 1.8) with Even-Shoshan as a variant form of מְצוּלָה (1989: 699).

90.   Though BDB presents the option of reading יאר as the Tigris, I read יאר as

ferent implications: he sees where Yahweh sent Jonah to and saved
Jonah from (Jon. 2.1-10), he sees where Yahweh will cast all the remnant's sins (Mic. 7.19), or from where, when Yahweh dries it up, the
sceptre of Egypt will depart (Zech. 10.11). Zechariah does not specify
at which of these locales he stands. It is possible that all of the references refer to the same locale. This allows one to import the implications of all three references into Zechariah.

'The deep' recalls Yahweh's promises to relent from his anger, return
(שׁוב) the remnant, return (שׁוב) himself, be compassionate (רחם) with
the remnant and cast their sins into the מצלה (Mic. 7.17-19; Zech. 10.9-
11). From this the vision implies, when Zechariah gazes upon the מצלה,
that Yahweh has, at least in the vision, returned, is having compassion
on the remnant, will return the remnant, and has cast their sin into the
מצלה. Zechariah sees the place from which it all begins: the מצלה at
which start both forgiveness and a return to the homeland.

I am inclined to translate עוד in the phrase 'and Yahweh will עוד
relent [with] Zion' as 'yet' or 'still' rather than 'again' because I cannot
find an incident in the Tanakh where Yahweh previously relented (עוד)
concerning Zion. If one translates נחם as 'relent' rather than 'comfort'
this problem is avoided. Yahweh Sebaoth thus answers quite literally
with relenting words: he yet relents concerning Zion, that is, he ceases
to be indignant with it.

נחמים only occurs three times in the Tanakh and is almost universally
translated 'comforting'. Petersen notes this word is rare as an adjective,
is a noun in Isa. 57.18 and is usually emended in Hos. 11.8 (1984a:
137). In fact, it only occurs once as an adjective: Zech. 1.13. Because of
its infrequency, and Zechariah 13's sense—Yahweh changes his orien-
tation towards the remnant—I propose to read it as 'relenting' focusing
on the relenting or repenting aspect present in the verb נחם (see BDB,
636-37). Furthermore, in Zech. 8.14 Yahweh uses נחם in reference to
how he has not relented from doing evil since he was first angry with
the forefathers. For other occurrences of נחם as 'relent' in the minor
prophets see Joel 2.13, 14; Amos 7.3, 6; Jon. 3.9; 4.2.

A near parallel passage exists in Amos 7–8. There Yahweh relents
[נחם] twice, but concerning Israel and the sanctuary at Bethel and not
Zion. Perhaps the עוד ('again, still, yet') in Zech. 1.17 refers to Yahweh

a referent to Egypt in Zechariah because it is paired with Egypt throughout the
minor prophets (see Amos 8.8; 9.5; Nah. 3.8 [linked with an Egyptian locale];
Zech. 10.11), and appears to only, possibly, refer to the Tigris in Daniel.

relenting over Jacob: as Yahweh relented over Jacob, thus he relents over Zion. If this intertextexual line is pursued, Yahweh sets a plumb line in the midst of Israel in order to desolate Isaac's high places and send the people into exile (Amos 7.8-9). Curiously a line, albeit קָוֶה (Zech. 1.16) rather than אֲנָךְ (Amos 7.8), occurs in close context with Yahweh's relent. Does the symbolic import of the line imply further desolation awaits Zion in Zechariah 1? This reading seems at odds with the text, but that the cities are yet to be scattered from good in Zech. 1.17 adds further weight to this reading of yet more woe awaiting Zion. The passage is very difficult to understand. It seems most 'natural' to read Zech. 1.16 in the larger intertextual context of Jer. 31.39, where a measuring line is associated with the rebuilding of the city. One wants to read the symbolic import of the line positively as associated with restoration, but elements in the text, and intertextual elements outside the text, resist this reading.

The first sight Zechariah sees is a man riding a brown horse, with brown, sorrel and white horses behind him.[91] Much ink has been spilled identifying the exact colours of these horses. Brenner astutely points out that identifying the horses' colour depends on whether one reads the text as operating under a mandate of verisimilitude, in which case the colours reflect colours of horses in the world (1982; see Seybold 1974b: 100; Richter 1986: 97 n. 9; Petersen 1984a: 142), or a mandate of the imaginary, in which case the horses' colours are not restricted to colours which horses possess in the 'real' world (Brenner 1982: 70). Brenner, operating under the mandate of verisimilitude, see the horses as brown (1982: 71), white (1982: 85) and sorrel (1982: 115). Hertzberg recon-ciles the riders in Revelation 6 with Zechariah 1 and Arabic colours of horses, for a reading of 'pale' ['fahl'] for שְׂרֻקִּים (1953: 180). That the horse colours do appear to exist on real horses suggests verisimilitude should be the operating mandate, but one is cautioned in this reading. The book of Zechariah is such a surreal text, that it is silly to literalize in this sense. After all, Zechariah contains talking horses (again com-mentators attempt to literalize these),[92] disembodied horns(?), a vision

91. Jones (1962: 58); Mason (1977a: 37); Petersen (1984a: 142); Ackroyd (1962: 647) inter alia attach no particular importance to the horses' colours.

92. It is curious how resistant readers are to allowing these horses to speak. So much so, that Savran claims animals only speak twice in the Tanakh (Gen. 3.1-5; Num. 22.22-35) and fails to mention 'hide nor hair' of these talking horses in his article on animal speech in the Hebrew Bible (1994).

of a divine council, stones with eyes, mountains levelled, flying scrolls of ridiculous proportions which are the physical perpetrators of justice, individuals who speak with God, and horses which inquire (בקשׁ) of Yahweh to go and walk in the earth. Applying rules of verisimilitude is as inappropriate a response to Zechariah 1–8 as it would be to apply them to *Alice in Wonderland*.

To throw an idea into the fray of competing of ideas, perhaps these colours are puns on directions of north, south and west: אדמים ('red') could be a pun on אדום 'Edom' which is southwards שׂרקים ('sorrel') could pun on שׂרק which is westward (Judg. 16.4), and לבנים (white) could pun on לְבָנוֹן which is northwards. Despite how far-fetched this reading may appear, there is no mention of the direction 'east' with this interpretation, nor is there in the much commented on absence of an expected chariot bound eastwards in 6.6.[93]

If the horses are the same ones that occur again in Zechariah 6, then they are the winds/spirits of heaven. The problem with this interpretation is that chariots occur in Zechariah 6, whereas only horses are present in Zechariah 1. Do the horses need to be harnessed to be the spirits/ winds of heaven? Perhaps the chariots are not the spirits/winds of heaven, but they are driven by the individuals who are the spirits/winds of heaven. There still is the option that these are the horses that will be harnessed to the chariots, and thus Zechariah sees a divine corral in Zechariah 1 (so Petersen: 'The garden functions rather like a pasture or corral' [1984a: 143]).

Up to this point in the minor prophets, numerous images have been applied to horses: Yahweh will not deliver Judah by horse or horsemen [Hos. 1.7]; Israel is implored to promise Yahweh they will not ride on horses so that Yahweh will turn his anger from them (Hos. 14.3); an advancing army's appearance is like the appearance of horses (Joel 2.4); those who ride horses will not save their lives on Yahweh's day (Amos 2.15); Yahweh slew Israel's captured horses with the sword (Amos 4.10); Yahweh will cut off horses (Mic. 5.10); the Chaldeans' horses were swifter than leopards, came for violence and were appointed by Yahweh to judge and correct (Hab. 1.8-12); Habakkuk prays for

---

93. Though, see McHardy for a clever reading in which, based on his theory that abbreviations have been misinterpreted by later redactors, he argues all four directions were present in the text (1968). Reider postulates that the text once contained all four compass directions, but a line has dropped out of the present text (1926: 110). He believes the difficult אחריהם originally read ארץ הים (1926: 110).

Yahweh to ride on his horses, trample the nations and save his people (Hab. 3.8-13); and Yahweh will overthrow horses and their riders when he destroys and overthrows the thrones and power of kingdoms and makes Zerubbabel like his signet ring (Hag. 2.22).

Which image should the reader keep in mind, if any, when reading Zechariah 1? Do the horses Zechariah sees suggest more divine judgment for the remnant like the Chaldeans' horses of Hab. 1.8-12 or the advancing army of Joel 2.4? That the horses are for the most part riderless might be taken to signify the returned horses of those who attempted to save their lives on horses but failed to (Amos 2.15)? It is ambiguous whether the horses are mounted or not, and some commentators find it objectionable that they are not. Since the text mentions no rider for these horses, it seems most likely to conclude that they are not mounted, except for the one, and thus it is the horses which speak in v. 11 and not some assumed riders.

Do these horses recall Yahweh's steeds which Habbakuk wants Yahweh to mount to save his people and symbolize that salvation is about to begin? Is Yahweh then in the act of saving his people? Are they horses which Israel has captured and Yahweh is about to slay with the sword? If one assumes Israelites are riding on these horses, then Yahweh's anger is not assuaged (Hos. 14.3). The especially close context of Hag. 2.22 might suggest these are the horses of the nations which have not been caused to go down (ירד) as of yet. Does this suggest that the foreign powers still rule and Haggai's prophecy has not taken place yet? This context makes it startling that Zechariah first sees a horse and a rider beside the deep. One almost expects the horse to be an evil agent whom Yahweh will destroy beside the deep. Perhaps this idea is played off to frustrate readers' expectations when the horses turn out to be agents of Yahweh.

That this section is dated by a foreign king precludes the notion that all the kingdoms of the world are overthrown. The militaristic expectations evoked by Haggai's horse imagery seem deliberately frustrated and misleading. Ruffin offers an ingenious interpretation of what these horses may signify by looking forward in Zechariah. He combines Yahweh's promise to make the house of Judah as his majestic horse in battle in Zech. 10.3 with the theme that Yahweh dispersed the people into exile (Zech. 2.10; 7.14; 10.9) to suggest that the horses represent the house of Judah. Yahweh thereby sent the house of Judah into exile to quite literally roam the earth (Ruffin 1986: 137). I am unsure which

of these symbols I should apply to this scene, but am unsatisfied with
accepting only the interpretation given later in the scene, and ignoring
the surplus of meaning inherent in the symbols.

Zechariah shares my confusion and must ask the messenger who
speaks with him the meaning of this appearance. The messenger replies
to Zechariah's question by promising to show (ראה) him its significance
(1.9). Oddly, it is the rest of the vision that shows Zechariah the identity
of the rider, the horses, and their significance; it is the dialogue in the
rest of the vision that shows Zechariah the vision's importance. Since
the rest of the vision shows Zechariah the initial sights' importance,
how can one say the messenger shows Zechariah the meaning of this
initial sight? This mixture of auditory and visual aspects to the prophets
leads Marks to comment that:

> from a Freudian perspective prophecy could be described as 'archaic' or
> 'regressive'—a displacement of thought by hallucination along a meta-
> phorical chain which begins with sensations and proceeds via mnemic
> images through words to verbal complexes or thought. If mnemic images
> are more primitive than words, we can understand the tendency of the
> prophets, oriented ethically as well as psychologically toward the pri-
> mordial, to displace or confuse word with vision. Thus, in the first vision
> of Zechariah, seeing and showing are interwoven with speaking and
> answering in what seems, semantic flexibility notwithstanding, like a
> deliberate synesthesia: the 'vision' being prompted by an initiatory
> 'word of YHWH' and having at its center a dialogue and a command to
> 'cry out' (Zech. 1.7-15) (227).

Marks notes that Zechariah 'marks an important step toward the full-
fledged apocalyptic prophecy of Daniel, Second Esdras, and the Book
of Revelation. These works were the models for the view of prophecy
as "visionary theater"' (1987: 226).

A musical is also a productive analogy for Zechariah. As the performers in a musical know when to begin and spontaneously express
their thoughts in song, even when it seems strange for a particular character to sing, so the man standing between the myrtles, as well as the
horses, speaks on cue. Likewise, the viewer suspends logical continuity.
It is the sequence of events combined with the lyrics that provide
coherence and implant meaning in the viewer's mind. Though they start
on cue, from the viewer's perspective the characters in a musical are
still free to act dynamically and dialogue with their co-performers. The
situation is the same in this vision. The issue is not the causal relationship between the messenger and the scene which ensues that places sole

responsibility for the rest of the character's actions in the vision on this messenger, but rather, the issue is that the scene continues. The messenger's promise to show Zechariah what these things mean is the link that perpetuates the vision. In essence, the messenger says, 'let the show begin'.

It is strange that the messenger who bears the epithet 'the one who *speaks* with me' promises to *show* the sights' meaning to Zechariah, whereas the man standing between the myrtles, whom Zechariah *sees*, *speaks* and directly answers Zechariah's query. He reports that the horses were sent by Yahweh to התהלך 'roam' the earth. The horses reply to the man's declaration by reporting that all the earth is sitting and quiet. כל־הארץ ('all the land/earth') may indicate a specific geographic region, for example, the land from Geba to Rimmon (Zech. 14.10), and it is therefore difficult to know whether to translate it as 'all the land' (that is, this specific geographic region) or 'all the earth' (that is, the entire world, as the phrase indicates in Mic. 4.13 and Zeph. 3.8). I interpret כל־הארץ as referring to the entire world in Zech. 1.11, because the vision later speaks about Zion and Jerusalem in relation to the secure nations (vv. 14-17). The secure nations seem synonymous with all the world that is sitting and quiet. This suggests the purpose of their walking in the earth was to gather information on the world's current state.[94] That they walked through all the earth demonstrates the compass of their mission and the extent of the present condition. Not just one country is quiet; rather the entire world is quiet.

May reads 'between the mountains' with the LXX instead of 'between the myrtles' of the MT and believes Babylonian New Year's coronation and ordination rituals are the background to much of the symbolism in Zechariah. He believes the man in 2.5 is 'Yahweh, in the role of Shamash' (1938: 174).

Seybold also attributes the origins of some of the elements in Zechariah to the Babylonian New Year festival and the myth which surrounded it (1974b: 93). Whether an emendation or not, which seems unlikely in three verses (1.8, 10, 11), as the text stands it is stressed that these are myrtles, as הדסים occurs three times. If one deletes myrtles (הדסים) from the text of Zechariah one loses two word-plays: one with

---

94. A similar sense for התהלך ('walk around') is when Joshua sends three men of each tribe to walk in the land and describe it in order to divide up the land among the remaining tribes (Josh. 18.4, 8). As is often noted, Satan acts similarly when he roams (התהלך) the earth (Job 1.7, 2.2).

the stork (הסידה); and another with the word 'lovingkindness' (חסד). In the Hebrew Bible, the stork is an animal which knows its times (מעדה): this idea of the stork knowing its time resonates with the emphasis on the times of the feasts in Zech. 5.9. The concept of 'lovingkindness' reminds one of the intertextual clusters of mercy and restoration in 1 Kgs 8.23; Isa. 54.8, 10; 55.3; Joel 2.13; and Mic. 7.18. 'Lovingkindness' is also connected with 'relent' (נחם) in Jon. 4.2. In addition to these intertextual links, the myrtles resonate with Isa. 41.19; 55.13 and Neh. 8.15. Isaiah 41.19 resonates with several themes in Zechariah. The making of a threshing sledge to pulverize and make hills like chaff (Isa. 41.15-16) uses similar imagery of bovine empowerment as is found in Micah 13 which may be the symbolic picture underlying Zech. 2.1-4 (see above). That the mountains (הרים) are threshed, winnowed (זרה) and stormed (סערה) away by the wind (רוח) is parallel to Zerubbabel making the great mountain (הר) a plain (Zech. 4.7). It is also a reversal of the exile in which Yahweh stormed (סערה) the ancestors away (Zech. 7.14).

Myrtles appear in the wilderness in Isa. 41.19 so 'that all may see and know, all may consider and understand, that the hand of the LORD has done this, the Holy One of Israel has created it' (NRSV). Again this explanation of these events ties into the title: Yahweh remembers. That Zechariah sees the myrtles may provide a setting for this first vision: in the wilderness where the myrtles have been made to grow.

Isaiah 55.13 depicts the emergence of the myrtle in places where nettles grew before, indicating Yahweh is showing compassion (רחם). This will take place after the implied audience obeys and returns (שוב; Isa. 55.7) to Yahweh (compare Isa. 55.1-7). Perhaps this indicates that the return of the audience in Zech. 1.6b is followed by Yahweh showing compassion and making the myrtles grow in these places. Furthermore, it subtly validates Yahweh's declaration that he has already returned to Jerusalem with compassion (רחמים) (Zech. 1.16).

The final intertext of Neh. 8.15 lists myrtle branches among those branches used to make the booths for the feasts of booths in the seventh month (Neh. 8.14). For Zechariah, the seventh month still functions as a fast (8.19). Zechariah is very much a text about feasts. That the myrtles are there suggests they could be used in a feast, but are not. It hints at the final conclusion of the booklet of Zechariah 1–8, and the entire book of Zechariah.

The image of the myrtles unites many texts and provides Zechariah with a much richer meaning than if it is omitted. I find it difficult to surrender these readings, and cling to them. I therefore cannot write them out of the text as is done if one substitutes mountains for myrtles.

There is ambiguity about which individual the horses address when they answer the messenger (מלאך) of Yahweh standing between the myrtles in Zech. 1.11, because two individuals bear the epithet 'messenger' (מלאך) in this vision: the messenger who speaks with Zechariah in 1.9, 13 and 14 and the messenger of Yahweh in 1.12. This creates further confusion: whenever the man riding the horse in 1.8 is mentioned, he is further identified as standing between the myrtles (vv. 8, 10). When the horses speak to the messenger standing between the myrtles, they could be addressing one of three figures: the man riding the horse, the conversing messenger or the messenger of Yahweh.

If the horses refer to the man, they reveal that he is more than just a man: he is Yahweh's messenger as well (Baldwin believes this use of מלאך designates a superhuman individual because of 'his ability to disclose information normally hidden from men [sic]' [1972: 96]). If the horses address the conversing messenger, they specify his location: the conversing messenger also stands between the myrtles. If they address Yahweh's messenger, they identify his location and inform the reader that two individuals stand between the myrtles: the messenger of Yahweh and the man. That the conversing messenger consistently bears the epithet 'the one who speaks with me' inclines me to discount him as the addressee of the horses: there is a standard epithet the author could choose to place in the mouths of the horses if he wanted positively to identify the horses' addressee as the messenger who speaks with Zechariah. Two options remain. Instead of choosing between the two, I see the text as recording Zechariah's progressive realization of the identity of the enigmatic character who he first sees riding a red horse standing between the myrtles. The second time he sees this character he calls him the man standing between the myrtles. The fact that the man stands between the myrtles is mentioned twice. The reader should by now grasp the point that the character standing between the myrtles is the man riding the horse. When the horses address this figure who stands between the myrtles, Zechariah finally realizes his identity: the horse rider of v. 8, the man standing between the myrtles in v. 10 and

Yahweh's messenger of vv. 11 and 12 are one and the same individual.[95]

The phrase 'and they answered the messenger of Yahweh who stands between the myrtles and they said' is Zechariah's speech and reflects his views. One does not know if the horses know that the figure who stands between the myrtles is Yahweh's messenger or not, since they are reticent on this issue. The important issue is that Zechariah realizes the man is Yahweh's messenger when the horses speak. After this realization, Zechariah can refer to this individual as Yahweh's messenger. The conversing messenger's promise to show Zechariah what these are (1.9) rings true: Zechariah realizes the horses' import and the identity and import of the rider as he sees more. This gradual realization of the identity of the rider is passed on to the reader through Zechariah's use of shifting epithets to portray Yahweh's messenger, in contrast with the static epithet used to portray the messenger who speaks with Zechariah. The character of Zechariah is portrayed as progressively realizing the identity of the man between the myrtles (Sternberg discusses how the narrator can align a character's discovery with the reader's discovery [1985: 243-46]). This teaches the reader that progressive realization is one of the techniques occurring in Zechariah: once again, the character Zechariah stands for the reader.

Further implications arise from the identification of the man riding the horse as Yahweh's messenger, because three entities are associated with the messenger of Yahweh in the minor prophets: the house of David, a priest and Haggai. The house of David is associated with the messenger of Yahweh when Yahweh promises that the house of David will be like Yahweh's messenger in Zech. 12.8. Then Mal. 2.7 identifies a priest as the messenger of Yahweh Sebaoth. Although the priest is identified as the messenger of Yahweh Sebaoth (מלאך יהוה־צבאות) in Malachi (Mal. 2.7), the distinction between the messenger of Yahweh Sebaoth and the messenger of Yahweh may be important identifiers of specific individuals. I concede that the term 'messenger of Yahweh' may generally refer to any individual who relates Yahweh's message, or may identify a specific individual of the divine court, but it may also identify Haggai. The text is ambiguous, and it is up to the individual

---

95. Similarly, Baldwin (1972: 93, 95); Clark (1982: 215); Feinberg (1940b: 436); and Mitchell (1980: 118). Van der Woude goes further and identifies the man between the myrtles, the messenger of Yahweh, and the conversing messenger as the same individual (1988: 245 n. 2; likewise Press [1936: 43-44]).

interpreter to decide this point, and determine the implications that arise from this choice. If one accepts the identification of Yahweh and Yahweh Sebaoth, then a priest may be riding the red horse. Joshua is positively identified as a priest (Hag. 1.1, 12, 14; 2.2, 4; Zech. 3.1; 6.1). Is one to see the individual raising the lament as Joshua? The lament may then be read as centred on priestly activities.

Finally, Hag. 1.13 identifies Haggai as Yahweh's messenger. Is Haggai to be seen as the individual raising the lament? Perhaps he is frustrated that the horses have not been thrown down yet; and the rest of his prophecies are as yet unfulfilled? Haggai thereby demands Yahweh to stop procrastinating and fulfil his promises. Haggai, etymologically, means 'my feasts'. Perhaps the time for the feasts come upon the house of Judah after they have roamed the earth and realized the earth is quiet. But the problem with this interpretation is no feast occurs in the eleventh month. It may be noteworthy that the final feast called for in Zech. 8.19 is in the tenth month. Thus a whole year's cycle of feasts has not been carried out by this eleventh month of the second year of Darius. Maybe the horses simply recall past events—they were in the respective countries during the festival times and now meet to discuss the fact that the countries did not celebrate the feasts. Perhaps that is the problem—the earth is not joyously celebrating Yahweh's feasts and a world-wide cacophonous ritual is required. The vision then foreshadows that prophesied highlight of the ancient Near Eastern travel agents' year: the annual feast of booths[96] in Jerusalem in Zechariah 14.

The conversation between the horses and the messenger of Yahweh results in the latter raising the lament 'Yahweh Sebaoth, how long will you lack compassion for Jerusalem and the cities of Judah with which you have been indignant these seventy years?' (Zech. 1.12). If all the earth is sitting and quiet, how does Yahweh Sebaoth specifically lack compassion for the cities of Judah and Jerusalem?[97] Zechariah 7 shows the results of Yahweh's 70-year indignation. This is shown only if one assumes that this vision takes place in Zechariah's present time and is not a vision of things to come or things that were; that is, the content in

96. One of the materials used to make these booths in Neh. 8.15 is myrtles, forming yet another connective.

97. Meyers and Meyers believe that this passage shows Zechariah to be concerned with the political state of the 'traditional Davidic territory': 'the two terms together apparently have a direct political reference, as a designation for the realm of a Davidic sovereign' (1992a: 123-24).

the vision occurs on the twenty-fourth day of the second year of Darius
and relates to that time.[98] Now Jerusalem seems incompletely inhabited
(see Zech. 2.11; esp. 8.4-8). That Jerusalem is uninhabited, or at least
only partially inhabited, and scattered throughout the world is implied
in many passages in Zechariah: the horns scattered Judah so that no
man lifts up his head (2.4); Jerusalem will be inhabited as open country
(2.8); Yahweh dispersed some people (presumably Jerusalem or Judah)
to the land of the north (2.10); Zion lives with Babylon's daughter
(2.11); the nations are still plundering the addressee of chapter two
(presumably Jerusalem or Judah), etc. (see esp. Zech. 8.4-8). While the
central issue in ch. 7 is the fasting and mourning for 70 years, it is
implied that the people of the land fasted, and continue to fast, because
they want to return to pre-exilic conditions: before the exile Jerusalem
was inhabited (יֹשֶׁבֶת) and its surrounding cities were quiet (שְׁלֵוֹה; Zech.
7.7).

This starkly contrasts with the state of the world presented in the
horses' report: it is inhabited (יֹשֶׁבֶת) and quiet (שֹׁקָטֶת). The messenger
of Yahweh reacts because Yahweh Sebaoth appears to favour the rest
of the world over Jerusalem and the Judaean cities: Yahweh Sebaoth's
indignation prevents Jerusalem and the Judaean cities from experienc-
ing the 'bliss' they once possessed and which the rest of the world possesses: populous and tranquil territories. The messenger of Yahweh
demands Yahweh Sebaoth to show compassion: רחם. Yahweh's compassion (רחם) results in him treading down the remnant's iniquities and
casting all their sins into the depths (מְצֻלָה) of the sea in Mic. 7.19. The
messenger wants Yahweh to show the type of compassion, like that of
Zech. 10.6 and Mic. 7.19, which restores Jerusalem and the Judaean
cities to their pre-exilic state after casting their sins into the deep. The
messenger of Yahweh in his outburst shifts the focus from all of the
world onto the cities of Judah and Jerusalem, and raises some issues

---

98. That the term 'seventy years' is used in both the second and fourth year of
Darius suggests it is an approximate number which comes close to an exact number
of years (Jeremias 1977: 131; Orr 1956: 306; Petersen 1984a: 149; 'when the number is used, it should not be taken in a rigidly literal way'). Contra Whitley (1954)
who believes it refers to the exact 70 years of the desolation of Jerusalem and the
temple from 586–516 (and must infer 7.5 is an interpolation by an editor to support
his exact use of the term); similarly Ackroyd who considers that 518 may be the
end of the 70 years (1958: 26; see Jeremias who engages on a lengthy discussion of
the term 'seventy years' (1977: 130-39).

which the rest of Zechariah's visions will address: the fate of Jerusalem and Judah and their moral state.[99]

Yahweh Sebaoth's imputed indignation (זעם) with Jerusalem and the cities of Judah recalls the forefathers' confession that Yahweh Sebaoth did with them as he purposed (זמם) to do (Zech. 1.6). The forefathers' proclamation and the messenger of Yahweh's outburst have similar implications: the fate of the forefathers, the remnant, and the cities of Judah and Jerusalem are ultimately in Yahweh's control. Only when Yahweh decides to show compassion will the status quo change.

Curiously, Yahweh answers his messenger's outburst by addressing the conversing messenger instead. The conversing messenger then proceeds to pass Yahweh's message on to Zechariah. The conversing messenger commands Zechariah to proclaim Yahweh's speech in vv. 14-17. Zechariah 1.3-6 established that the former prophets called (קרא) to their audience, the present generation's forefathers, and their words overtook the forefathers, that is their words came true. The efficacy of the prophetic proclamation is asserted. Zechariah, who is also a prophet (Zech. 1.1, 7), is now commanded to perform the same act as the former prophets and call (קרא) to his audience. By implication, his words harbour the same efficacy the former prophets' words contained. Zechariah's readers are assured that whatever Zechariah proclaims is Yahweh's words and his audience should thus heed his words.

Yahweh's response directly answers the messenger of Yahweh's complaint. Yahweh demonstrates he is responding to this messenger's lament by specifically using the title by which his messenger addressed him: Yahweh Sebaoth. Whereas the messenger of Yahweh lamented Yahweh Sebaoth's lack of compassion for Jerusalem and the cities of Judah, Yahweh diminishes the equal focus between the two locales in his messenger's lament and focuses attention upon Jerusalem (Meyers and Meyers 1987: 120-21). Yahweh Sebaoth is zealous (קנא) only for Jerusalem and Zion (v. 14) and omits any reference to zeal for the cities of Judah (v. 14). In addition, only Jerusalem is specifically mentioned as the recipient of compassion (רחם)—Yahweh states he returns to Jerusalem with compassion (v. 16). Yahweh eventually promises to show compassion for the house of Judah in Zech. 10.6. Yahweh's declaration that he has returned to Jerusalem with compassion (רחם) rebuts the messenger of Yahweh's allegation that Yahweh lacks com-

---

99. Meyers and Meyers develop this theme in relation to Yahweh's speech (1987: 120-21 and elsewhere).

passion (לא תרחם) with Jerusalem and the cities of Judah.[100]

It is as if Yahweh says to the messenger (v. 12), 'You accuse me of lacking compassion for Jerusalem, but look, I have already compassionately returned there—I am thinking, and acting, ahead of you'. This alludes to the events in Haggai where Yahweh declares (on his own [2.4, 5] and through Haggai [1.13]) that he is with Joshua, Zerubbabel and the people and that his spirit is standing in their midst. Yahweh has been with the people for some time. Now Yahweh reveals their location: he is with Zerubbabel, Joshua and the people in Jerusalem. Yahweh did not wait for the remnant to return to him physically before he returned to them (see v. 3). Part of the ambiguity of v. 3 is removed; the remnant now know that Yahweh is in Jerusalem and that they can match Yahweh's physical return to Jerusalem and perform Yahweh's demand to return (שוב) to him (v. 3) by physically returning to Jerusalem.[101]

Yahweh at least mentions the cities of Judah—they seem identifiable with Yahweh's designation 'my cities' in v. 17—but he does not speak kindly or at length about them: they will still be scattered from good. It is Yahweh alone who introduces the concept of Zion—the messenger of Yahweh does not mention Zion in his lament. Zion frequently occurs parallel to Jerusalem in the minor prophets (Joel 3.5; 4.16, 17[H]; Amos 1.2; Mic. 3.10, 12; 4.2; Zech. 8.3; 9.9; see esp. Zeph. 3.16 where Jerusalem is addressed as Zion). By using the term 'Zion' Yahweh Sebaoth conjures up images of Zion's role in his other promises in the minor prophets: Yahweh returns to Zion (Zech. 8.3) and will dwell there (שכן; Joel 4.17, 21), after which his Law will go out from there. The participle שכן ('am dwelling') is used in Joel 4.17 and 21(H). The passage as a whole refers to future events, so I interpret the participle in these passages to indicate Yahweh's constant dwelling in Zion in the future. Yahweh is concerned about Zion because it is where he will return to live and where his house is located (see Mic. 4.1-7). This conclusion is

---

100. The verb שבתי is problematic. While practically all agree it is a qal first-person singular perfect, whether or not it refers to the past, present or is a prophetic future is a debated point (Mason 1977a: 38; Meyers and Meyers 1987: 123; see Waltke and O'Connor 1990: 31.6.2b). I read it as a preterite.

101. See Petersen 1984a: 131 for the geographical sense of Yahweh's demand for the remnant to שוב ('return') to him. Marinkovic views 'the return of YHWH *and* his people to Jerusalem and their living together there' as one of the three central themes of Zech. 1–8 (1994: 93; see 91ff.).

based on Micah's treatment of the terms 'Zion', 'house of Yahweh', and 'mountain of the house of Yahweh'. That Yahweh's house is located on a mountain is shown by the phrase 'the mountain of the house of Yahweh' (Mic. 4.1). The only mountain specifically identified in Micah is Mt Zion (Mic. 4.7). Though a loose conjecture, it seems that Zion is the location of Yahweh's house. Yahweh's focus on Jerusalem and Zion reflects his desire for the completion of his house in the rest of his message (see also Haggai).[102] By not talking much about the cities of Judah, introducing Zion and talking about Jerusalem, Yahweh shifts the focus away from Judah and Jerusalem and onto Jerusalem exclusively and the activities which will take place there.

Yahweh Sebaoth changes the objects of his anger as well. Whereas he was angry with the remnant's forefathers in v. 2, now, he is angry with the secure nations. His use of the adjective שַׁאֲנָן—'secure/at ease'—recalls the horses' report in which the entire world was sitting and quiet and identifies the secure nations as the entire world. The phrase 'the nations at ease' is unique to Zech. 1.15. שַׁאֲנָן neither carries negative connotations nor does it positively identify these nations. In Amos 6.1, the only other occurrence of this root in the minor prophets, those at ease in Zion are those who do not grieve over the ruin of Joseph and consequently are sent into exile. Perhaps this indicates a negative connotation for this term in the minor prophets. The root does carry positive connotations in the Tanakh and describes Jerusalem's undisturbed idyllic state (see Isa. 32.18; 33.20). Thus, whether שַׁאֲנָן carries negative or positive connotations is contextually determined, and not inherently lexicographic. It seems present in Yahweh's speech to identify the secure nations with those aforementioned in the horses' report rather than to condemn the nations for their security.

Yahweh Sebaoth is angry with the entire world. He is not angry because they are at ease (which is a morally neutral act in the Tanakh, if any morally neutral acts truly exist in the entangling webs of complicity present in all relations), but because they helped to bring about evil (or

102. Zion is sometimes even synonymous with the temple (see *ABD*: VI, 1096). On Zion and Jerusalem, Meyers and Meyers say, 'the terms should be viewed as complementary designations rather than as synonymous expressions. Jerusalem is a somewhat broader term, although it frequently assumes the characteristics of its chief component Zion, the mountain of God's temple. The two words together signal the religious and political centrality of the postexilic capital of Judah (Yehud)' (1992a: 124).

calamity—רעה) when he was only a little angry (v. 15). While the text
does not explicitly denote the evil that the nations commit, that the next
pericope about the nations tells how the nations scattered Judah implies
the scattering and plundering of Judah and Zion is the evil the nations
committed (Zech. 2.3, 12). This is intertextually confirmed in Joel
4.2(H), where Yahweh declares he will gather all the nations to judge
them in the valley of Jehoshaphat because they scattered Israel among
the nations and divided up the land (the verb חלק ['to divide'] in Joel
4.2(H) parallels Yahweh inheriting Judah as his portion [the noun חלק]
in Zech. 2.16). Further evils that Joel records are that the nations cast
lots for Yahweh's people (ידי in Joel 4.3 parallels Zech. 2.4 and the
throwing down of the horns), traded them (one infers as slaves), and
took Yahweh's silver and gold (parallel to the plundering of Israel,
Judah and Jerusalem?).

Micah tells of another evil the nations committed which may bear on
Zechariah. In Mic. 4.11 many nations assemble against Zion and say
'let her be polluted and our eyes will look on Zion'. In Mic. 5.14 Yahweh says he will do vengeance with anger and wrath on the nations
which did not obey (presumably Yahweh), so perhaps the nations' evil
is disobedience. While all of these are possible allusions and interpretative options, they are not clearly linked, and only a reader may judge
whether she equates these deeds with the nations' evil.

How did the nations help for evil? Later in his speech Yahweh mentions that his cities are scattered from good. The opposition of good and
evil may indicate that the evil which the nations caused (v. 15), or one
aspect of the nations' evil, is that they scattered Yahweh's cities from
good. The implication of Yahweh's speech in v. 15 is that he would not
have committed evil on his own and his anger would have had less
severe effects if the secure nations did not help Yahweh to bring about
evil. Yahweh Sebaoth is shifting the blame for the current state of
Jerusalem and the cities of Judah away from himself and onto the
secure nations. In essence Yahweh is saying, 'It is not my seventy-year
indignation which brought about these conditions; rather, it is those
secure nations that helped for evil'. Rather than simply admit he was
angry for 70 years and will be angry for 70 more if he pleases—after
all, he is God—he patronizes the remnant by blaming the nations for
placing the remnant in a condition which he is ultimately responsible
for.

Is Yahweh justified in condemning his employees? Both Yahweh and the nations played the same game—they scattered the ancestors (Zech. 2.4; 8.14)—yet the nations are condemned for their role in this act while Yahweh absolves himself of guilt in this matter. If we were speaking about war crimes, Yahweh, as the authority figure, would be responsible and condemned.

To whom should Zechariah proclaim this message? Presumably the same audience whom Zechariah addressed in v. 3; but who composes this audience? House equates the minor prophets' implied audience with the postexilic remnant (1990: 239-40).[103] That the remnant is the book's implied audience is indicated in Zech. 8.6, 11. This remnant appears to live in both Jerusalem (6.10) and abroad (8.7). The text still does not specify where Zechariah is to proclaim this message—to the remnant abroad or in Jerusalem? Perhaps it is simply a general message that should be proclaimed to both the remnant in Jerusalem, and the remnant outside it. No audience is specified because this message is pertinent to more than just one locale's audience; it pertains to both the Jerusalemite remnant and the Diaspora remnant.

Yahweh's anger resulted in the punishment of the forefathers (Zech. 1.2-6), a punishment that dispersed them among all the nations. Now that he is greatly angry with the nations, what will the outcome of his anger with them be? If Yahweh deals with the nations as he dealt with Israel and Judah, will he send the nations into exile in Judah? This is indeed the prophetic outcome of Zechariah's book, if read as a whole: in Zechariah 14, after a plague the nations will annually celebrate the feast of booths and worship Yahweh in Jerusalem, under threat of another plague if they abstain (Zech. 14). The nations are temporarily exiled to Jerusalem every year. As a consolation, they can avoid these plagues and do get a chance to see the holy land (2.16), and during a festival as well. On the downside, that they worship under duress suggests they may not wish to worship Yahweh of hosts and lack religious freedom.

If the nations helped Yahweh, do Yahweh's motivations overlap with the nations' motives, and if so, where do Yahweh's motives end and the nations' motives begin? What was Yahweh doing when they were helping for evil? No matter how they helped for evil, and no matter what Yahweh did while they helped, the implication of Yahweh's

103. House does not identify the minor prophets' implied audience as solely the remnant and also includes the nations and 'sinful Israel' in this designation (1990: 240).

rhetoric is that he incompletely controls the situation and is susceptible to outside influences. Moreover, in Zechariah 7 and 8 Yahweh Sebaoth directly contradicts his statements here: in 7.12 Yahweh Sebaoth, via Zechariah, describes his previous anger as a great anger (קֶצֶף גָּדוֹל) and in 8.14 Yahweh Sebaoth declares he purposed to cause evil (רעע) on the forefathers and the remnant. The nations that helped for evil or calamity only did so in accord with, and as an extension of, the divine will. So why is Yahweh Sebaoth angry with them? What kind of artisan blames his or her tools?

The book of Zechariah does not even attempt to address this issue and is completely reticent on how the nations might feel about being condemned. There is no assurance that performing Yahweh Sebaoth's will results in gaining his favour, especially if one is not a member of his privileged camp. That Yahweh later contradicts himself raises the suspicion that he changes his recollection of history to match the moment's rhetorical demands. Yahweh wants the people to return to him in Jerusalem and build his house. Haggai shows the remnant's reluctance to do so. Thus, Yahweh whitewashes himself to appear as the remnant's best friend—someone who would never of his own accord let such atrocities afflict the remnant as those events which had transpired. Only after two years of time, and the possibility that Yahweh has partially achieved his goals and work is well under way on the temple, can Yahweh say he was angry and purposed to do evil to the remnant and their fathers. Yahweh contradicts himself and his word is not completely reliable. Why should any character believe Yahweh Sebaoth's words or promises? The efficacy and potency of the deity's prophets' words, which some elements of the text strenuously attempt to affirm, is rendered impotent: the prophets' words are, after all, only as reliable as their ultimate source.

Faced with this crux in reliability, how should both the characters in the text, and readers, both implied and present, react to the rest of the work? If I may, I will briefly enter a highly speculative realm for a moment and speak about a possible original purpose for this work. The lack of recorded responses to demands in the book of Zechariah intimates that the work as a whole may be propositional and that it aims to elicit a response from its initial audience, who may have been the work's implied audience, the remnant. If the remnant picked up on this inconsistency, they may be very reluctant to respond to Yahweh's demands in this work. But perhaps Yahweh's unreliability is part of the text's rhetoric. The depiction of Yahweh as a crafty, wily, perpetually angry, capricious figure furthers the moment's exigency: everyone fears, and fairly automatically obeys, a tyrant. Turn to Yahweh while you may, because his offer's expiry date is unknown, to say nothing of his next judgment day. The effect is that while Yahweh promises yet to relent concerning Jerusalem and the cities of Judah, the implied audience should not delay too long in responding to his demands because his past record shows he can, and will, cause great calamity for lengthy amounts of time when angered: 'Don't make him angry. You wouldn't like him when he's angry.' Furthermore, it is Yahweh's explanation of events which is unreliable and not his ability to perform his promises. Perhaps it is simply a post-Aquinian view of God as the unmovable mover and the unchanging God, which casts a negative shadow on Yahweh's shifting explanations and attributions of his deeds.

There is a problem of speaker in v. 16: is the phrase, 'therefore, thus says Yahweh', Yahweh's speech or the conversing messenger's interjected comment? Alternatively, the conversing messenger only interjects the phrase 'thus says Yahweh', and 'therefore' (לכן) is part of Yahweh's speech. Another option is that the entire phrase is part of Yahweh Sebaoth's dictated speech which the conversing messenger relates to Zechariah so that Zechariah can proclaim Yahweh's speech to the remnant. Yahweh Sebaoth, via the conversing messenger, is Zechariah's speech writer, and dictates the entire speech, including the conversing messenger's interjections, to ensure the precise message is delivered verbatim.

Yahweh promises that his house will be built in Jerusalem. He depicts the menial labour of temple building as a blessing by speaking about it in the same breath as he speaks about his compassionate return to Jerusalem. His use of the niphal form יִבָּנֶה ('will be built') implies he will not be personally undertaking this task. In Haggai, Yahweh had to incite the remnant to lay the foundations for his house by explaining their economic situation was the result of his displeasure with the remnant because he lacked a house (Hag. 1.9-10). Perhaps their apathy has returned. That Yahweh here presents building his house as a positive activity suggests the remnant still does not want to rebuild Yahweh's house. But this text is reticent on the remnant's feelings as it is reticent on how the nations feel about Yahweh's unjust treatment of them. Yahweh has compassionately returned to Jerusalem, yet his house is still incomplete—it has only been founded (Hag. 2.18; Zech. 8.9) and

no stones are yet laid (Hag. 2.15).[104] Yahweh has no house and is therefore a Jerusalemite vagabond. In his desire to obtain a home, Yahweh
tries a new approach to get a house built. Instead of commanding the
people to build his house, he promises future weal for the remnant if
they build his house. As it is sometimes easier to make children perform
tasks if the tasks are made to look attractive, so Yahweh tries another
approach with the remnant. He nudges the audience to remind them that
there is work to do and tries to persuade them that building his house is
desirable. This text appears to attempt to persuade the remnant to build
his house; if the house does get built it proves its rhetoric worked. It is
self-fulfilling prophecy.

Once one recognizes that Yahweh's plan is focused on Jerusalem, his
statement 'while my cities will be scattered from good' is comprehensible. The cities which Yahweh calls 'my cities' are contextually
identifiable with the cities of Judah about which the messenger of Yahweh lamented. That Yahweh Sebaoth calls them 'my cities' shows that
he is personally concerned about them. But his statement about them is
far from 'relenting'. While the preposition מִן may bear a causative
meaning 'because of' (Waltke and O'Connor 1990: 213), it more often
means 'from' when it follows the root פּוּץ ('spread') and the sense is
usually one of separation from that object or idea. That Yahweh's cities
are 'scattered from good' means they are removed from good (see
1 Sam. 13.8; 2 Sam. 20.22; 2 Kgs 25.5; and, slightly differently, Gen.
11.8 and Ezek. 46.18, where the מִן does not immediately follow פּוּץ).
Thus I read with Ruffin 'while my cities are scattered from good'
(Ruffin 1986: 139).[105] Ruffin rightly observes that this reading suits the
context well (1986: 139), as numerous verses in Zechariah hint that the
cities of Judah, as well as Jerusalem, lack inhabitants (see Zech. 7.7).
Yahweh Sebaoth's agenda for the immediate future of the cities is not
promising. He postpones showing compassion for the Judaean cities,
though he will eventually restore them too (see Zech. 2.16; 10.6). Per-

---

104. Gelston demonstrates that יָסַד 'need not mean literally to "lay a foundation"...it may have a more general meaning—"repair, restore, rebuild", with the
emphasis on the idea of firmness and durability' (1966: 235; see Eybers's discussion of this [1975: 19-20]). Thus Zerubbabel does not necessarily lay a foundation
stone in 4.7, but is simply 'the leader under whom the work of restoration was
begun' (Gelston 1966: 235).

105. For an example where מִן following פּוּץ is best translated as 'because of'
see Ezek. 34.5.

haps this is to facilitate his plan more rapidly. Yahweh wants the returning exiles to settle in Jerusalem to build his house. After this portion of
his agenda is taken care of, and Jerusalem is inhabited, then his blessings can flow into the Judaean cities.

Yahweh's promise to choose Jerusalem augments his case for
rebuilding his house. Yahweh Sebaoth previously chose Zerubbabel
and promised to make him like a signet ring on the day in which he
overthrows kingdoms and the power of the nations (Hag. 2.23). He has
chosen the person he wants to exercise his authority (as signet ring); he
now promises that Jerusalem is the city he will choose to exercise this
authority from. I translate עוד in ובחר עוד בירושלם as 'again' and view
this sentence as an allusion to the idea found in Kings (and elsewhere)
which stresses that Yahweh chose Jerusalem as a place for his house
and his name (compare 1 Kgs 11.13, 32, 36) and then rejected it (2 Kgs
23.27). Zechariah is the sole prophet to attribute Yahweh with choosing
Jerusalem (De Vaux 1969: 286). In Zech. 1.17 Yahweh alludes to his
rejection of Jerusalem and promises he is either in the act of choosing
again, or will again choose Jerusalem. The selection recalls Yahweh's
choice of Jerusalem in Deuteronomy and in 1 Kings as a place for his
house and his name (see 1 Kgs 11.13, 32, 36) and his rejection of it just
before the exile in 2 Kgs 23.27. By promising to choose Jerusalem
again, Yahweh is restoring Jerusalem's pre-exilic status as 'his place'.

The building of Yahweh's house, combined with his choosing of
Jerusalem, develops the opening scene by the deep (מצלה). Deuteronomy 16.13-17 commands all males to assemble before Yahweh on the
feast of booths in the place which Yahweh chooses and to give according to how Yahweh has blessed him. Zechariah's further development
of this theme in ch. 14 depicts the plunder of the surrounding nations,
followed by the entire world celebrating the feast of booths. If all males
in the entire world celebrate the feast of booths by bringing gifts in
accord with their harvest, the tribute from that festival will be enormous, not to mention the economic influx of tourist shekels. Perhaps
this is how Yahweh will fulfil his promise in Hag. 1.7-8 to fill his house
with glory—silver and gold.[106]

106. Carroll says the temple in Haggai, Zechariah and Malachi is 'the economic
centre of the community' (1994: 44): Haggai depicts 'the new temple as a potential
storehouse or treasury of the empire. It is hardly a holy place for worship or the cel-
ebration of cultic rituals, but it is to be a place for the generating of great wealth.
With its building the economic welfare of the community will be trans-

The nations will be initially plundered, and much gold and silver and many garments will be gathered. Not content with a single plunder, Yahweh proposes a sustainable influx of capital. The temple will annually receive the world-wide tribute for the feast of booths. In order for these events to occur a temple needs to be built to hold the gold. Yahweh provides the best incentive possible to build his house, and one which directly addresses human concerns—enormous economic growth centred on a world-wide festival. Not only does economic growth occur, but they get a party, perhaps an ancient equivalent to *Mardi Gras*, as a bonus. In the future, Jerusalem will annually be filled with tourists bearing much cash and vacation spending mentalities. This tourist industry will further help the Jerusalem economy.

When Yahweh Sebaoth's speech is finished, little about the current world situation is changed. Most of the statements Yahweh makes are promises with no action. Yahweh only performs three acts: he was/is zealous for Jerusalem and Zion, angry with the secure nations and has returned to Jerusalem with compassion. Yahweh's return is hardly a new act, since he was already present with the remnant in Haggai. All Yahweh does here is specify the location he returned to, which was implied in Haggai anyway.[107] The fate of the Judaean cities is still to be determined as Yahweh only states their present condition and affirms that this condition will be unchanged in the (immediate?) future, or will recur. As to how long they will be scattered from good, Yahweh is here reticent. Perhaps he will address this issue later in the vision sequence. That Yahweh is angry with the secure nations hints that revenge may lie in the future for the implied audience's suffering at the hands of these nations, even though the nations may hardly deserve this punishment. Still, Yahweh promises no explicit revenge for their evil. Concerning

formed...Zechariah 8.9-13 also represents the temple as an economic centre, and the burgeoning of the economy is associated directly with the building of the temple' (1994: 41-43).

Berquist discusses the role of the temple: 'the construction of a temple allowed for a variety of functions to be met in a single building: imperial government, financial administration and renewed worship of the people's deity' (1989: 165). He strikes a balanced view of the temple when he says 'a substantial portion of the populace would interpret the building of a temple as a sign of God's favor. This view may have been held instead of or in addition to an interpretation of the temple as the administrative tool of the Persian empire' (1989: 162).

107. Marinkovic points out that Yahweh's return is to 'the whole city of Jerusalem' and not solely to the temple (1994: 93).

the future in general, Yahweh focuses on Jerusalem and promises his house will be built there, a line will be stretched over Jerusalem and he will yet show compassion for Zion and choose Jerusalem. Yahweh has shifted the focus of his messengers' query onto Jerusalem and Zion, and specifically onto the building activity.

Reading one of Zechariah's visions in conversation with the minor prophets (with 'dips' into other intertexts) does provide a reasonable interpretation of some of the textual elements. Yet, the interpretations it provides depend on repression of knowledge of other texts outside of the minor prophets. Most readers, I hazard, are aware of the story of the Exodus. When the other images in Zech. 1.8 are combined with the horse imagery in Hag. 2.22, they recall Moses' song in Exodus 15. In Exodus 15 Pharaoh's army, including horse (סוס) and rider (רכב; Exod. 15.1) descend (ירד) into the deep (מצלה; Exod. 15.5). This theme is similar to Yahweh's promise in Hag. 2.22, the most recent reference to horses in the book of the Twelve, that the horses (סוסים) and their riders (רכביהם) will go down (ירד) by the sword of another. Does this mean that Zechariah sees the aftermath of a second Sea of Reeds in which all the horsemen of the nations have been dismounted and drowned in the מצלה with a solitary rider emerging from the carnage between the myrtles? In essence, do the remnant stand at the sea of Reeds before Pharaoh's army is defeated, or after? Zechariah's first vision incorporates the Exodus motif to portray the end of the Exile as a new Exodus. Another element of the Exodus motif carried further in Zechariah is that in Exodus it is for a feast that the Hebrews left Egypt (Exod. 10.9; 12.14). In Zechariah 14, after a plague, a feast is celebrated. These connectives remain dormant if one solely uses the minor prophets as the interpretative text by which to read Zechariah.

This reading involves repressing the roles of the myrtles. These are also significant in that they were used in postexilic times to celebrate the feast of booths (Neh. 8.15)—a feast which commemorates the Exodus and how Yahweh made the sons of Israel live in booths when he brought them out of Egypt (Lev. 23.43). The interpretation also leaves unexamined the stretching of the line over Jerusalem in Zech. 1.16 because a line (קו) is not stretched out in the minor prophets (although note the near parallel text of Amos 7.8). Petersen discusses the use here of the ambiguous metaphor of 'stretching a line': it is a symbol of both construction or destruction (1984a: 156-57). That a negative assessment is given to the cities in 1.17 might imply the line is being stretched in its destructive capacity here (see 2 Kgs 21.13; Isa. 34.11; Lam. 2.8). Petersen notes the intertexts of Ezek. 47.3 and Jer. 31.38-39, in which stretching the line 'is to measure the extent of Yahweh's restorative blessing' (1984a: 157). The intertext of Lam. 2.8, in which the walls of בת־ציון ('the daughter of Zion') are ruined, is particularly enlightening in the context of Zech. 2.8, in which Jerusalem will be inhabited as an open city as Yahweh will be its walls. The line may be stretched over Jerusalem again to completely eliminate the walls to ensure it remains an open city (פרזות). Both constructive and destructive images may be merged in the metaphor to suggest the city is rebuilt, but the walls are to remain devastated. But to read this way we must expand our context further. Reading in the context of the minor prophets demands the repression of too many intertexts. Thus, the intertextual net must be spread further.[108]

---

108. Jer. 31.39 and Ezek. 40–44 provide intertextual help in understanding the symbol of a line.

Chapter 5

ZECHARIAH 1–8 AND ITS INTERTEXTS

The confusing nature of Zechariah 1–8's narrative encourages readers to expand their horizons in their quest for meaning: readers are forced to look for meanings in intertexts if they want to satiate their curiosity. These intertextual contexts are then imported back into the narrative of Zechariah, with the images generated in the readers' minds for both the intertext and Zechariah: new pictures are created as the mental pictures are merged.

Since Zech. 2.1-4 was *unsuccessfully* analysed in the previous chapter, this chapter will return to that passage in a second attempt to master the beast. After this analysis, I will examine the overt intertextual phrase found in Zech. 3.2. An attempt will be made to understand the symbolism which surrounds this difficult phrase. Finally, some conclusions will be drawn about how the intertextual mingling helped, or did not help, to enlighten this reader in the impenetrable darkness surrounding the narrative in Zechariah.

New Growth on Horns: Zechariah 2.1-4 in an Intertextual Frame

This passage has already been extensively dealt with in the previous chapter. The reader is referred to the section, 'The Second Vignette: 2.1-4' for a discussion of the difficulties of this passage. The confusing nature of the interpretation given for the horns has already been explored on an intratextual level. The intratextual connections do not provide an unequivocal interpretation for the hypertext. Yet another matrix is formed when the reader re-asks the questions, already posed, what is a horn[1] of a nation and how does it scatter or winnow Judah, Israel and Jerusalem? Once these horns are identified, what does it

1. For an in-depth discussion of the metaphor of horns in the Bible and in the ancient Near East, see Süring's works (1980, 1985).

mean that they, collectively, scatter or winnow them to such an extent that no one can lift up their head? How do all of these disparate symbolic elements combine to infuse me, as reader, with meaning?[2]

Süring cautions against interpreting the horns necessarily as a bull motif (Rudolph [1976: 82 n. 1] says the image of a wild stampeding bull scattering a crowd may lie behind the image), or an animal motif, as 'horns' occur in both literal and metaphorical contexts (1985: 327; Rudolph [1976: 82] believes these horns are too long to be animal horns). She lists senses outside of the animal imagery for the word horn:

> (1) Depiction of literal horns (such as on altars), without any sort of explicit reference to their meaning; (2) depiction of horns, with functional aspects or dimensions indicated in the context; and (3) the use of the terms 'horn' and 'horns' in a purely metaphorical sense (Süring 1985: 327; see her discussion of horn[s] used as a pure metaphor [335-40]).

That 'horn' may be used in a purely metaphorical sense suggests a sense of endless substitution surrounds the term: it can be a pure signifier.

Süring also suggests connotations such as salvation, safety, security, an invisible messianic kingdom, political or national domination, and the use of the term as a cryptic device for a kingdom or kings (1985: 337-40). She cautions that one cannot prove the four horns represent totality (contra Rudolph [1976: 83] who sees the four horns as representing the totality of the known world power preventing Yahweh's lordship) or four successive (or definite) world powers, but they may represent four kings or contemporary kingdoms like the horns of Daniel (1980: 386). Galling interprets this way to see the four horns as a 'Bild für die Herrschaft der Babylonier, wobei die Vierzahl sich unschwer aus dem alten Königstitel: "Herr der vier Weltgegenden" erklärt' ('picture of the Lordship of the Babylonians, where the number four is easy to explain as [coming] from the old king's title "Lord of the four world regions" ') (1964: 112).

---

2.   Rudolph depicts the horns as stuck in the ground in a quadrant (1976: 82) He takes חריד here not to mean 'make afraid' but to physically shake (1976: 81 n. 4f). The artisans come, one for each horn, and each takes hold of a horn and 'shakes' it until it falls to the ground (1976: 82). As to the symbolism of the horns, he suggests they do not symbolize the foreign people, but only their might and strength (Rudolph 1976: 82).

Freer provides one of the more interesting definitions of horn: '"horn" can also be used to connote a man's progeny (1 Chron. 25.5) or even a fertile hill (Isa. 5.1). It may be that when the word is used in these contexts it has sexual or even phallic overtones' (Freer 1975: 126). The metaphor in 1 Chron. 25.5 is קרן הרים ('cause his horn to be raised'): Heman's horn is 'raised' and he has many children. This strongly supports Freer's phallic reading. Is the idiom of raising (רום) a horn in 1 Chronicles 25 synonymous with the idiom of raising (נשא) a horn in Zechariah 2? If so, what is implied by the horns of the nations being raised so a man of Judah cannot lift his head in Zech. 2.4? Are the nations engaged in sexual cavorting while the man of Judah cannot raise his head, that is, he is impotent? This is hardly sustainable, though, because 'head' nowhere signifies 'phallus' in classical Hebrew literature. Perhaps though the nations are sexually ascendant while a man of Judah is in shame. The metaphor deflates quickly though, as it is senseless for a phallus to winnow people (though it's an image worthy of Rabelais). Freer sees a similar use of horns in Zechariah 2 and Daniel 7–8: they are 'symbols of nations which have oppressed Israel and the destruction of those horns as the symbol of the downfall of those nations' (1975: 127).

Jeremiah 17.1 reads 'The sin of Judah is written with an iron pen; with a diamond point it is engraved (חרושה) on the tablet of their hearts, and on the horns of their altars' (NRSV; חטאת יהודה כתובה בעט ברזל בצפרן שמיר חרושה על-לוח לבם ולקרנות מזבחותיכם). It is presumably an artisan who engraved these horns. Engraving, albeit פתח rather than חרש, is an activity in which artisans engage (Exod. 28.10). Even if artisans do not merely, or even necessarily, 'engrave' (חרש),[3] the identical root is a connective to a reader cognizant of both texts.

There is an ambiguity as to whether the horns are something upon which the sin of Judah is engraved or are themselves the product of the engraving process. The resolution depends on how metaphorically one reads the engraving in Jeremiah. That the sin of Judah is engraved on the tablet of their hearts alerts one quite quickly to the presence of metaphor in this verse. Is the engraving on the horns a literal engraving, a metaphor, or both? The engraving could metaphorically read when attributed 'on their hearts' but read literally for 'on the horns of your

---

3. Three texts which may be helpful in determining the profession of one who חרש (as a verb) are Gen. 4.22; 1 Sam. 8.12; and 1 Kgs 7.14. Unfortunately these are all fairly vague texts.

altars'. Perhaps the sin of Judah is simply horns which have been engraved. Either way, the horn is a symbol of Judah's sin. The artisans of Zechariah 2 may come to remove this engraving of sin: to chisel out the sinful inscription.

Amos 3.14 contains a similar motif: 'On the day I punish Israel for its transgressions, I will punish the altars of Bethel, and the horns of the altar shall be cut off and fall to the ground.' In Lamentations 2 Yahweh hews off the horn of Israel and raises the horn of Zion's adversaries (vv. 3, 17). The implication is that the symbolic logic underlying the symbol 'horns' requires the horns of one nation to be raised at the expense of the horns of another nation. Psalm 75 may echo a similar motif as the horns of the wicked are cut off while the horns of the righteous will be exalted. Jeremiah 11.13 and Hos. 10.1 speak of Judah and Israel multiplying gods and setting up many altars. This symbolic logic can be taken to provide a background to Zechariah 2. The symbolic logic displays an understanding of history and portrays the historical condition which led to the proliferation of altars which the artisans come to redress.

Zechariah 2 is a partial reversal of the situation in Lamentations 2—the horns of the nations are cast down. Oddly, the horns of Israel, Judah and Jerusalem are not portrayed as being raised in Zechariah. A reader familiar with these other texts may condense them to create an explanation of the symbolic system underlying Zechariah. Are the horns of the nations an altar of a foreign god? If the horns זרו (scatter) Judah in Zechariah 2, perhaps it is best to read the piel of זרה here with the causative sense, so that the horns of the nations caused Judah, Israel and Jerusalem to be scattered. Yahweh is often the subject who זרה (Israel as object in 1 Kgs 14.15; those who cut the corners as the object in Jer. 49.32; Elam in Jer. 49.36; foreigners dispatched by Yahweh scatter Babylon in Jer. 51.2; Yahweh scatters the remnant of Jerusalem to every wind in Ezek. 5.10; the mountains of Israel in Ezek. 6.5, the prince in Jerusalem and the house of Israel [cf. Ezek. 12.10; 15]; and Egypt and the Egyptians in Ezek. 29.12; 30.23, 26). That a similar phrase is used for both Yahweh's action and a similar action by the horns might suggest the activity is synonymous and Yahweh is complicit in the scattering of Judah by the horns. At any rate, the horns of the nations represent the worship of foreign gods by Judah, Israel and Jerusalem. This resulted in their being scattered.

Though Amos 3.14 is only concerned with one altar, the artisans of

Zechariah 2 come to fulfil a similar role and cast down foreign altars. This concept is nearly synonymous to Amos 3.14's horns being cut off and falling to the ground. There are other pre-texts where the destruction of altars is part of the restoration. In Isa. 27.9 crushing the altars as chalkstones results in the removal of Jacob's sin (חטא). This is a connective with Amos 3.14 and the sin of the altars. The textual construct formed by this and Zechariah is the artisans coming to crush the altars into stone. The artisans then come to hew off the horns of the nations, perhaps crush them and throw them to the ground.

If the reader takes the time to read the context of Jeremiah 17 (Jer. 16–17) she will quickly notice many connectives between Jeremiah 17 and Zechariah 1–8. Yahweh promises people will not go into the house of feasting to eat and drink (16.8). He promises to remove (שׁוב) from this place 'the voice of mirth (שׂשׂון) and the voice of gladness (שׂמחה)' (NRSV). These acts are undone in Zech. 8.19: the fasts are turned into feasts, 'seasons of joy (שׂשׂון) and gladness (שׂמחה)' (NRSV). In Jer. 16.13 Yahweh promises to 'hurl you out of this land into a land neither you nor your ancestors (אבותיכם; see Zech. 1.2-6) have known (אשׁר לא ידעתם)' (NRSV; see Jer. 17.4). This concept is akin to Zech. 7.14 where Yahweh storms them (presumably the ancestors of 1.2-6) to all the nations they did not know (אשׁר לא־ידעום). After this act in Jeremiah, Yahweh says he will bring up the sons of Israel from the land of the north (מארץ־צפון).[4] Zech. 2.6's command to flee from the land of the north (מארץ־צפון), if obeyed, is a fulfilment of this prophecy.

Other connectives abound: Yahweh's inheritance is spoken of (Jer 16.18; Zech 2.16); nations will come to Yahweh (Jer. 16.19; Zech. 2.22); Judah will serve their enemies in a foreign land (Jer. 17.4; Zech.

---

4.   See Childs (1959) for a discussion of the merger of the concept of the land of the north and the chaos traditions which takes place in exilic and postexilic texts. He argues that רעשׁ ('quake') is integral to the chaos tradition (so Hag. 2.22; 1959: 188-90). Perhaps this is related to the problematic Zech. 4.7 where the great mountain is made into a plain before Zerubbabel (see Zech. 14.10; see also Ezek. 38.20; Nah. 1.5; and Jer. 51.25). Rost sees this mountain as Persian world power (1952: 220). Stuhlmueller sees the mountain being made into a plain as representing 'the mountains around Jerusalem leveled to a plain as workers quarry rock from these hills' (1970: 393). In many ways Zech. 1–8 connects with the 'enemy from the north' tradition and may hint at a reversal of the situation which is brought about by the enemy of the north. Childs notes the enemy from the north 'comes from "afar"' (see Zech. 5.26; 6.15), speaks in a 'foreign tongue' (see Zech. 7.14 and 8.23) and is 'a storm coming from afar' (see Ezek. 1.4 and Zech. 7.14; 1959: 190-91).

2.13); Judah will be plundered (Jer. 17.3; Zech. 2.12); and Yahweh promises to give according to their ways (דרך) and deeds (מעלל; Jer. 17.10; see Zech. 1.4, 6). In Jeremiah 17 the wealth of Judah is given away and the Judaeans are made to serve their enemies in a land they do not know because of Yahweh's anger. This is a situation that is reversed later in Zechariah 2 where the daughter of Zion is the servant of foreign nations who plunder her. After the horns are cast down this situation is set aright and the daughter of Zion will plunder those who previously plundered her. The situation in Jeremiah 17 is described also in Zechariah—the nations take their wealth (Jer. 17.3; Zech. 2.13). As to being scattered in lands they do not know, this is exactly the situation that is described in Zech. 7.14. Perhaps the question of the location of the ancestors in Zech. 1.5 is to verify that the situation described in Jeremiah has indeed occurred, and the prophecies of a former prophet have indeed overtaken their addressees.

A particularly potent connective is found in Jer. 17.2. That this verse begins with כ ('as, while') links it to the preceding verse in a temporal sense.[5] The NRSV translates this continuity in its translation of 17.1-3:

> The sin of Judah is written with an iron pen; with a diamond point it is engraved on the tablet of their hearts, and on the horns of their altars, *while* their children remember [זכר] their altars and their sacred poles, beside every green tree, and on the high hills, on the mountains in the open country (emphasis mine).

The connective is not with any specific verse in Zechariah, but with the name of the book: זכריה. The exact translation of the name is unimportant.[6] What is important is the connotation evoked by the recurrence of the root זכר. A further connective is present in the assertion that the sin of Judah is written and engraved on the horns of their altars as long as their children (בניהם) remember their altars. The children of Jer. 17.2 contrastingly resonate with the fathers of Zechariah. The remembrance of the altars metaphorically, and perhaps literally, engraves the sin of

---

5.   On the semantics of the inseparable preposition כ, and specifically with the infinitive (as it is found in Jer. 17.2), see Joüon (1991: 133g): 'Before an infinitive…כ means *like the action of* …(= as when…, *as if*)…or, with a temporal meaning…*just as, when, as*'. Similarly Waltke and O'Connor, 'The *temporal* use of *k* is related to its sense either as a marker of approximation ("about that time") or of correspondence ("at the [same] time"…) and is found with the infinitive construct' (1990: 11.2.9e; see 36.2.2b).

6.   See my section 'Fluctuating Lists' for a discussion of the name Zechariah.

Judah onto the horns. Perhaps it is the remembrance of Yahweh that will end this process. When the children remember Yahweh rather than the foreign altars they will be restored to the land of their fathers (see Jer. 16.15).

Lamentations 2.1 also contains the connective זכר (remember), but in a very different sense. There, Yahweh, in his anger, does not remember his footstool (the daughter of Zion or the glory of Israel). Zechariah also portrays Yahweh once again remembering his footstool and presumably ending his anger (this interpretation is well supported by Zech. 1). In Lam. 2.6 Yahweh causes to be forgotten (שׁכח) the appointed time (מועד) and sabbath. In Zech. 8.19 the fasts are turned into appointed times (מועד).

Perhaps it is the symbolization underlying Micah 4 that informs the symbolic motif of the horns in Zechariah. Micah 4.11-13 reads:

> Now many nations are assembled against you, saying, 'Let her be profaned, and let our eyes gaze upon Zion.' But they do not know the thoughts of the LORD; they do not understand his plan, that he has gathered them as sheaves to the threshing floor. Arise and thresh, O daughter Zion, for I will make your horn iron and your hoofs bronze; you shall beat in pieces many peoples, and shall devote their gain to the LORD, their wealth to the Lord of the whole earth.

A reader familiar with Micah may assume that Yahweh is fulfilling this promise. A picture of warring horns is created: the horns of the daughter of Zion versus the horns of the nations. The situation at the beginning of Zechariah presupposes that the horns have initially won the battle and have forced the horns of Judah, Israel and Jerusalem into submission, recalling the hewed off horn of Israel and the raised horn of Zion's adversaries (Lam. 2.3, 17). That each one[7] cannot lift his head may indicate the horns of Judah are unable to battle the horns of the nations, perhaps because they were hewn off. The artisans in Zechariah come to redress this situation—to transform the daughter of Zion's horn into iron and her hoofs into bronze, thereby enabling her to thresh the nations. Perhaps they make artificial horns to replace the ones which were hewn off.

An ironic situation is latent in the agricultural motif which underlies Micah and Zechariah. In both of these texts horns are used for agricul-

---

7.   BDB translates אישׁ as both animals (Gen. 7.2) and inanimate objects (Exod. 36.4; see BDB, 35-36).

tural purposes: threshing and winnowing.[8] Though this may exist purely as a metaphor, this imagery may provide insight into ancient agricultural practices. Perhaps animals, presumably cattle, were used in harvesting: in winnowing and in threshing. Were devices attached to the animals to facilitate this process? Were artisans employed to attach these devices that would harness a threshing sledge or a winnowing fork to the respective feet and heads of these animals? The horns of the nations winnowed (זָרָה) Israel, Judah and Jerusalem; that is they began the processing of the harvest: they intended, and indeed started, to harvest Israel, Jerusalem and Judah. Ironically, it is not the horns of the nations which complete the process, but the horns of the daughter of Zion. Furthermore, they obtain the wealth of these many peoples by threshing them. The horns are connected with harvesting motifs in both Zechariah and Micah. Where the nations were winnowing Judah in preparation for threshing, it is Zion who completes the process and threshes the nations. This ties into the Zechariah theme of the nations being plunder for their servants (2.12-13).

Readers may bring with them intertexts in which the horns clearly belong to an animal. Deuteronomy 33.16-17 contains a similar metaphor:

> Let these come on the head of Joseph, on the brow of the prince among his brothers. A firstborn bull—majesty is his! His horns are the horns of a wild ox; with them he gores the peoples, driving them to the ends of the earth; such are the myriads of Ephraim, such the thousands of Manasseh.

This scene describes the horns of a wild ox which are metaphorically attributed to Joseph. The scene is reversed in Zechariah where horns scatter Israel, Judah and Jerusalem. In a reverse image of the horns of Joseph, Israel, Judah and Zion have been driven to the ends of the earth. Elsewhere in Zechariah 2 Zion is scattered to the four winds of heaven (2.10).[9] Horns are connected with the dispersion of people.

---

8. Good says of this vision 'We must recognize that the scene unfolding before Zechariah is bucolic' (1982: 58). Good argues that the הרשׁים are 'ploughmen' who 'come to startle beasts of burden' which have overrun the uninhabited cities (1982: 59). Good bases his arguments on the grounds that this form is theoretically possible, yet unattested, in biblical Hebrew (1982: 58-59). I support his reading as one possibility, but do not stand by it as the only possible reading. This is one more example of the agricultural theme present in this vision.

9. Driver translates this 'I have made you to fly as the four winds of heaven' (1930–31: 252-53).

If one recalls Jer. 48.25, the removal of the horn of Moab is equated with judgment. According to this, the nations are being judged if their horn is being cast down here.

Military,[10] economic, agricultural and animal symbolism are all united in the image of the horns. All these intertextual interpretations of horns are held in tension when Zechariah 2 is read and one reading cannot be definitively chosen at the expense of ignoring the rest, as there are elements of Zechariah which support all of them. The elements of Zechariah that support one reading involve clusters of connectives which appear in both Zechariah and the pre-text. Examples of these are legion, but only a few of them will be pointed out here.

While the multiplicity of connectives between Jeremiah 17 and Zechariah 2 might support the use of Jeremiah 17 to control the metaphor, the same thing could be said for many of the intertexts. Lamentations 2 shares the motifs of Yahweh's anger (2.1), and Yahweh's purposes for Jerusalem (2.17). Micah 4 also shares motifs with Zechariah: people sit under their own vines and fig trees (v. 4), those who have been driven away are gathered (v. 6), and the nations planning to assemble against Zion have their plans upset when they become plunder for Zion. The overlap of the motifs teases me even more.

What does the idiom כְּפִי־אִישׁ לֹא־נָשָׂא רֹאשׁוֹ mean?[11] What if the idiom is taken to be the key to the activity of the nations rather than the scattering of the horns? This opens anew the question of what man (אִישׁ), lift (נָשָׂא) and head (רֹאשׁ) mean. Freud teaches the necessity of interpreting figures of speech literally to understand dreams (1991: 532-33). Since the material in Zechariah is very dreamlike, perhaps the same method of interpretation would be valuable here. Though many, following BDB (805b), read כְּפִי as a particle meaning 'as' in Zech. 2.4,[12] other occurrences of כְּפִי often suggest viewing the mouth as literal (see Jer. 15.19; 1 Chron. 12.23). The phrase is literally כ (as, like), פֶה (mouth), (of), אִישׁ (a man), לוֹא (negative particle), נָשָׂא (lift, bear, forgive), (of), רֹאשׁוֹ (his head; so Chary [1969: 66]). Does this phrase mean

10. Seybold, on the analogy of Isa. 54.16 and Ezek. 21.36, reads these as armourers (1974b: 104).

11. Meyers and Meyers argue from Jer. 52.31; Gen. 40.20-21; and Num. 1.2, 49; 26.2; and 31.49 that the idiom represents the lack of 'individual autonomy of deported Judeans' (1987: 141). See Rignell for a discussion of various viewpoints concerning this phrase (1950: 66-68).

12. For example, Rudolph (1976: 81 n. 4d).

they could not raise their mouth to their head, that is they could not lift
their jaw? Does the phrase indicate some state of utter shock on the part
of those winnowed? Might it mean they are speechless at the extent of
their winnowing—they cannot raise their mouth to speak?[13] Might this
phrase be related to the idiom פתח פה which also relates to speechlessness (Ezek. 24.27; 33.22; Job 33.2; Dan. 10.6)?

Similarly, the idiom פתחון פה ('open [your] mouth') relates to speech
(Ezek. 16.63; 29.21). In Ezek. 16.63 the idiom is related to shame (בוש
and כלמה), forgiveness and remembrance (זכר), which are similar concepts to those in Zechariah. Ezekiel 29.21 forms a fascinating intertextual cluster of connectives with Zechariah 2. In Ezek. 29.21 Yahweh
causes 'a horn (קרן) to sprout up (צמח) for the house of Israel' (NRSV)
and opens the mouth of the people, after which they will know (ידע) he
is Yahweh. The artisans cast down the horns of the nations (Zech. 2)
leaving room for the horn to sprout up. The image is similar to garden-
ing: it is as if the horns of the nations block the sunlight from the
emerging horn of the house of Israel (see Dan. 7.8 where three horns
are uprooted to make room for the little horn which possesses a mouth
and Dan. 8.8 where four horns grow when the big horn is broken). If
the clauses in Ezek. 29.21a and 29.21b are consequential rather than
autonomous, that is if the opening of the mouth is consequential on the
horn sprouting, then perhaps the horns are cast down in Zechariah to
make room for the horn of the house of Israel to sprout, which will
enable the house of Israel to speak. This is like the horn of Dan. 7.8
which speaks once it grows. To read Zechariah 2 in the penumbra of
Ezek. 16.63; 29.21; Dan. 7.8; and 8.8 creates a picture in which the
house of Judah cannot speak because of its shame (Ezek. 16). When the
horns of the nations are cast down, the horn of the house of Judah may
grow (this is a gap which the reader familiar with the symbolic universe
of these idioms might construct), providing the house of Judah with the
pride necessary to speak. The house of Judah is thereby a marginalized
presence in Zechariah lacking the necessary power to voice its dissent.

Horns grow on the head. Further, one lowers the head to use them in
battle. That the head could not be raised might imply Judah is in a state
of constant battle and cannot raise its head, that is lift it up in ascendancy after gaining victory in combat.

13. So Ischodad of Merv translated and quoted in Rignell (1950: 67).

The idiom may be a conflation of two idioms or collocations which occur in the Tanakh: ראשׁ נשׂא (lift a head) and פי־ראשׁו (mouth of his head/opening). In Prov. 12.14; 13.2; 18.4 and 20 the phrase 'the mouth of a person' (פי־אישׁ) is used to denote the words of a speaker. The same metaphor is used in Zech. 2.4 to describe what a person cannot raise. Does the scattering result in speechlessness? Another interpretation for this idiom might be reached by combining a few passages. In Josh. 14.1; and 19.51 the heads (ראשׁי) of families distribute inheritances (נחל in the piel). In Num. 35.8 אישׁ כפי נחלתו is used to designate an inheritance. Perhaps the entire idiom relates to a person of Judah not being able to obtain the inheritance distributed by the head of his family? If one ignores the maqqeph between פי and אישׁ then one might view the כפי as relating to the head. In Exod. 28.2 the high priest's robe has an opening for the head (פי־ראשׁו). כפי is used to indicate the openings on other garments (see Exod. 28.32; 39.23; Job 30.18). Perhaps the idiom כפי־אישׁ לא־נשׂא ראשׁו means someone could not put on a garment. The picture of the re-clothing of Joshua in ch. 3 comes to mind. But there Joshua was wearing a garment. Perhaps the idiom then means the man (Joshua) could not put (that is, 'lift') his head through a garment: therefore he could not change clothes and assume his priestly office. That the idiom פי ראשׁו is used of the high priest's garments in Exod. 28.32 might suggest that the man could not put on priestly robes. כפי is also used of the opening of a corselette (Exod. 28.32; 39.23). This provides a martial context. Perhaps the artisans come to fashion a coat of mail for him to wear so that he can battle the horns.

If one looks at the other idiom which may contribute to this metaphor (נשׂא ראשׁ), a different interpretation emerges. The idiom has many uses. It can refer to taking a census (for taxes: Exod. 30.12; or for military duty: Num. 1.2-3; 4.2, 22; 31.49). Lifting a head is an idiom for counting in Numbers (see 4.2; 7.2). Perhaps in Zechariah Judah has been scattered so extensively that the people cannot be counted: they are far too dispersed to count. The census in Numbers 4 and 7 is performed to see who qualifies to work for the tent of meeting. The parallel to Zechariah may imply that temple service may not begin if the quantity of individuals eligible to work in the temple cannot be determined because the population as a whole cannot be counted. Would this make the idiom of Zech. 2.4 hyperbole: they were scattered so much that not even one person could be counted? The abundance of people and cattle in Zech. 2.8 is thus a symbolic reversal of this situation.

Alternatively, it means they could not ascertain their own military strength and therefore could not wage war against the horn. In 2 Kgs 25.27 the idiom means 'freed from prison'. Perhaps all of Judah is pictured as imprisoned. In Judg. 8.28 Midian is said to not lift their head. Previously Midian destroyed produce and stole the livestock of Israel (see Judg. 6.1-6). That they no longer lifted a head after being subdued suggests that their lifting a head was waging war and oppressing Israel. Judah is thus depicted in Zech. 2.4 as being oppressed or incapable of oppressing others.

Micah 4.1-4 provides a different understanding of 'head', as well as a cluster of intertextual connectives which relate to understanding 'head', and many other themes in Zechariah.

> In days to come[i] the mountain of the LORD's[ii] house shall be established as the highest of the mountains (בראש ההרים), and shall be raised up (נשא) above the hills. Peoples shall stream to it, and many nations[iii] shall come[iv] and say: 'Come, let us go up to the mountain of the LORD, to the house of the God of Jacob; that he may teach us his ways and that we may walk in his paths.' For out of Zion shall go forth instruction, and the word of the LORD from Jerusalem. He shall judge between many peoples,[v] and shall arbitrate between strong nations[vi] far away; they shall beat their swords into ploughshares, and their spears into pruning hooks; nation shall not lift up sword against nation, neither shall they learn war any more; but they shall all sit under their own vines and under their own fig trees,[vii] and no one shall make them afraid;[viii] for the mouth of the LORD of hosts has spoken.

Intertextual connections between Mic. 4.1-4 and Zechariah 1–8:

i.   באחרית הימים ('in the days to come' [NRSV]) stands antithetically to כימים הראשנים ('as in the former days') in Zech. 8.11. Perhaps this is to signal a looking forward to Zechariah by the reader of Micah, or a looking back to Micah by the reader of Zechariah.

ii.   הר יהוה צבאות ('the mountain of Yahweh Sebaoth') occurs in Zech. 8.3. This appears synonymous with the הר בית־יהוה ('the mountain of the house of Yahweh') in Mic. 4.1 and the הר־יהוה ('the mountain of Yahweh') in Mic. 4.2. This passage shares many concerns with Zechariah 8. Principally, both are concerned with a 'pilgrimage' of nations to Jerusalem which seeks the word of Yahweh.

iii.   גוים רבים ('many nations') is a connective with Zech. 2.15
where many nations are joined to Yahweh and will become his
people.

iv.   Nations הלך ('walk') to the mountain of the house in Mic. 4.2
(which appears to be in Jerusalem; see 4.2b) and to Jerusalem
in Zech. 8.21, 23.

v.   עמים רבים ('many peoples') is a connective with Zech. 8.22.

vi.   גוים עצמים ('strong nations') (Mic. 4.3, 7) is a connective with
Zech. 8.22 which only occurs five times in the Tanakh (the
other occurrences are Deut. 9.14 and Isa. 60.22).

vii.   A future state of prosperity designated by the image of a man
(איש) sitting under a vine (תחת גפן) and under a fig tree (תחת
תאנה) is shared with Zech. 3.10.

viii.   The verb here is the hiphil of חרד ('tremble'), which is the
same root of Zech. 2.4.

In Micah 4 the elevation (נשא) of the mountain of Yahweh results in
it being the ראש (head) of mountains (so also Isa. 2.2). By this reading
the house of Yahweh is not established as the pre-eminent mountain in
Zechariah: it is not lifted as the head of mountains yet.

There is even a possible allusion to the artisans in Micah 4: who else
would beat the swords into ploughshares? The horns of Judah are not
elevated in Zechariah 2 to put a final end to this military activity: the
swords will be beaten into ploughshares and spears into pruning hooks.
If Judah were to raise its horns, military oppression would still be
occurring, only they would be the oppressors. Zechariah signals the end
of war.

Yet another option presents itself. In Isa. 58.5 the head of an individual fasting is bent down like a bulrush. Perhaps this is the image that
lies behind Zechariah 2: the man cannot raise his head because he is
fasting or deprived of food. This ties into the end of the fasts at the end
of Zechariah 1–8 (8.19).

Which of these interpretations should be applied to this idiom? Perhaps it is a conflation of all of these readings. Perhaps that is why the
two idioms appear to be mixed. Many of these readings work to explain
the metaphor in some ways, but fail in others. A sense that one has truly
figured out the metaphor is not reached after pursuing this analysis.
Lifting a head could be read in conjunction with 2 Kgs 25.27 and Gen.
40.13 and 20 where it signifies freeing an individual from prison. Read

this way the horns are responsible for Israel, Judah and Jerusalem's imprisonment.

There are many paths by which one can reach an understanding of what 'head' may represent in Zechariah. In what appears to be a post-exilic situation in Hos. 2.2 (1.11e)[14] the descendants of Judah and Israel will appoint for themselves a head (ראש) and go up from the land in the day of Jezreel. Perhaps this is the type of situation in mind in Zechariah. That a man cannot lift his head means there that Judah cannot gather themselves together to appoint a leader (ראש) to take them out from their lands of exile.

Micah 2.12-13 contains a similar motif of a 'head', gathering the remnant of Israel and Jacob. Yet, in Mic. 2.13 it is Yahweh who is the head, or leader. Yahweh is also exalted (hithpael of נשא) 'for a head' in 1 Chron. 29.11. Perhaps it is Yahweh who they cannot raise as their leader, or exalt, in Zechariah because of their oppression.

In Mic. 3.1 and 9 the heads are the rulers of the people (ראש also signifies leaders in Josh. 14.2; 19.51). Zechariah may signify that the men of Judah were not ruling themselves, but were subject to foreign rulers: they could not raise a head of their own.

Amos 2.7 depicts economic depression and moral depravity. Those who are selling the righteous (read 'selling people'?) for money and sandals (2.6) are metaphorically (and literally?) trampling the head (ראש) of the poor into the ground (2.7). So does the image of a man not being able to raise his head signify he is poor and subject to being sold? In Joel 4.1-8(H) the nations are depicted as trading the people of Israel, Judah and Jerusalem (similar motifs are found in Nah. 3.10, where lots are cast for the honourable ones of No-Amon, and in Obadiah 11, where foreigners [נכר] cast lots [ידו גורל] for Jerusalem). Perhaps this is the image in mind in Zechariah. If so, it is a fitting reversal for the horns as the nations are depicted casting lots (ידו גורל) for Yahweh's people.[15]

When Yahweh turns back the captivity of Judah and Jerusalem he

---

14. This is at odds with many commentators who date Hosea much earlier. The reference to the return of Judaeans strongly suggests a much later date, at least for this verse, than the eighth century. If one does not assume redaction of this text, Hosea is much later than is generally acknowledged.

15. While לידות is problematic, Even-Shoshan views ידו as a shortened form of יידו (1989: 431) thus making ידו a piel form of ידה and not a qal form of ידד. He lists it in the same semantic group as ידות.

will gather all nations which have cast lots (ידו גורל; see Zech. 2.4) for his people and divided (חלק) his land.[16] Is a parallel meant to be set up between the horns and lots? Thus the artisans throw the nations as easily as one throws lots? There is a certain irony in that the nations who once cast lots for Jerusalem and Yahweh's people will themselves be cast. If one assumes that they are thrown to the ground in the casting, then the irony is further developed; the nations who lift up a horn will have their horn thrown down like a lot.

How do artisans make a horn tremble? When a horn is made to tremble, has one left the realm of the symbolic; that is, is it the people which comprise the nations which will be made to tremble, or does causing the horn to tremble belong with the symbolic world of the horn, that is the horns themselves will be made to tremble? If it is a musical horn one is tempted to say they blow the horn to make it sound, that is to vibrate (to tremble). This interpretation would belong to the symbolic world. Do artisans strike the horn to make it tremble by resounding from the blow (as a percussion instrument, rather than a wind instrument)? It is strange that the artisans come to terrify 'them' in Zech. 2.4. What might this action signify? In Hos. 11.10-11 Yahweh will roar like a lion: 'When he roars, his children shall come trembling from the west. They shall come trembling like birds from Egypt, and like doves from the land of Assyria; and I will return them to their homes, says the LORD' (NRSV). Yahweh's roaring results in the undoing of the exile. By this interpretation, the terrifying is not directed at the nations, but at the exiles and its aim is to cause them to return: the artisans come to terrify the exiles back to their homeland. While this passage speaks primarily about Ephraim, that in the next verse (Hos. 11.12) Yahweh mentions his dispute with Judah in the same context as Ephraim suggests Judah's children may be included in Hos. 11.10-11's gathering of children. Judah (2.2), Israel (2.1) and Ephraim (9.13) possess children in Hosea.

One can read an irony into the situation depicted in Zechariah 2 if Amos 3.6 is read as the primary intertext. There the blowing of a trumpet (שופר), which is a curved horn (see BDB, 1051; *LVT* 957; Josh. 6.4, 5) causes people to tremble (this reading assumes the rhetorical ques-

---

16. If Joel 3 is kept in mind while reading Zechariah, this concept forms another intertextual construct. After the horns of the nations are cast down, Yahweh inherits (נחל) Judah as his portion (חלק; see the verb of this root in Joel 3.2) in the holy land (2.16).

tion of this verse is answered affirmatively). The irony consists of horns
being made to tremble, when usually the opposite occurs: the blowing
of horns makes people tremble. In musical terms, does the blowing of a
horn make it tremble when it vibrates?

In Nah. 2.8-14 Nineveh, personified as a lion, is plundered and no
longer has a den free from terror (חרד). A similar situation occurs in
Zechariah: the nations are terrified (2.4) and subsequently plundered
(2.13). Yahweh's manner of overthrowing a nation is consistent in
Nahum and Zechariah. Zephaniah 3.13 contains a similar motif. It envi-
sions the returned remnant: There is no one who will make the remnant
of Israel tremble (reading Zeph. 3.8-13). The lack of one to make them
tremble is a picture of peace and security in both Zephaniah and
Nahum.

The use of חרד to describe the effect of the artisans coming may be
vague to allow multivalency. Artisans terrify Judah to scare them home,
and terrify the nations to end their oppression of Judah.

Isaiah 3–4 possesses a cluster of terms that form an intertextual construct with Zechariah 1–8. Zechariah 1–8 might be construed as a symbolic reversal of Isaiah 3. The symbolism of Isaiah 3 is of the judgment
of Yahweh on Jerusalem and Judah (Isa. 3.1, 14) and the ensuing
removal of people and items from Jerusalem and Judah (Isa. 3.1) and
their replacement by what the text constructs as less desirable elements
(Isa. 3.4-8, 12). Artisans (חרשים) are among those removed from the
land (Isa. 3.3). In Zechariah 1–8 artisans return (Zech. 2.4). The people
of Yahweh are crushed and the faces of the poor are ground (Isa. 3.15).
This may be construed as the symbolism underlying the expression
כפי־איש לא־נשא ראשו ('so that a man could not lift his head') in Zech.
2.3. The artisans thus come to undo this 'grinding'. Finally, luxurious
robes (מחלצות; BDB translates as 'robe of state' [323] but there is not
enough evidence to say more than this appears to be a luxury item; see
Petersen 1984a: 196) and turbans (צניף) are removed from the daughters of Zion (Isa. 3.16-24).

Joshua is clothed with robes (מחלצות) in Zech. 3.4. Zechariah's
demand to set the turban on Joshua's head may symbolize the renewal
of the presence of these luxurious items and beauty in the land. If the
reading 'festal apparel' is accepted for מחלצות (NRSV; NASB reads
'festal robes') this may symbolize the re-establishment of feasts which
may accompany these clothes (bearing in mind Thomas's criticism that
מחלצות means a clean or pure garment rather than a festal robe [1931–

32: 279-80]; likewise VanderKam 1991: 556-57; if this reading is accepted, the intertextual connection with Isaiah remains unbroken by this criticism, only the connection with feasts is banished). The only evidence in Zechariah which might allow this costume to be related to festivals is the changing of the fasts into feasts at the end of ch. 8. Perhaps Joshua is clothed in ornate clothing to take part in the feast.

On another level, the vocabulary emphasizes the relatedness of Isaiah 3 and Zechariah 3 as these are the only two chapters in the Tanakh in which צָנִיף ('turban') and מַחֲלָצוֹת ('festal robes') are found together (these two occurrences are the only occurrences of מַחֲלָצוֹת in the Tanakh; צָנִיף is a rare word only occurring 4 times in the Tanakh [Isa. 3.23; 62.3; Job 29.14; and Zech. 3.5]). Isaiah 62.3 calls Jerusalem and Zion a צְנִיף מְלוּכָה (a royal diadem; NRSV) in the hand of their God when Jerusalem is restored. Whether the royal connotations are transferable to Zechariah 3 is debatable. Why the צָנִיף ('turban') is in the hand of their God is confusing: should it not rest on his head? It is very difficult to transfer this symbolism over to Zechariah: how does one set Jerusalem (which is the צָנִיף in Isa. 62) on Joshua's head. Perhaps this passage allows one to distinguish between a royal turban (צְנִיף מְלוּכָה) and an ordinary one, which most likely occurs in Zechariah. It may be significant that in both Isaiah and Zechariah צָנִיף is used as a symbol of restoration.

Job's צָנִיף ('turban') is a metaphor for justice (מִשְׁפָּט; Blocher 1979: 267). Koch defines מִשְׁפָּט ('justice') as something which 'must continually be established anew in the gate of the city...*Mišpāṭ* means, rather, the institutional order, the intact but dynamic form of community, its specific characteristics and actions, the positive order of existence *per se*' (1978: 59). The turban can be seen as a symbol of justice in Zechariah, so that Joshua's clothing signifies his justice and the beginning of institutional order. The activities of Joshua can be seen to be a partial restoration of the justice which was removed from the land in Isaiah (3.4-7). Joshua is to judge in the temple rather than the whole land (for a discussion of how this judging might overlap with royal prerogative see Mason [1982: 147]). Day sees בַּיִת ('house') as designating the Israelites and so reads this entire passage as indicating that Joshua will judge, in a legal context, 'my people' (that is, the house of Israel [1988: 111-12]). This means to her, 'the high priest is to ensure that the legislative and forensic responsibilities of the priesthood are properly carried out, namely interpretation of *tôrâ* (Hag. 2.11-13) and the deciding of cases that could not be settled by civil process' (1988: 112). Zechariah depicts the return of these people and objects to Jerusalem and Judah, and a small scale restoration of justice (Zech. 3). That Joshua might be a priest on the throne (depending on how one reads 6.13) might suggest a much larger restoration of justice in the land: perhaps the complete restoration of justice is accomplished then in Zechariah 3.

Isaiah 4 contains a cluster of parallel thoughts to Zechariah too. In Isa. 4.1 seven women grasp (hiphil of חזק) a man (איש) in that day (ביום ההוא). This loosely parallels ten men grasping (hiphil of חזק) the hem of a man (איש) of Judah in those days (בימים ההמה) in Zech. 8.23. Isaiah 4.2 is one of the three occurrences of the use of צמח ('branch') as a title outside of the book of Zechariah (the other two being Jer. 23.5 and 33.15; so Barker [1977: 41]).

Unfortunately, the intertextual analysis of Zech. 2.1-4 has not established data which will control the metaphors in Zechariah 2. Instead, it has expanded the interpretative options. The clusters of connectives suggest significance may be found in that interpretative option. Unfortunately, the clusters often point in various directions and this creates a tension in the text as to which intertext should control the metaphor. As an example, are the horns being cast down to allow a horn of Judah to sprout, or are they cast down by the construction of a bronze horn for the daughter of Zion? The significance is not clearly indicated by the text, and the reader is free to choose her own interpretation, or to let various interpretations float in her consciousness.

Snatching Texts from the Fire: Zechariah 3.2

In this example the book of Zechariah is the hypertext. When Zech. 3.2 is read:

> And the Lord rebuke you, O Satan! The Lord who has chosen Jerusalem
> rebuke you! Is not this a brand (אוד) plucked (מצל) from the fire (מאש)?

I am immediately reminded of four themes which occur elsewhere in the Hebrew Bible: Yahweh's rebuke (Isa. 17.13; 54.9; Nah. 1.4; Mal. 2.3; 3.11; Pss. 9.5; 106.9; 119.21), 'Satan' or 'adversary' (Num. 22; 1 Sam. 29.4; 2 Sam. 19.22; 1 Kgs 5.4; 11.14, 23; Pss. 38.21 (20E); 71.13; 109.4, 6, 20, 29; Job 1–2; 1 Chron. 21.1), Yahweh's election of Jerusalem (1 Kgs 11.13, 32, 36; 14.21: 2 Kgs 21.7; 23.27; Zech. 1.17; 2.16; 2 Chron. 6.6; 12.13; 33.7), and a parallel phrase in Amos 4.11 about a brand plucked from the burning.

Day, drawing on the work of Johansson, asserts that interpreters must understand the role of הַשָּׂטָן in Zechariah 'in the context of Joshua's investiture' as high priest, as well as in relation to the role of 'the heavenly *mēlîṣ* (16.20; 33.23) or *mal'āk* (33.23) of the book of Job...[who is] a celestial intermediary who acts both as intercessor and witness' (1988: 123). In this setting,

> an individual stands accused by a *śāṭān*. The case is heard by the heavenly tribunal. For the case to be decided in the accused's favor, a celestial advocate is necessary...the heavenly council has convened in Zechariah 3 to hear an individual case pertaining to a particular circumstance (Day 1988: 124).

Thus, 'the *śāṭān* of Zech. 3.1-7 is the mythological medium through which the author of the passage expresses the conviction that the objections to Joshua's investiture had been voiced in the heavenly court' (Day 1988: 126).

Zechariah 1–8 is full of connectives to Job 1.7 and 2.2: Whereas the Satan roams (שׁוּט and הִתְהַלֵּךְ) the earth (בָּאָרֶץ) in Job, in Zechariah the horses and chariots 'walk up and down in the earth' (הִתְהַלֵּךְ בָּאָרֶץ; 1.10, 11; 6.7; NRSV's translation of הִתְהַלֵּךְ in Job 1.7 and 2.2), and the eyes of Yahweh 'range' all the earth (מְשׁוֹטְטִים בְּכָל הָאָרֶץ; 4.10). In Job the Satan presents himself to the divine council, and, as Day and others have established, so this also happens in Zechariah 3. It appears as if many 'divine' functionaries in Zechariah perform the same tasks as the Satan does in Job. The similarity of their tasks might be attributed to all of these entities being part of the divine council. As the sons of God present themselves before Yahweh in Job (הִתְיַצֵּב עַל־יהוה; 1.6; 2.1), so the chariots present themselves before the Lord of all the earth in Zechariah (הִתְיַצֵּב עַל־אֲדוֹן כָּל־הָאָרֶץ; 6.5). If one equates the Lord of all the earth with Yahweh, then the horses and the chariots are the sons of God. All of the actions specifically attributed to the Satan in Job are presented in Zechariah, but through multiple agents (see Oppenheim [1968: 176] who also links Zech. 1; 3; 6 and Job 1–2). As the attributes of the prophet are split in Zechariah, so are the tasks of the Satan.

I will not analyse the role of the Satan in depth here as it has been done many times before. Instead of analysing all four intertextual constructs of Yahweh's rebuke, the 'Satan' or 'adversary', Yahweh's election of Jerusalem, and the parallel phrase in Amos 4.11 about a brand plucked from the burning, I will focus on tracing only one intertextual path: the brand plucked from the burning.

I, along with others, see a link between Zech. 3.2 and Amos 4.11.

Zech. 3.2

ויאמר יהוה אל־השטן יגער יהוה בך השטן ויגער יהוה בך הבחר
בירושלם הלוא זה <u>אוד מצל מאש</u>

Amos 4.11

הפכתי בכם כמהפכת אלהים את־סדם ואת־עמרה ותהיו
<u>כאוד מצל משרפה</u> ולא־שבתם עדי נאם־יהוה

The phrase מ מצל אוד ('a brand snatched from') is a connective be-tween these texts.[17] Another connective is the synonymous relationship between the final word of these two phrases אש ('fire')/שרפה ('burning fire') which results in a nearly identical meaning for the two phrases. (NRSV translates אוד מצל מאש 'a brand plucked from the fire' and כאוד מצל משרפה 'like a brand snatched from the fire'.) The same imagery that is applied to Joshua in Zechariah is also applied to Israel in Amos: they are both brands plucked from burning/fire.[18] But another inter-textual force is at work in Amos—simile. Sodom and Gomorrah are compared to the brand plucked from the burning. Sodom and Gomorrah are intrinsically linked with the overturning which resulted in Israel being likened to a brand snatched from the fire. In order to understand what the brand plucked from the fire signifies in Amos, it is necessary to examine how a brand plucked from the fire relates to Sodom and Gomorrah, that is, how Amos depicts Israel as similar to Sodom and Gomorrah. How is God's overturning of Sodom and Gomorrah like the overturning described in Amos 4? Are Sodom and Gomorrah somehow

17. Day (1988: 122) and Fleming (1989: 198) see this phrase as a proverb. To Fleming, 'it signifies Yahweh's prerogative in pronouncing an acquittal by answer-ing a multitude of objections with one defense' (1989: 198). Day discusses the function of proverbs and concludes it here deals solely with the individual, Joshua, (rather than the whole community) and 'is intended to counter objections to Joshua becoming high priest' in the divine assembly (1988: 122, 124). Chapter 3 'informs us that the objections to Joshua's investiture had been heard by the highest possible court, the divine council, and were overruled' (1988: 126). Further, 'any attempt to elucidate the referents to which the proverb is applied must be conjectural... The genius of the *mal'āk yhwh*'s response is that it is capable of countering a wide vari-ety of objections, and therein lies its utility' (Day 1988: 123).

18. Craig view the fire in Amos 4 and in Zechariah 3 as the fire of judgment (1991: 116-17). He says the phrase 'snatched from the fire' is closely related to Yahweh's judgment (1991: 118; see his discussion of Zech. 3 and its relation to Amos 4 [110-25]).

like this brand snatched from the fire? The reader will then read texts in which Sodom and Gomorrah play a role, such as Genesis 18–19; Deut, 32.32; and Isa. 1.9. When examining Genesis, Deuteronomy and Isaiah, the hypertext becomes Amos. Two hypertexts exist: Amos 4.11 and Zech. 3.2. Yet, at the same time, the reader is ultimately reading Genesis, Deuteronomy and Isaiah in order to understand Amos, which the reader is reading to understand Zechariah. An intertextual chain is formed which directs me from Zechariah to Amos to texts about Sodom and Gomorrah.

While reading Amos, Deuteronomy, Genesis or Isaiah the reader may encounter other phrases or concepts that occur in Zechariah. This invites play between the texts and an intertextual dialogue occurs in the reader's mind between these concepts. In this way the symbolic order surrounding the connectives from Genesis, Deuteronomy and Isaiah is transported into Zechariah via Amos.

The use of the software programs MacBible and acCordance to examine Zechariah is very much a hypertextual style of interpretation as words from Zechariah are entered into the search driver. Once the search results are viewed, other signifiers discovered in the search results which may help to eventually interpret Zechariah are pursued. Chains of associations are constructed, as in this example under consideration.

Nothing in the pre-texts to Amos is snatched, נצל, from Sodom and Gomorrah, as the brand is snatched from the fire. But Lot and his family are dragged out by the hand and urged to escape, the mental picture of which is akin to snatching (Gen. 19.16; another connective between Gen and Amos is overthrow [הפך; Gen. 19.29; Amos 4.11]).[19] In a sense, Lot and his family are exiled from Sodom: they are dragged out of it and it is impossible for them to return to their city (Gen. 19). They are forcibly removed from the land and are not even allowed to look back on it. Day suggests, 'perhaps the *mal'āk yhwh* is arguing that Joshua's family had survived the conflagration of Jerusalem in 587 BCE, and that this should be understood as a sign of divine intervention and favor' (1988: 123).

Deuteronomy 28–29 draws out these implications of Lot's forcible removal from Sodom when it depicts the exile using imagery of the

19. One problem presents itself. Never in the Tanakh is נצל ('snatching') performed with the hand. But Hos. 2.12 and Zech. 11.6 both mention that no one will snatch [anything] from the hand of someone else.

overturn of Sodom and Gomorrah. Deuteronomy 29.22 compares the
land, presumably of Israel, after the exile with the overthrow of Sodom
and Gomorrah using the same word for burning (שׂרפה) as Amos does.
This word for burning (שׂרפה) creates another node and stronger link
between the two texts in this reader's mind. It is an indicator of how
symbolic orders follow words. Somehow the writer of Deuteronomy or
of Amos, whichever came first, had read the other text and subconsciously or consciously associated שׂרפה with Sodom and Gomorrah.
Thus the word makes its appearance in both texts. Deuteronomy says
'the whole land [is] brimstone and salt, and a burnt-out waste (שׂרפה),
unsown, and growing nothing (לא תצמח), where no grass can sprout'
(and following, RSV).[20] The overthrow of Sodom and Gomorrah in
Deut. 29.22 is an almost entire annihilation, especially agriculturally.
(In a similar desolation Yahweh rains sulphur and fire on what grows
on the ground [Gen. 29.24]. The writer of Genesis paints a picture of
desolation when he shows Abraham comparing the smoke rising from
the land to the smoke of a furnace [Gen. 19.27-28].) In Genesis, Lot
and his family are the sole survivors of the destruction.

The story is further elaborated in Deut. 29.27 where the exile is
described in terms of uprooting in great wrath, 'so the anger of the
LORD was kindled against that land, bringing on it every curse written
in this book. The LORD uprooted them (נתש) from their land in anger,
fury and great wrath (קצף גדול), and cast them into another land.' Both
the destruction of Sodom and Gomorrah, and the land of Israel are
described in terms of the depopulation of both plants and people.

Jeremiah 50.40 further develops the theme of Sodom and Gomorrah,
'As when God overthrew Sodom and Gomorrah and their neighbouring
cities, says the LORD, so no man shall dwell there, and no son of man
shall sojourn in her'. Again, in Jeremiah, Sodom and Gomorrah are
pictured as depopulated.

Merging all of these intertexts produces a composite story. Out of a
massive destruction, few survived. By implication from Lot's experience of Sodom and Gomorrah, both Israel in Amos and Joshua in Zechariah are survivors of mass destruction which involves the destruction
of the food chain right down to the agricultural level. Read back into
Zechariah, Joshua is one of the few left, snatched from the fire. All

---

20. There are many lexical connectives between Gen. 19.24-26 and Deut. 29.22:
sulphur (גפרת), salt (מלח), overturning (הפך) and the synonyms שׂרפה/אשׁ.

three—Lot, Israel and Joshua—are saved by the hair of their 'chinny-chin-chins'.

But what is the fire Joshua has survived? Joshua being soiled and 'barely saved from destruction' is 'a veiled reference to lapse into apostasy' (Blenkinsopp 1984: 238). Blocher bases his reading on Deut. 4.20 and Amos 4.11 to conclude that the fire from which Joshua, the brand which has been uprooted, has been plucked from is 'la fournaise de l'exil' ('the furnace of the exile') (1979: 265). VanderKam, following Petersen, while noting the 'saucier' readings of the 'filthy' garments, sees it as a reference to Joshua's clothes being damaged by the fire (VanderKam 1991: 555; see Petersen 1984a: 193-94). But the connotations of the nominal cognates (צֹאָה and צֹאָה; see VanderKam 1991: 555) suggest a much more grotesque reading of the use of the phrase here, as they are always used with bodily refuse (dung [Deut. 23.14; 2 Kgs 18.27; Isa. 36.12; Ezek. 4.12]; vomit [Isa. 28.8; perhaps Isa. 4.4]). Likewise Fleming, 'it is as though the clothes were covered with human excrement...service is hindered until cleanness is achieved by council functionaries' (1989: 199 n. 136). The sheer number of connectives with Isaiah 3–4, especially the same terms for garments, suggests one read Isaiah 3–4 as controlling the metaphor in Zechariah 3. As Petersen notes, fire serves a very different function in the two: it cleanses in Isaiah 4 but appears complicit in the 'filthiness' of the garments in Zechariah 3. The suggestion of the two is that Yahweh has not yet washed the filth from Jerusalem.

Another connotation is carried if one reads Isaiah 28 as controlling the metaphor. There priest and prophet vomit because of their drunkenness (vv. 7-8) and do not teach knowledge. Perhaps Joshua is being portrayed as just such a priest and the suggestion is he should teach knowledge (as in Mal. 2.7). Joshua is then perhaps rightfully being accused, but Yahweh is ignoring the adversaries complaints in the interest of re-establishing a priesthood.

If Ezek. 4.12 controls the metaphor, it may suggest that even the priest had to cook his food over excrement and perhaps soiled his garment in the process. The metaphor then alludes to the appalling conditions of the exile.

The metaphor of the fire also begs the reader to identify Joshua's ordeal with a stick nearly consumed by fire. But how does fire function as a metaphor? Fire is often identified both literally and metaphorically with Yahweh's anger; that is, Yahweh's anger is frequently portrayed in the prophets as burning like fire (see Amos 5.6; Isa. 30.27; Jer. 4.4; 15.14; Zeph. 3.8, and a multitude of other references, too numerous to begin to list comprehensively—anyone who has failed to notice this theme has probably never read a prophetic book). The metaphor of the fire of Yahweh's anger becomes a literal fire in Jeremiah. As in other prophetic works, Yahweh's wrath is repeatedly described as fire in Jeremiah (Jer. 4.4; 5.14; 15.14; 21.12). In Jer. 5.14 this fire is equated with the prophet's words and the people are equated with wood. Joshua could be part of this wood, and the fire he is snatched from is thereby the fire of the prophecies, such as Jeremiah's. The final result of Yahweh's anger in Jeremiah is the literal burning of the house of Yahweh, the king's house, and all the houses of Jerusalem (Jer. 52.13; see 2 Kgs 25.9). This connection between Yahweh's anger and fire is more explicitly spelled out in Jer. 21.10-12.

> 'For I have set my face against this city for evil and not for good,' says the LORD: 'it shall be given into the hand of the king of Babylon, and he shall burn it with fire.'
>
> And to the house of the king of Judah say, 'Hear the word of the LORD, O house of David! Thus says the LORD: "Execute justice in the morning, and deliver [נִצָּל] from the hand of the oppressor him who has been robbed, lest my wrath go forth like fire, and burn with none to quench it, because of your evil doings."'

This passage speaks of both the burning of the city with fire and the wrath of Yahweh going out like fire.

The relationship between the metaphors of fire and wood is elaborated further in Ezekiel 15 and 19. The imagery of Ezekiel 15 and 19 is somewhat parallel to the brand being burnt by fire. Ezekiel 15 uses the metaphor of the wood of a vine which is nearly useless before being consumed by fire, and after it is burnt at both ends and scorched in the middle, it is even less useful (v. 4). One implication of the passage is that it is not the vine which is useful, but the fruit it produces. The metaphor is also an allegory for the inhabitants of Jerusalem which Yahweh has given up to the fire to be consumed (vv. 6-7). After they are consumed the land is desolate. Ezekiel 19.10-14 re-uses this burning vine motif, albeit for Israel:

> Your mother was like a vine in a vineyard transplanted by the water, fruitful and full of branches by reason of abundant water. [11]Its strongest stem became a ruler's scepter; it towered aloft among the thick boughs; it was seen in its height with the mass of its branches. [12]But the vine was

plucked up in fury, cast down to the ground; the east wind dried it up; its
fruit was stripped off, its strong stem was withered; *the fire consumed it.*
[13]Now it is transplanted in the wilderness, in a dry and thirsty land.
[14]And *fire has gone out from its stem, has consumed its branches and
fruit, so that there remains in it no strong stem, no sceptre for a ruler.*

The symbolism underlying Ezekiel 15 and 19 may inform the symbolic motif of the brand in Zechariah. The vine in Ezekiel is plucked up
(נתש) in anger. If you remember, Yahweh in his anger uprooted (נתש),
the people, sending them into exile in Deut. 29.27. Another connective
is formed. Plucking up is symbolic of the exile. So, plucking up the
vine in Ezekiel 19 also represents the exile. The strong stem which
came out of the vine in Ezekiel 19 stands as a metonym for a ruler. This
strong stem is consumed in the fire of exile (v. 12). Afterwards, there is
no strong stem left in the branch for a sceptre. To interpret the symbols:
Israel, after the exile, remains without a ruler and without potential
leadership (v. 14). Unlike the vine in Ezekiel, which was burnt out, and
did not possess leadership potential, Joshua, the brand, is snatched from
the fire which would have left him like the vine—unable to sustain
leadership and useless, bearing no fruit. However, Joshua still retains
the potential for leadership. Incorporating the larger context of
Zechariah 1–8, a diarchy between priest and governor is the form of
leadership Zechariah depicts (cf. Zech. 6), so this metaphor hints at
Joshua as a ruler. Joshua, as a brand plucked from the fire, is thereby
plucked out from Yahweh's anger, the exile, in order that a strong stem
may still remain to stand as a ruler.

Other intertextual constructs create other impressions. In Isa. 7.4
Rezin and Pekah are attacking Jerusalem. They are portrayed as two
smouldering stumps of firebrands (NRSV; זנבות האודים העשנים). Why
are they depicted as smouldering firebrands? Is it because they are
angry (Isa. 7.4)? Is it because they inspire fear (Isa. 7.2, 4; 8.5), and
thus a burning firebrand is to be taken as one that instils fear? Is it
because they have plotted evil against Ahaz (7.6)? If it is their anger,
then Joshua is depicted as an angry individual. Or perhaps the angry
individual is the adversary, the Satan, and it is from the anger of the
adversary that Joshua is saved.

This intertextual journey through these portions of the Hebrew Bible
was begun by the observation of a text parallel to Zechariah. This parallel text sent the reader on another journey as she chased the signifier
through the Hebrew Bible. Along the way she noticed many parallels to

Zechariah which fed back into the interpretational matrix that formed in
her head. When she returned to Zechariah these parallels came with her.
When she read Zechariah 1–8 after going on her intertextual journey,
she saw many things she had never seen before. Joshua is plucked from
the fire, and this made her think of the exile. The exile is not only a
destruction, but also a deliverance. The brand snatched from the fire is
that saved from the destruction. The fire that it is snatched from is the
exile. It also recalls the desolation of the land described in Deuteronomy: a land in which nothing can grow (לא תצמח).

Yet Joshua has been snatched from the fire and is back in the land.
The land is not a desolation like Sodom and Gomorrah. With this reversal comes the possibility that something will grow. This expectation of
fertility takes place on various planes: literally for the restoration of the
land and metaphorically for leadership and repopulation. Agriculturally,
Yahweh's great wrath, his קצף גדול, the same phrase used to describe
Yahweh's anger in Deut. 29.27, in Zech. 7.12-14 results in a desolate
land which was infertile because Yahweh would not allow things to
grow. As Sodom and Gomorrah were desolate, so is the land in
Zechariah. But things are different now as Yahweh promises in 8.11-12

> but now I will not deal with the remnant of this people as in the former
> days, says the Lord of hosts. [12]For there shall be a sowing of peace; the
> vine shall yield its fruit, the ground shall give its produce, and the skies
> shall give their dew.

Yahweh is instigating a 'Green policy'. The vine which was burnt in
Ezekiel has become useful again: it will yield fruit. The depopulated
city will be repopulated (cf. Zech. 7.7; 8.5). In front of Joshua, on the
leadership front, a branch will be brought in who will build the temple
and rule in a diarchy (6.12-14).[21] Perhaps one is to picture this branch
metaphorically as growing out of the wood plucked from the fire, that
is, Joshua.

This walk through a small portion of Zechariah's intertextual matrix
has demonstrated that Zechariah is a pastiche which has drawn on many
textual traditions in its composition: from Genesis, Deuteronomy,
Jeremiah, Ezekiel, Amos, and others. The readers familiar with these

---

21. See Petitjean for a discussion of the word 'branch' and its relation to fertility
(1966: 64; see his treatment of the topic [63-71]). Petitjean takes the branch to refer
to Zerubbabel and indicates he is the 'legitimate successor to the royal throne'
(1966: 71).

texts can recognize them in Zechariah. The writing strategy of alluding to these predecessors is pervasive. In a sense, the author of Zechariah has created a text which directs the reader to Amos via the image of the brand. Amos then directs the reader to the broad range of Sodom and Gomorrah stories. These stories in turn lead the reader to stories about the exile. The reader is encouraged to mix together all of the metaphors from these pre-texts in their interpretational matrix. The metaphors all contribute to the symbolic chain which surrounds the phrase 'is not this a brand plucked from the fire?' When the reader returns to Zechariah, she realizes how intricately laced Zechariah is with the thought worlds of these other texts. She is forced to admire the artistry of Zechariah— to realize that Zechariah is a master weaver.

Seeing so many verbal and conceptual interrelationships between Zechariah and these other texts invites the reader, or at least this one, to ponder over the symbolic logic at work in these texts. There is a certain non-linear dimension to the symbols. Once readers consult the other texts, they realize that an intricate structure is at work in the hypertext. The elements of the pastiche, like Lacan's symbolic chain, carry a plethora of connotations from their previous texts to Zechariah. To begin to grasp some of these, the reader is compelled to follow the signifier, the intertext, to the pre-texts. Of course this chase after the signifier will never completely satisfy the desire to understand a text, as there are always more chains of associations to follow. This section began by citing three intertextual dimensions present in Zech. 3.2: the near quote of Amos, Yahweh choosing Jerusalem, and the concept of Yahweh's rebuke. There is still the task of performing a similar analysis on the other two intertexts to comprehend this verse. But for the moment, the urge to ponder the text is satisfied and the sense of incomprehension in the face of the text will remain repressed. Even having made this intertextual construct, it is very difficult to understand exactly what is the point of Zechariah quoting Amos 4.11. New possibilities are constantly being constructed, but none of them offer themselves as obvious interpretations of Zech. 3.2. Yet, on its own without the intertexts Zech. 3.2 remains very difficult to understand.

Winging Women: Zechariah 5.5-11

Finally, I will examine the slightly longer passage of Zech. 5.5-11. I assume that by this point you have an understanding of the intertextual strategy(ies) I am using to read the text and will not explicitly spell out every move. I will simply draw attention to connections, comment on them and then move on.

In Zech. 5.5-11 Zechariah sees a woman in an ephah. Something is referred to as 'wickedness' and the woman is thrust back into the basket. Subsequently, winged women carry this basket-enclosed woman to Shinar where a house will be built for her. This image is extremely condensed and the intertextual threads, as always in Zechariah, lead in many directions.

To begin with, the women are referred to as having wind in their כנפים ('wings/skirts'). This is a punning use of the noun כנף, for the reader on first reading the text thinks the women have wind in their skirts. At least to modern readers, this is a somewhat sexy image reminiscent of a shampoo commercial. The next clause suddenly frustrates this line of thought as the image changes when the reader realizes the women have wings and not skirts: the next clause states 'and their כנפים [wings or skirts] were like the wings of the stork' (5.9b). At the beginning of this story the reader is made aware that the author is playing with language.

Comparing the women's wings to the wings of the stork makes for some interesting intertextual associations. The wings of the ostrich are enjoyable or delightful (reading אם as an interrogative particle [see BDB, 50; Joüon 1991: 610-11; 619; CHD reads '*is it (the) wing?*, i.e. is it like the wing?' [115]) like '*the wing (of) the stork and (her) plumage*' [CHD, 115; Job 39.13]). This implies that the stork's wings are enjoyable to behold. The reader can then read the women of Zechariah 5 as possessing beautiful wings.

One option is to link חסידה ('stork') with חסד ('lovingkindness'), because of the similarity in the their spelling, and therefore read some kind of tender affection into this description of women with stork's wings. The word-play encourages this kind of reading. At the same time, this seems an anachronistic reading of the connotations which 'stork' carries in modern Western culture. In the Tanakh, storks are unclean animals, to be detested (Lev. 11.13) as they are unsuitable for human consumption (Lev. 11.19; Deut. 14.18). The stork knows its times (מועד; Jer. 8.7). They also build their homes in Lebanon (Ps. 104.16-17). All of these connotations create many connectives with Zechariah that tear the reader to view the stork simultaneously as both a negative image and as a positive image and suggest that the stork may be a condensed image.

That the stork knows its appointed times plays off the theme of the fasts being turned into feasts (מוֹעֵד; 8.19). The *kethib* of Jer. 8.7 contains a curious statement that a horse (סוּס), along with a turtledove and crane, observe their migration time. This is usually read with the *qere* to be סִיס. The *kethib* creates a link with Zechariah: the horse migrates to Jerusalem (Zech. 1.7-17) when the stork migrates to Shinar. (Perhaps the writer of Zechariah is playing with the reader's knowledge of the *kethib* and *qere*.) Does this suggest the implied audience of Zechariah does not realize the time for feasting has arrived. This is suggested by Zechariah 7–8. Might the link between the stork and migration (Jer. 8.7) relate to the movement from Babylon/Shinar to Jerusalem and vice versa: the stork-women know the time to migrate to Shinar has come. Does this imply a return to Jerusalem is appropriate in the future, as with all migrations, or should the symbolism not be pushed that far?

The stork is also an appropriate animal to convey the woman and build a house for her, as they are accustomed to building houses, albeit in treetops. These trees are in Lebanon: northwards. So the storks are appropriate to take the ephah northwards and build a house for it there. The trees in which the storks make their homes, cypress (בְּרוֹשׁ), produce desired wood which is appropriate for temples (see 1 Kgs 5.8, 10). Perhaps this provides semantic slippage between the building materials of the house they are making for the woman in Shinar and the building materials of the temple in Jerusalem.

Petersen notes that this vision has contacts with the primaeval history (for example, Gen. 3's 'tradition about the feminine as evil', the contamination of the daughters of God by the sons of man in Gen. 6.1-4, and the plain of Shinar [1984a: 257-58]). Tollington suggests that 'behind this vision of all humanity drawing together before God there may lie the ancient story of the confusing of the tongues at Babel' (1993: 241).

Many connectives exist between the story in Gen. 11.1-9 and Zechariah 1–8: כָּל־הָאָרֶץ (פְּנֵי) ('[the face of] all the earth') as a recurring theme (Gen. 11.1, 4, 8, 9; Zech. 1.11; 4.10, 14; 5.3, 6; 6.5); שִׁנְעָר בָּאָרֶץ ('in the land of Shinar', Gen. 11.2; Zech. 5.11); שָׁם ('there', in reference to being in Shinar; Gen. 11.2, 4, 7, 8, 9; Zech. 5.11); בנה ('build', Gen. 11.4, 5, 8; Zech. 1.16; 5.11; 6.12, 13, 15; 8.9); אָבֵן (as 'brick'; Gen. 11.3; Zech. 3.9?; 4.7?, 10?; 5.4); פּוּץ ('scatter', 'Gen. 11.4, 8, 9; Zech. 1.17); בָּבֶל ('Babylon', Gen. 11.9; Zech. 2.7; 6.10); זמם ('purpose', Gen. 11.6; Zech. 1.6; 8.14, 15). In both texts people are building structures. In Genesis they are scattered over the whole earth as a consequence of this building. Though the phrase 'all the earth' is not used to depict the return, in Zechariah people are brought from all over the earth to work on the temple (6.15) or to seek Yahweh Sebaoth (8.20-23). In Genesis 11 the people speak one language, which is divided into many languages, and they are then scattered throughout the earth. As Burgess phrases it, 'The confusion of tongues means the confusion of all civilised endeavour. This confusion is genuine, and it lies wholly in the slippery, devilish, disobedient organ known as the tongue' (1993: 31). In Zechariah people from all the languages come to seek Yahweh in Jerusalem (8.23; this verse is a connective with both Isa. 4.1 and Gen. 11).

Tollington believes the number 10 is used to indicate completeness and takes the phrase 'ten men from the nations of every tongue' to indicate the 'whole human race' (1993: 241). Is this a new beginning for civilized endeavours? Curiously, or not, the ten men who will grasp the hem of a Judaean will speak to him in Hebrew or Chaldean? (our nomenclature betrays our political agendas) (Zech. 8.23bβ). Does this imply a reversal of the division of the languages in Genesis 11? In Zechariah 8 the languages are reunited by the *lingua franca* of Hebrew (maybe not so strange if one thinks of the prominence of Chaldaean around 500 BCE).

This entire depiction seems to be a symbolic reversal of the event which occurred in Genesis 11: the people were scattered over the earth from one city in Genesis; in Zechariah they are reunited in the city of Jerusalem. Does this imply the activity in Genesis 11 may have been the right activity at the wrong place, or maybe the right activity (building) of the wrong structures (a tower and city instead of a house for Yahweh). Might this allusion to Shinar be construed as a reference to the confusion of languages there and thereby bare the device and hint at the confused nature of language in the text of Zechariah? If so, at the same time as the text is suggesting the end of the confusion of languages, it is denying this solves the problem in asserting the extremely confused nature one language can manifest. Might this deconstruct itself and assert that the cessation of multilingualism need not mean the end of misunderstanding.

Zechariah sees the woman in this vision in an ephah. Many have noted that an ephah is not large enough to contain an adult woman (Clark 1983: 440; Delcor 1975: 138; Marenof 1931–32: 264). Because of the problem of squeezing a woman into an object so small, Marenof draws on the Zikkurat of Lagash called an *E-pa* to assert that the איפה in Zechariah 5 refers to 'one of the edifices of the deities that existed in Palestine during the period after the destruction of the first temple' (1931–32: 266). He further explains that Zechariah uses the phrase זאת עינם בכל הארץ (lit. 'this is their eyes in all the land') to signify that the ephah is a Zikkurat, which was called a 'conspicuous house' (1931–32: 266). He equates the woman sitting with a figurine of a seated woman identified with Astarte (1931–32: 266-67; Delcor also associates the woman with Ištar/Astarte [1975: 137]; Galling sees her as Ištar [1964: 120]). The whole passage thus 'implies that Zechariah is objecting to a temple of Astarte in Palestine and is suggesting that this temple will be removed from Palestine and restored to Babylon where it rightly belongs' (Marenof 193–32: 267). This reading integrates well with the image of the stork and its role in building discussed above.

This said, I do not accept the premise that an ephah is not big enough to contain an adult woman as truly justifiable given the surreal nature of Zechariah 1–8. We already have talking horses, messengers of Yahweh and flying scrolls of immense proportions performing preternatural deeds. Why not a woman in an ephah? Is it such a great stretch of the imagination to picture either a small woman or a large ephah? As I said, I'm more interested in the associations that arise rather than establishing any principles of verisimilitude.

In Zech. 5.8 the woman is labelled 'wickedness' (though other referents are possible for the wickedness) and thrust into the midst of the basket. It is a violent image of a messenger manhandling a woman and then slamming a stone down. Mitchell believes the wickedness is idolatry and is represented as a woman in accord with the prophetic traditions which 'denounce this offence under the figure of prostitution' (1980: 173). This is extremely complicated to analyse. At any rate, Mitchell is justifying violence against a woman, violence against a prostitute, or perhaps both at the same time if some kind of temple prostitute is imagined. Petersen counters this assertion claiming 'this contention is not warranted on the biblical usage of the term [רשעה]' (1984a: 257). The text states she is a woman, nothing more. The messenger casts her down into the ephah and throws a lead stone on its (the ephah's) or her (the woman's) mouth. Apart from the usual interpretation that views this as closing the lid on the ephah,[22] the ambiguity between the feminine referent of 'mouth' allows one to attribute the mouth to either the ephah or the woman (both are feminine as is the suffix on 'mouth'; Meyers and Meyers 1987: 304). If it is the woman's mouth which is referred to, throwing a stone on her mouth could be viewed as symbolic (literal?) silencing.

Glazier-McDonald, who comments specifically on the woman in the ephah in *The Woman's Bible Commentary*, notes that this figure is 'bottled up' (1992: 231). Another notable observation she makes is that 'ephah also designates a Mesopotamian cult room. Thus, the woman 'Wickedness (= idolatry) may represent a goddess in her shrine and so symbolise non-Yahwistic worship' (1992: 231). She also suggests that they may represent 'foreign women (in this case Babylonian wives brought back from exile by returning Judaeans) [who are] purveyors of alien culture threatening Yahwism's integrity' (1992: 231). She condenses the two images to suggest this figure 'may be both a foreign woman, denoting the explicit historical danger of foreign cultural integration, and a goddess, the result of such integration, that is, idolatry' (1992: 231). If this reading is adopted Zechariah is a culturally exclusive, racist text which marginalizes portions of the community. Personally, as someone in an interracial relationship living in a foreign country, I find this ideology in Zechariah extremely offensive and worry about what the results might have been if this kind of thinking caught on among the implied readers: ethnic cleansing supported by religious ideology? Sounds familiar (no more need be said).

In the narrative, the wickedness might be that she is 'their eyes in all the land' (עינם בכל־הארץ); reading 'eye' (עין) with the MT rather than 'iniquity' (עון) with the LXX and the Syriac (see *BHS*). The collocation עין ב often signifies sight (1 Sam. 12.3; Isa. 52.8; Ezek. 10.19; Pss. 17.8; 141.8). But does the ב here symbolize the object of their sight (as in Ps. 141.8) or the subjects who are looking? That is to say, are their eyes looking on all the land, which would make the ephah symbolically synonymous with the eyes, or are the eyes of all the land looking at the ephah? If all the eyes of the land are looking at the ephah, the ephah

22. Delcor uses Hittite myths as the controlling intertexts through which to interpret the ephah in Zechariah (1975: 140). These intertexts contain lead lids with magical properties which are used to enclose spirits (1975: 142-43). It is likewise appropriate to shut in the 'wickedness' (which he relates to idolatry and specifically Ištar represented as a female) in these baskets as is done in Zechariah (1975: 143).

may be depicted as an object of desire. If so, then the woman is depicted as an object of desire, and is removed from the sight of those looking on her. This seems a case of punishing the victim for the crimes of the accused.

The woman is depicted as sitting in, or inhabiting, the ephah (see 2 Sam. 7.2; Jer. 29.32; 39.14). If one reads יושבת in 5.7 as 'inhabiting', the woman is living in a state of constant assessment: she is living in a place where she is dealt with as a commercial object.[23] An איפה is used to measure an item to trade it (Petersen discusses the occurrence of איפה ['measure'] and אבן ['weight'] as units of trade; 1984a: 258-59). A word-play with נשא seems present in Zechariah 5. Ezekiel 45.11 suggests one lifts an ephah to assess the weight (האיפה והבת תכן אחד יהיה לשאת; Job 6.2 employs נשא ['to lift'] as part of the weighing process for balances [מאזנים]). Lead is a commodity which is traded (see Ezekiel 27.12-13). ככר is a unit used to measure precious metals to indicate their value, and to use in transactions (see 1 Kgs 9.14, 28; 10.10, 14; 16.24; 2 Kgs 15.19; 18.14; Prov. 6.26). It seems very unlikely that it should be translated as 'lid' in Zechariah, as everywhere else it occurs with metals it indicates a commodity. The lead ephah (ככר עפרת) in Zechariah is more likely to represent a unit of trade like the ככר זהב ('gold unit') and the ככר כסף ('silver unit'). That the ephah is lifted up suggests the content of it is being assessed. Zech. 5.7 (והנה ככר עפרת נשאת וזאת אשה אחת יושבת בתוך האיפה) may then be translated, 'and behold a lead weight was lifted up [that is, weighed] and this is (the price of) one woman'. This explains why the cardinal number is present in this passage—to specify the rate of exchange. If one wants to buy one woman, one will have to pay a lead ephah. Is this a metaphor of slavery or prostitution?

---

23. The Targum interprets the passage as relating to the banishment of those who are 'trading with false measure' (so translate Cathcart and Gordon [1989: 196]) and so links the ephah with economic malpractice. See Cathcart's and Gordon's translation of this entire passage for an example of how these symbolic texts invited decoding from an early stage (1989: 196-97).

In an ingenious article, Barker follows the Targum and links the wickedness with trade (1978: 18). She reads עינם בכל־הארץ as 'This is their hostile attitude towards the whole land' (1978: 22). She further links the woman with idolatry, but 'not the worship of alien deities' (1978: 22-23). Rather, she symbolically represents both disregard for the Law and Jerusalem (1978: 24). The idolatry is thus 'the idolatry of a corrupt economic system' and the 'religious zeal of the exiles' for the new Jerusalem and its (corrupt) new economic system (1978: 22-25).

Wallis takes the figure in the ephah to be a prostitute (1978: 388). A word-play may also present with Prov. 16.3. There the 'going rate' for a prostitute is a כבר ('unit') of bread. Is the wickedness the abysmal economic state in which women must prostitute themselves to obtain bread? Is this what the eyes of all the land are on: they are lustful eyes ogling women? The women who take her away to the land of Shinar save her from this state of commerce and establish her in her own house. This sounds like a happy ending for the woman. If this reading is followed the text is somewhat redeemed. Rather than portraying the victim as wickedness, perhaps her oppression is 'the wickedness' and she is given her own house to provide her with economic independence. But the context of Zechariah 5 may argue against this 'happy ending' reading. In Zech. 5.1-4 those who lie and steal are cleansed from the land. This might suggest that it is the woman who should be viewed as the wickedness. Either way, it appears that a happy ending is achieved in the end, at least from the woman's perspective. Unfortunately, her thoughts on the matter are not disclosed. If she is a foreign wife of a returned exile, perhaps it isn't a happy ending at all.

It is strange that the solution to the land's wicked desire, is to silence the victim, enclose her in an ephah and carry her away. Pippin, writing on the 'Female in the Apocalypse of John' says, 'the female that is displaced as subject in this political fantasy is the female that reflects (mirrors or mimics) aspects of the prevailing social order (both good and evil) and ideology' (1992: 68). This woman is being displaced in two ways: both in the text and in modern readings of the text. What is being displaced in ancient Israelite and Judaean society and what does that displacement say about that culture? What are modern commentators displacing and what does that displacement say about modern culture(s) and the modern culture of criticism? There is a lack of confrontation or condemnation of this act of the messenger among the scholarly community. What are we implicitly accepting by not challenging this type of thinking? Why do we fail to see this when we would readily see it in (m)any other text(s)? Just what kind of ideology is being presented and what kind of ideology are readers subconsciously performing and accepting by not analysing the implications of their readings? What does it say about us as commentators that we gloss over the sexism of this text by identifying the woman with a foreign goddess? Are we suffering from denial? She is displaced from being a woman to being an idol, and thereby we sanction the violence against her character by displacing the woman and making her an idol: we use a defence mechanism to avoid confronting the violence before us. But the text never calls her an idol, or calls her the figure or appearance of a woman: it calls her אשה ('a woman'). The violence perpetrated against her is violence against a woman.

Bach calls for readers to become conscious of 'gender-differentiated systems of ancient religion' (1993: 202). It is notable in the vision of the ephah that all of the actors are female. If one does read the woman as Ištar or Astarte, it depicts a form of female religion. In the so-called 'legitimate' religion in Zechariah, the functionaries are all male: Zechariah stands as the prophet consulted in the house of Yahweh (7.2-3) and Joshua is the high priest. The actors in positions of power are all males: Joshua, Zerubbabel, Zechariah, the *men* which are signs, Heldai, Tobiah, Jedaiah, Josiah, Helem and Hen. The only women mentioned in Zechariah are the old women sitting in the streets of Jerusalem (8.4), the girls playing in the streets (8.5), probably women comprise the inhabitants and peoples of the nations (8.20-22), and those women who appear in the vision of the ephah. One need only note the occurrences of איש ('man') throughout Zechariah to see that 'male' performers are stressed (1.8, 10; 2.4, 5; 3.8, 10; 4.1; 6.12; 7.2, 9, 10; 8.4, 10, 16, 17, 23). That men comprise the new order is almost stressed throughout the text: 16 out of the 121 verses of Zechariah contain the singular or plural of איש. That is, 13 per cent of the verses of Zechariah 1–8 deal with 'manly' issues. And that only deals with specific attestations of the root איש and does not incorporate all accounts of male activity in Zechariah, which would encompass over 95 per cent (only excluding 5.6-11). Compare this with אשה in the singular and plural, which occurs twice in Zechariah 1–8: that yields 1.6 per cent. Women are marginalized in the text, rarely occurring, and when they do occur, their forms of religious expression are banished. But moreover, this may be an attack on feminine religions and feminine religious expression. It seems very similar to the mistrust associated with the religion of Bachus in Greece. Pippin's comments are once again pertinent to Zechariah: 'the Apocalypse is not a tale for women… Women of the past as well as the present are going to have to be about the business of creating their own apocalyptic tales, their own utopian narratives' (1992: 79).

I am somewhat confused about where to proceed from here in the analysis of this phenomenon of female oppression in the text of Zechariah. Moi says 'male feminists cannot simply *repeat* the words and gestures of female feminists. Speaking as they do from a different position, in a different context, the "same" words take on different meanings' (1989: 183). Moi says further that it is necessary to take into account the power position of the speaker.

My power position is very ambiguous. Currently, I work in the margins of Biblical Studies—I am an English teacher by profession, living as a minority in a foreign country. As a speaker in Biblical Studies, I am relatively, if not completely, unknown. Should I consider the motivations underlying describing what I see as sexism in a text? Of course these are legion and, as with spirits, contain both positive and negative aspects. That I, as a male reader, see sexism where many others do not may also be conceived as some sick kind of voyeur-ish wish-fulfilment. To be quite honest, I have no idea about what my underlying intentions are in this observation, as I am unsure of the underlying intentions of all of my observations. I do not intend this comment to be defensive posturing; it is a dreadfully honest reflection on a matter that I've seriously tried to consider deeply. I am uncertain of how it relates to my authoritative position as a teacher (and yes, it is very authoritarian as I teach in a Confucian country) as I never teach Biblical Studies. As mentioned in Chapter 1, I am unsure of where my interpretative strategy derives from. That I see oppression (and liberation) where many female readers do not causes me some consternation: why do only I see it and write about it? Am I somehow 'way off base'? In addition to challenging racism wherever I see it, I guess my principal concern is to raise awareness and let other interpreters do what they will with that awareness.

As with the other intertextual examples, the chase after the intertexts did not end my search and simply led to more multivalency.

Reflections on Zechariah's Intertextuality

The nonsensical or surreal nature of Zechariah 1–8's narrative, and its lack of explanation of these surreal elements on intratextual grounds, sent me on a journey through various intertexts instigated by Zechariah 1–8's own references to these precursors (its connectives). Yet the map is misleading. I hoped to discover some 'core' meaning to the symbolism which would explain each symbol, some line of thought which would return me to the focused text and explain the symbols in an allegorical manner. Yet no one-to-one correspondences were established in this quest for meaning. The symbols in Zechariah often recall uses in more than one intertext and thereby defy being intertextually explained. When one explanation for the symbols is accepted, the reader cannot completely repress the other possible meanings. The overdetermined nature of the symbols in the intratextual reading is multiplied manyfold in the intertextual reading. Many possible readings are held in tension when reading the text and one definite reading cannot be chosen. The text has once again toyed with the reader. It describes a bizarre event, suggests to the reader that the key to interpretation is found in the inter-texts, 'knowing' all the while it is not. It suggests the chase after the intertext will centripetally return the reader to Zechariah 1–8 with understanding, yet sends the reader away from itself in a centrifugal fashion. When the reader returns to the text her goal to determine a single meaning for these symbols is frustrated. The reader is tossed to the four winds in search of an understanding that does not exist, that is 'blowing in the wind'. The text remains opaque and impenetrable.

Why Zechariah Uses Pastiche Rather than Quotation: A Suggestion

The author of Zechariah, as a late writer, must pay a price for using the prophetic persona; he must account for those aspects of the prophetic corpus hostile towards prophecy. In appealing to their authority, he appeals to an ambiguous authority which carries both positive and neg-ative connotations (see Isa. 29; Jer. 5; 11; 14; 25; 27; 29; 35; Ezek. 13; Hos. 4; 9; Mic. 3; Zeph. 3). The author of Zechariah anticipates the inherent risks involved in using the prophetic type and therefore strenu-ously attempts to establish the character of Zechariah as a reputable prophet.

One can read Zechariah's attitude to prophecy in the light of Joel 3.1. In Joel all flesh is to be silent because Yahweh is about to pour out his spirit on all flesh (כל בשר), the result of which is that the sons and daughters will prophesy, the old men dream dreams, and the young men will see visions. Perhaps the happenings Zechariah sees are not called 'visions' in order to differentiate them from what will happen when Yahweh pours out his spirit on all flesh.

One of the texts that attributes negative connotations to certain prophets' activities is Jeremiah 23. It seems that the author of Zechariah has anticipated, or reacted to, some negative connotations inherent in prophecy in Jeremiah 23 and, in building the character of Zechariah, has deliberately tried to avoid using any of the characteristics by which the author of Jeremiah negatively characterizes prophets. This is to circumvent the criticism that the character of Zechariah is a false prophet.

Examples of the interrelation of these texts abound. Jeremiah negatively depicts some prophets as those who walk in falsehood (והלך בשקר; Jer. 23.14) whereas Zechariah, though never directly opposing false prophecy, criticizes those who swear falsely (Zech. 5.4; including by Yahweh's name [הנשבע בשמי לשקר]; 8.17 [ושבעת שקר]). While swearing falsely appears to carry economic connotations in the Tanakh (for example, Lev. 19.12; Jer. 5.2), it may also do so in Jer. 23.14 and is a negative depiction of the prophets of Jerusalem. Jeremiah's false prophets speak a vision (חזון) of their own heart (Jer. 23.16) and prophesy falsely in Yahweh's name claiming to have a dream (Jer. 23.25). Though they do not swear falsely, that they prophesy falsely 'in my name' is a close link with the prohibition of swearing falsely by Yahweh's name in Zech. 5.4.

Given the content of Zechariah 1–6, it is conspicuous that the words for vision, חזון, and dream, חלום, are both absent from these chapters (North 1972b: 48). The text of Zechariah teases the reader by employing a vocabulary stock which suggests dream activity: these events occur at night (הלילה; Zech. 1.8), Yahweh is aroused/awoken from his holy place (2.17); in 4.1 Zechariah describes how the messenger 'roused me as a man who is awakened from his sleep' (NASB; ויערני כאיש אשר־יעור משנתו), and the occurrence of חלם. It is as if the book is aware of how close the material is to a dream, but refuses to acknowledge it is a dream, while admitting the intense similarity between a dream and the material contained in its pages. North says of Zechariah 1–8, 'characteristic of dream however is the combination of images never experienced together in real life: flying scroll v 1; girl inside bottle v 7; horns without heads (which may be unnoticed behind the myrtles, i 18); green horses i 8' (1972b: 48). He says elsewhere, 'the explicit night-visions of First-Zechariah are doubtless intended to represent *dreams*, but as a purely literary vesture' (1972b: 71).

Wallis discusses this dreamlike nature of the book and concludes that the book means to depict the prophet in the waking state (1978: 377-79). Tollington discusses these issues and in relation to dreaming and prophecy concludes, 'as the prophets gained ascendancy and the community came to expect Yahweh to address them through prophets, then dreams as a means of divine revelation were devalued' (1993: 88; see 87-91).

By not using the words 'vision' or 'dream', the implied author of
Zechariah seems to not want to be accused of speaking a vision of his
heart not from the mouth of Yahweh or a dream that is not from Yahweh, by scroll-thumping Jeremians linking his prophet with the false
prophets decried in Jeremiah 23. סערת ('storm') and זמם ('purpose') are
connectives between Jeremiah 23 and Zechariah (סערת in Zech. 7.14;
Jer. 23.19; Yahweh's purposes [זמם] in Zech. 1.6; 8.14, 15; Jer. 23.20).
Yahweh's word also has a primacy in Jeremiah 23: it is as fire (Jer.
23.29). Because of both the negative connotations of dreams and
visions in Jeremiah and the positive primacy of Yahweh's word in
Jeremiah 23, Zechariah claims to possess Yahweh's word and labels as
Yahweh's words rather than visions or dreams what for all extensive
appearances seem to be visions and dreams. By not putting any of the
language associated with false prophecy in Jeremiah into the mouth of
his character, Zechariah avoids any association between the two types
of prophets and prevents his character from being maligned.

The false prophets in Jeremiah would have turned Yahweh's people
from their evil ways and deeds if they had stood in the council of Yahweh and heard his words (Jer. 23.22). Though Zechariah never uses the
word סוד for council, as Jeremiah does (23.18, 22), he depicts Zechariah as both having appeared in the council of Yahweh in ch. 3 and as
having not only heard Yahweh's words, but also seen them. If one reads
Zech. 1.6b intertextually with Jeremiah and as the statement of the
implied audience, Zechariah is depicted as having succeeded from the
beginning of the book in turning the remnant from their evil ways and
deeds, thereby proving he is a prophet and that he has stood in the
council of Yahweh. Zechariah's eagerness to iterate and reiterate how
he is sent by Yahweh (Zech. 2.13, 15; 4.9; 6.15) recalls Yahweh's
claim that he did not send these prophets in Jer. 23.21. Yahweh furthermore did not speak to these prophets, yet they prophesied. Perhaps
that is why Zechariah does not perform the verb 'prophesy', but constantly claims that Yahweh's word came to him and depicts Yahweh as
speaking to him. Zechariah's references to the former prophets may be
meant to recall Jer. 23.20's iteration that in the latter days (הימים
באחרית) you will understand this. Zechariah writes in the latter days
recalling the former prophets. Zechariah 1.6b is therefore a tacit recognition that the remnant now understand Yahweh's anger as Jer. 23.20
predicted would happen. Zechariah further strengthens the former
prophets' authority by this allusion and ultimately strengthens his own

rhetorical force; the efficacy of the former prophets' words is further demonstrated, further empowering Yahweh's emissary Zechariah who speaks with the same authority, that is, the word of Yahweh.

A challenge to the authority of Yahweh is constituted by the false prophets. Yahweh is against the prophets who steal (מגנב) Yahweh's words from their neighbours (Jer. 23.30-31), presumably because they are not sent and this activity will cause the oracle of Yahweh to be forgotten, literally, not to be remembered (Jer. 23.36), because it has been mixed with the words of others who prophesy words (cf. Jer. 23.25-40). Perhaps this is a reason Zechariah has a curse go out on the thief and the person who swears falsely by Yahweh's name. He thereby cleanses the land of false prophets. But the curse which goes out over the land only truly exists in the book of Zechariah. In reality, there is no flying scroll, but only the scroll of Zechariah, or the scroll of the minor prophets. The book itself is the curse. This curse is directed against those who steal and swear (falsely by Yahweh's name?; v. 4).[24] Jeremiah 23.28 may provide the background for the command to love truth in Zechariah. By loving truth, the command in Jer. 23.28 to speak Yahweh's word in truth can be obeyed.

When Zechariah 5 is read in conjunction with Jeremiah 23, one can see the curse in Zechariah 5 as addressed against hypothetical false prophets that the scroll is straining to establish have not written on its parchment. Perhaps that is a reason for the title of the book of Zechariah—a remembrance of Yahweh because his words have been forgotten and mixed with others. It also provides an explanation for the oracles in chs. 9–14: they are a reiteration of the forgotten oracles of Yahweh. That may be a reason why Zechariah does not quote other prophets verbatim very often. In order to avoid the charges of false prophecy, he keeps his distance from their exact words to build a fence around the law of not quoting other prophets. Ironically, this kind of quoting can produce exactly the result of modifying the prophets' words. An intertextual reading focusing on Jeremiah rather than Zechariah could bring out a reaction to the book of Zechariah. Jeremiah may oppose Zechariah's ideology, and even establish Zechariah as one who perverts pure prophecy by reincorporating previous prophecy into his literature; but Jeremiah is scarcely innocent in this regard, as his text

24. Jeremiah 23 contains other connectives with Zechariah: branch (צמח/Jer. 23.5/Zech. 3.8; 6.12), and the north as the place from which the remnant will return (צפנה/Jer. 23.8; Zech. 2.10; 6.8).

shares many common prophetic themes, as Zechariah does. Is para-phrasing another's words the same as stealing those words?

Excursus: The Fabricated Audience

Such a reading might be criticized on the grounds that it is the result of sustained research, with the help of a concordance and a computer with a search driver and *BHS* in digital form, which examines parallel themes, words, collocations, and so on, between the hypertext of Zech-ariah and its pre-texts, comprising practically the entire Hebrew Bible—I use the MacBible and acCordance software programs (the grammatically tagged text that acCordance uses is version 2.0 of *The Westminster Hebrew Morphological Database* which differs slightly in a few places from *BHS*; see their software manual, D-9 for notes on the text). Some critics may believe a reader could not be that cognizant and would not be able to recall these pre-texts from the entire corpus of the Hebrew Bible. This section aims to preempt that criticism.

Intertextual references in a hypertext are the result of conscious and subconscious activity on the part of the author and/or the reader; they may be expressions of either the personal or the social symbolic order.[25] My attribution of a personal and a social symbolic order, as far as I know, is an appropriation of the Jungian division between the collective unconscious and the personal unconscious (see Samuels 1985: 24). Writers and readers are not always aware of their influences. Readers/ interpreters are subject to these same conscious and subconscious pro-cesses when they read the hypertext. The intertextual references may not have any real existence in the author's conscious or subconscious, but may be pure constructs of readers' imaginations and their submis-sion to the intertextual drive.

Author's and reader's conscious and subconscious symbolic orders

---

25. For a small sample of writers who describe the unconscious element of writing and/or psychology's relationship to writing see Bakhtin (1990: 69); Dalton (1979: 26-28; and elsewhere throughout this work); Eco (1992b: 68-71); Freud; Jung; Kurzweil (1983: 68-70); Riffaterre (1990: 77); Samuels (1985: 12), and Wright (1982: 145-48).

Specifically relating to prophetic texts, Holladay, in his discussion of the sources Jeremiah uses, discusses deliberate and unconscious processes of citation and how 'it is usually not possible to distinguish between the more deliberate and the less deliberate use of earlier phraseology' (1989: 35-36). Holladay chooses to call these 'reminiscences' of earlier material (1989: 36).

are irrecoverable: only postulates and traces remain. One way to
attempt to recover these possible worlds of meaning is by following
Freud's, Bakhtin's and Lacan's theory of language and opening interpretation up to something akin to Freudian free association, complete
with the mechanisms of condensation and displacement.[26] Condensation is essentially the combination of two or more elements into one
element in the dream. The condensed element thus allows 'multiple
determination' and alludes to more than one element at the same time:
it is overdetermined (see Freud 1991: 402). Displacement is essentially
the substitution of one element for another. The reasons why displacement occur are much too complex to delve into here.

Interpretation becomes especially complex once one realizes these
mechanisms can both occur in the same image. The represented object
may be a displaced image. The image it displaces may be condensed.
Whatever a reader associates with a text, through condensation or displacement, be it a presence or a lack of a textual element, is valid interpretation.[27] One may view symbolism and imagery in literature as the
conscious representatives of this subconscious aspect of dream symbolism. This allows one to incorporate Freud's techniques of analysing
dreams into the interpretation of literature. That Zechariah is very
dreamlike (see above) further legitimizes this interpretational effort.
Ricoeur supports defining interpretations this way: 'all the connotations
that can fit are to be attached; the poem means all it can mean' (1974:
104).

Riffaterre also connects psychoanalysis, intertextuality and the role of
the connective, and even goes so far as to postulate an 'intertextual
drive':

> And, generally speaking, we are justified in drawing a parallel between
> intertextuality and the unconscious, since the text plays the role of a
> screen. Thus the intertext is to the text what the unconscious is to con-

---

26. See Freud for a discussion of condensation and displacement (1991: 383-
419); see also Wright (1982: 147-48) for a succinct discussion.

27. Freud's theory of free association sublimates the subject's associations
between words to the level of ultimate reality. Public perceptions of validity, which
demand concensus, are swept away in a move of supreme relativism which recognizes that reality ultimately resides in the subject and the associations that subject
has made throughout his or her life. Despite the grandiose claims to liberate the
reader characteristic of reader-response criticism, Freud's theory predates reader-
response criticism by at least 70 years.

sciousness. Reading, therefore, is not unlike analysis. Nonetheless, we must recognise that what impels the reader to pursue the search for the intertext, to experience the intertextual drive, as it were, is…consistent with, or a variant of, the ubiquitous mechanism of tropes. In a response rendered compulsive, and facilitated by this familiar model, as soon as the reader notices a possible substitutability, s/he automatically yields to the temptation to actualise it. The intertextual drive, therefore is tropological rather than psychoanalytical, a reader response dictated by the tantalising combination within each connective of the enigma and the answer, of the text as Sphinx and the intertext as Oedipus (1990: 77).

Even transference takes place in reading. The difference between the transference in reading and psychology is that the transference is from the reader to the assumed author (the entity the reader has constructed as author of the text under consideration based on attributing elements in the text to an authorial consciousness), whereas in psychoanalysis the transference occurs between the analyst and the analysand. This study is an attempt to construct a meaning for Zechariah 1–8. When a reader deals with associations which textual images invoke, she walks in Umberto Eco's twilight zone between the 'use' of a text, which is a personal appropriation, and the 'interpretation' of a text, which is more concerned with the text's cultural and linguistic background.[28] Unfortunately for Eco, the difference between the two is very difficult to define. It is nearly impossible to define scientifically a difference between 'use' and 'interpretation'.

This project attempts to stay within Eco's *interpretation*, as opposed to his *use* of a text, by setting (constructing) historical and cultural limits on which texts are used to chase the signifier(s) encountered in Zechariah. In this examination, the rest of the Hebrew Bible is viewed as the unconscious of the book of Zechariah: Zechariah is the conscious text and the rest of the Hebrew Bible the subconscious intertexts. The Hebrew Bible thereby stands as the gate to an unconscious for the author(s) and reader(s) of Zechariah, albeit an unconscious that is structured by me as just one reader. The original author's and reader's free associations, which are irrecoverable, are thereby displaced with my own. Through free associating words and images various readings are produced via my consciousness: my conscious and subconscious displace the author's conscious and subconscious. By chasing the signifier

28. Eco's difference between use and interpretation is that interpretation must respect the cultural and linguistic background of the text being read (1992b: 69).

through the Hebrew Bible, various contexts condense in my head. These other contexts are then brought back to Zechariah when I (re)read it. This is a scholarship of possibilities—but which form of scholarship is not?

Humans automatically make texts, acts and life mean, and no amount of theory will prevent humans from exercising this autonomy and, in Jobling's terms, bridging the gap between the texts and our world (1991: 182). Recognizing the plenitude of problems and ultimate subjectivity involved in historical construction, I will assert my humanity and determine how the fabricated author[29] of Zechariah has written this text (does this imply there is a historical drive that arises after the intertextual drive?). I use the term 'construct' rather than 'reconstruct', for this project to avoid the implication of objectivity implicit in the term 'reconstruct' which suggests that the artifice the interpreter builds is similar to the original 'construction'. Another reason to use the word 'construct' is because of the similarity between this work and the act of building. In building a structure the builder uses the materials at hand to erect a structure. Interpretation uses the material data at hand to construct a story and/or a history. Implicit in my statements is the belief that Zechariah is and always was a written document. It seems doubtful that the oracles were ever delivered in any form outside of their present ones, and faced with the lack of evidence that they ever were, the onus is actually on those who believe they pre-existed the compilation of the book to prove it, rather than vice versa.

The historical conclusions of this study are based on the identification of a plethora of intertexts in Zechariah. Due to the sheer quantity of intertextual references perceived in Zechariah, I have constructed a historical situation in which it may have been a prerequisite of good style to incorporate as many themes as possible into a classical Hebrew work. I am one of a long tradition of scholars who have recognized many other influences in Zechariah. This might be taken to relegate Fishbane's mantological exegesis to an earlier time. Recently, Nogalski has commented broadly on this phenomenon in the book of the Twelve:

> the tradent responsible clearly exhibits considerable ability in the art of prophetic intertextual interpretation, or *Schriftprophetie*. One of the

---

29. While some may choose to use the term 'implied author' I prefer 'fabricated author' to avoid the connotations that the author of the text is implied, that is latent, in the text. The view of biblical authorship I propose here is constructed on other grounds than solely the text of Zechariah.

intriguing questions raised by this observation affects how pervasive one perceives this practice of intertextual reflection. Some quarters presume this type of intertextual reflection must only be associated with later wisdom circles, but the utter familiarity of the tradents of the Book of the Twelve with prophetic traditions demands that one consider whether such a limitation is wise (1993b: 282).

Specifically regarding Zechariah, Blocher says, 'He was a child of the sacrificers of the exile who concentrated on studying [because] of the impossibility of [performing] sacrifices. His text is a fabric of allusions to oracles of the predecessors and it combines an anthological style of others [in] a refined composition.'[30] Zechariah has a very developed style. As Woody Allen films frequently exhibit allusions to other literature and film, specifically to Ingmar Bergman's films, the fabricated author of Zechariah in a high-brow manner alludes to previous Hebrew works. As discussed, the fabricated author of Zechariah constantly draws from an existing biblical corpus when writing this book.

Readers of Zechariah, who are fabricated as well, may have had a similar breadth of knowledge of their own culture and its texts. It is impossible to determine the breadth of knowledge of any reader. The sheer quantity of texts (from numerous traditions and times—English, French, German, Greek, Latin, Russian) that Bakhtin appositely uses as examples in his work is staggering. Perhaps the original audience of Zechariah could recognize the intertexts in Zechariah (then they would be allusions). The fabricated readers would then be extremely erudite and *intimately* familiar with the Hebrew Bible corpus. This is a realistic postulate if one considers that there is not a large extant collection of Hebrew texts from 1000 BCE to the turn of the common era.[31] If those are the only texts which did exist, they are the only works in their own tongue which the implied audience might read. How many pages does

30. 'Il était fils des sacrificateurs de l'exil que l'impossibilité des sacrifices avait concentrés sur l'étude. Son texte est un tissu d'allusions aux oracles des prédécesseurs, et il combine au "style anthologique" d'autres procédés de composition raffinés' (1979: 264).

31. Barton muses, 'Of course the suggestion that some prophecy may have been literary from the beginning does not in itself detract from its inspiration; but it does imply that the prophet was a learned writer rather than a simple and perhaps illiterate spokesman for Yahweh' (*ABD*: V, 494).

Carroll considers the term 'intellectual' 'a useful category for considering these poets [prophets who were]...social critics operating with a high level of theory' (1983: 26; parenthetical material mine).

the average literate person, let alone a scholar, read in a year? One could easily read the 1574 pages in *BHS* in a year. So these members of the intelligentsia probably have a small corpus of texts in their own language to read and re-read. Presumably these 'scholars' (literate individuals) are not only reading these texts, but copying them as well, perhaps many times (if they want their own copy they are certainly copying them, or are very wealthy and can afford to pay a scribe). If they are copying these texts, they most likely know them left to right, back to front.

The fabricated reader of Zechariah may well have belonged to a small audience of learned individuals (scholars?) intimately familiar with the Hebrew literature of their day (whatever it was that existed at that time—for the purposes of this study, it is heuristically assumed that the biblical canon existed in its current form). The best a modern can do is take the literary canon as we have it. Ultimately in interpretation the only canon which exists is that of the reader, as readers can only supply information to which they have access. For this fabricated audience, authors could raise themes mentioned in previous works and the allusions would be quickly picked up.

In some ways the readers have no choice but to notice links as they are 'machines' which process language and their reading activity is dictated by the language they read (see Lacan 1988: 43; Muller and Richardson 1988: 74). The ideal reader would reverberate the many intertextual links to view different aspects of Zechariah differently, depending on which intertextual thread she focuses on in her reading. More than one thread can be held in tension at once, a situation which allows this ideal reader to shift the intertexts in her mind as different elements in the text of Zechariah interact with different intertexts, allowing and causing the reader to pursue different quests for the sign; allowing the reader to see all the intertexts interacting synonymously at the same moment in the reading process. Readers thereby hold intertexts in their minds, and it is not until different words, themes and concepts trigger the intertexts that they are raised into conscious thought.

Another possibility is that these texts were written for a royal patronage, or a small group of influential people, like works in the Renaissance.[32] In this way Zechariah, or the author of the text of Zechariah,

---

32. For a discussion of renaissance poetry see Tompkins (1980b: 207-11).

Garbini postulates that in pre-exilic times 'the monarchy constituted the pivot around which all literary production gravitated' (1994: 181). Literature was thereby

would have been kept at court (Zerubbabel's or Joshua's?) and pur-posely wrote these texts with the courtly audience in mind. There cer-tainly is a sycophantic aspect of Zechariah in its flowery depiction of Joshua as the branch, in its portrayal of Joshua as being crowned and reclothed, and in its flattering direct addresses to Joshua (3.6-10) and Zerubbabel (4.7-10). One can imagine Joshua sitting on his throne say-ing: 'Oh look, Dear, he's identified *me* as "the branch". How very clever.'

This audience would enlarge and change as Zechariah became a doc-ument of the community. Since the communities this document has passed through occupy practically all of Western culture, one obviously cannot trace all the communities through which this text has passed. Nor can one trace the way the text allows a community to appropriate it, or how this text works in each society. These issues will be left for another study. It fulfils a different function for each community it passes through. But the intertextual dimensions of the text would not cease to exist in a larger community less aware of the entire biblical tradition. They would just be less active in the mind of an individual reader; that is the individual reader may not make as many intertextual connections as a more learned implied reader, but would still recog-nize/create some of these connections, depending on which texts this real reader was aware of. Between the time these texts were written and the time the 'secondary' audience reads it, new texts have entered into circulation (texts like 1 and 2 Chronicles; Daniel; Ezra and Nehemiah immediately come to mind; and who knows what is happening with Third Isaiah?). These 'secondary' audiences may make intertextual connections with these newer texts, in the same way that later Christian readers make connections between Christian Scriptures and the Hebrew Bible. How valid or appropriate these connections are depends on the goal(s) of the reader and the goal(s) of the community.

If you remain unconvinced by these arguments and believe that your fabricated readers could not have produced these interpretations, there

---

either produced by monarchic circles or a reaction against monarchic practices (Garbini 1994: 181-83). He believes that in the Persian period 'the literature of the court is now replaced by the literature of the temple' which focuses 'on the need for self-definition within the group in power, which had taken the place of the monar-chy' (1994: 184). Perhaps Zech. 1–8 appeals to Joshua as representative of the temple, as a local ruler, and Zerubbabel as representative of the higher court of the Persians, which had power over the temple.

are a number of reasons to still engage in this type of research. That readers could not have read in this manner does not negate the value of intertextual practices as an examination of current hermeneutics. Here we have a test case of a modern reader, one aware of poststructuralist theory, encountering text(s) from a foreign culture. The application of this theory limns our modern thought processes and how we make sense of the confusing. There is the possibility that it may help to illuminate this foreign culture's texts as well.

(IN)CONCLUSION

Chapter 6

THE ELUSIVE CRITIC

> The scriptures are unalterable and the comments often enough merely express the commentators' despair.
>
> Kafka 1968: 243

> A situation where everything is meaningful is certainly oppressive: the logical extreme of such an attitude is paranoia, ominously meaningful that its slightest fragments operate as signs in some sinisterly coherent text.
>
> Eagleton 1989: 187

Texts need interpretation. Interpretation is the job of the reader. As texts are judged by how they create enjoyment, likewise interpretation is to be judged by how it creates enjoyment.

Some may be dissatisfied with such a conclusion. Here is another. This work has been primarily concerned with demonstrating why, as readers have perceived Zechariah 1–8 to be incoherent or unreadable. The grounds on which this assertion is made have been dealt with extensively in this study and will not be fully rehearsed here. The initial reading of the text on narrative grounds alienated me. Confronted by this alienation, I desperately attempted to control the text using intra- and intertextual strategies in search for some clue which would explain the text. On reflection, this task resulted in multiple interpretational options which were not always mutually complementary.

The final readings, while lacking the elegance of Umberto Eco's writing, are analogous to the ever-shifting conspiratorial interpretations which Belbo, Casaubon and Diotallevi create in *Foucault's Pendulum* (1992a). Like those interpretations, these interpretations of Zechariah flip ever so slightly depending on which element is taken to control the metaphor(s). The final interpretation may look little like the initial interpretation, they may even be mutually exclusive, and the reader of this discourse may forget what the initial interpretation looked like. Nonetheless, the interpretation is the process: the malleable matrix of interpretation which inexorably mutates like a common virus. Hand says, 'the resolution of tensions between signs...is dependent on a principle of coherence in which the reader closes a circuit of illusion by meeting and eliminating obstacles to a coherent meaning' (1990: 84). I not only failed in the task of understanding Zechariah 1–8, I also multiplied the inherent confusion by introducing the evolution of nonsense precipitated by multivalency or overdeterminism: I did not produce a principle of coherence which would eliminate the semantic obstacles. This is a text in which the reader does not know which direction to take and does not know where to base her reading. There are no stable points in the text, as almost all of the textual elements are involved in a game of perpetual substitution. I was caught in the dream of Zechariah, and as Eco says, 'capturing readers' dreams does not necessarily mean encouraging escape: it can also mean haunting them' (1994: 72).

Lest you, reader, believe I am alone in labelling Zechariah incomprehensible, consider the following opinions. Jerome called Zechariah the most obscure book in the Bible (so Stuhlmueller [1970: 391]). Barker says, 'there are eight visions in Zechariah, all alien to our normal patterns of thought, experience and communication' (1978: 20). Ruffin phrases it thus:

> the message of the book is consistently inconsistent. That is, the desired happy ending is never achieved. If the reader cannot assimilate the value system of the book then the narrative is totally frustrating (1986: 221).

I agree with Ruffin's assertion that the book is 'consistently inconsistent' and totally frustrating, but question how he can understand the value system of the book, since one must first understand the book before one can assimilate its values. What are those values?

The task left for the reader is to confront the incoherence and read it as such, not to force it into some mould of coherent meaning into which it will not fit. Felman elaborates:

> The history of reading has accustomed us to the assumption—usually unquestioned—that reading is finding meaning, that interpretation—of whatever method—can dwell only on the meaningful. Lacan's analysis of the signifier opens up a radically new assumption...that what *can* be read (and perhaps what *should* be read) is not just meaning, but the lack of meaning; that significance lies not just in consciousness, but, specifically, in its disruption; that the signifier can be analyzed in its effects without its signified being known; that the lack of meaning—the discontinuity in conscious understanding—can and should be interpreted as such, without necessarily being transformed into meaning...what is

> analytical par excellence is not...the *readable*, but the *unreadable*, and
> the *effects* of the unreadable. What calls for analysis is the insistence of
> the unreadable in the text (1988: 149).

We must ask the question 'why is Zechariah unreadable?'

Claiming Zechariah is unreadable is a statement which needs qualifications. On what level is it unreadable? Was it the intention of the
author to deliberately create an unreadable text? Was this text once
readable, but we have lost the hermeneutical skills to read it? This is not
to claim it required an esoteric code to read it, but rather that these hermeneutic codes no longer exist. Cultures change, as do styles of reading
and writing. If it was once comprehensible, then it is modern readers
who are incompetent. In this postmodern climate of criticism, it is
widely accepted that author's intentions are irretrievable, but readers
may still construct an author who deliberately made the text unreadable.
This is a final attempt to master the text on the part of the reader who
has failed using other methodologies to probe the text. It projects
responsibility for failure from the reader to the text. This is, perhaps, a
final, vengeful thrust at the text in the vanquished death throes of this
reader's defeat. Regardless, the codes used in Zechariah 1–8 are so
alien to modern times that there is no competent reader alive today.
This unreadability must be confronted as it is the character of this text.
A hermeneutics of the unreadable must be established.

Long, while dealing with only Zech. 2.3-4; 4.1-6a, 10b-11, 13-14;
5.5-8; and 2.1-2, alludes to the unreadable nature of the text, but takes
the position that ancients did understand these 'Revelatory–Mysteries–
Visions':

> This type is a report whose basic intent is to convey in veiled form,
> secrets of divine activity and events of the future... The language, there-
> fore, tends towards allegory. Whatever 'message value' the report may
> have has to be first freed from its esoteric entrapment. Thus the
> prophet...is understood as one who receives and transmits esoteric reve-
> lations. The vision-report intends to instruct the cognizant, while mysti-
> fying those lacking proper keys (1976: 363-64).

Long includes Daniel 8 and 10–12 in this category and believes it oper-
ated under the same hermeneutic. Long represents a tradition of viewing these texts as bizarre to modern tastes because they are meant to
hide secrets from the uninitiated. In this viewpoint, these texts were
even bizarre to the writer's ancient contemporaries who were not privy
to the initiates' hermeneutic. This interpretation of the data is seriously

flawed in that it is an argument from silence that involves a grandiose construction of supposed mystery groups and cults and initiates. Where are the Hebrew or Aramaic texts (biblical or other) which describe such groups and their clandestine hermeneutics? Even if we should find such a text, how would we know if it was actually contemporaneous with the original writer(s) of Zechariah 1–8 and not a later appropriation or interpretation? Because of the absence of material supporting such an ambitious construction, I propose we all lack the proper keys, both modern and ancient, and the original implied audience did too. This suggests a reason for why these texts are impenetrable other than that they are this way to conceal their meaning from the uninitiated.

Craig is the only other author I am aware of also to investigate at length the unreadability of Zechariah.[1] He has shared my experience and notes, 'on first appearances, Zechariah 1–8 consists of an unrelated deluge of obscure symbolic visions and oracular interpretations' (1991: 48). Craig believes that while this text is confusing, the symbols collectively 'provide a "total effect"' (1991: 49).[2] The text 'calls for experiential participation': 'the multiple embedded metaphors of Zechariah create a similar affect of "trance induction" which indirectly provides a new way of seeing in the midst of the colonial domination of Judah' (Craig 1991: 50 n. 76, 50 n. 77). He describes the process thus:

> The surface-level conflict of styles and meaning in this text forces readers to search for meaning through the impasse of literal, grammatical meaning to another 'deep' or 'Figurative' level. Readers are prompted to separate themselves from the 'real-world' status of the colonial province of Judah and submit themselves to the other-worldly presence of YHWH. The text of Zechariah, it might be said, invites readers to participate in a symbolic process of transformation by entering into the liminal, visionary realm disclosed by the prophet (1991: 79).

Zechariah 1–8 is 'an invitation to transcend the world of societal conflict and poverty and participate in "a metaphysical movement from the here and now to the timelessness of the Other"' (Craig [1991: 81], quoting Edmund Leach).

---

1. A principal difference between his work and this thesis is that he accepts the difficulty of many of the elements, whereas I have set out to demonstrate how confusing these elements are.

2. Craig postulates, 'the redundancy and fractured syntax in the book of Zechariah, it may be said, simulate the prophet's "aural" experience of hearing the word of YHWH and the "visual" experience of his visions' (1991: 59 n. 101).

Stuhlmueller differs from Craig in focusing on understanding each symbol individually and claiming the writer is not concerned about the total effect, yet, ironically, comes to the same conclusion in seeing the effect of reading this text as the apprehension of the deity:

> These symbols are heaped one upon another—to an extent that seems weird and baffling to the modern reader but that may be congenial to the modern artist—for the apocalyptic writer is not at all concerned about the total effect. Each symbol must be appreciated independently of the others. The prophet has succeeded, in fact, if he has stunned the reader with the sense of the numinous (1970: 390).

What kind of a sense of the numinous is this? Incomprehensible, opaque, inarticulate, and soon. The resulting theology, presumably would be, that God is symbolic and very confusing. Fair enough—it sounds similar to Job's theology.

An issue that must be confronted in Craig's and Stuhlmueller's readings, that postulate the effects of the text on the reader, and which Stuhlmueller hints at in this quote, is whether it is the ancient reader, the modern reader, or both who experience this sense of the numinous or transcendence from the mundane world. Craig appears to be suggesting that it is the ancient reader who undergoes this experience as he says it is 'the everyday world of colonial Judah' which is transcended (1991: 78; see also 49, 79, 81). From such a brief discussion of this topic, it is difficult to be certain if it is ancient or modern readers that Stuhlmueller is discussing. Both of these writers postulate readers who have a far richer experience of the text than I do: to these readers the text functions as an opiate.

To see if it was just me who did not have this experience of the text, and might be missing out on a good fix, I asked some of my friends to read Zechariah 1–8. Stunned and confused they were, but they experienced neither a sense of the numinous nor the timelessness of the other.[3] Perhaps Stuhlmueller and Craig feel these things when they read the text. If so I could not refute their readings; and I here follow Borges, 'of course, if you don't see it, your incapacity will not invalidate what I have experienced' (1971: 25). But one must recognize this is not likely to be the experience of many (any?) in our culture. Furthermore, if it is an ancient who is supposed to experience this transcendence, are some

---

3. I thank Tara Ascott, John Jenkins and Graham Ovenden for lending their reading services. Of course, they may have had selfish motives, that is, escapist tendencies.

assumptions being made about the different mental states of ancient and modern readers? The most damning criticism is that already raised above: where is the ancient textual evidence for these assertions? Where is the inscription which reads, 'and behold, I read Zechariah and I escaped from this dreadful world of colonial servitude'. Either more concrete testimonial evidence is required, perhaps in the style of Holland's research into how readers read,[4] or some other explanation.

But 'explanation' is not the name of this game. Unlike most modern 'response-readers' I resisted my own premature readings, followed every clue, every option, every signifying chain, tempted by the multiplicity of options into deferring my desire for closure. I constructed an author who created this abundance of signification. I became a modernist reader, seeking *the* coherent meaning of a text constructed by a meaning author.

It was only this search for determinate meaning that delivered a determinate lack of meaning. I *have* found an author, and I feel I have understood the game he has invented. This author is one who has deliberately avoided discovery. In a sense, this is an ancient form of postmodernism. Because of its milieu, perhaps we should call this 'postpropheticism'.

In both the postmodern and the postprophetic, the confidence of the previous age has collapsed and we see the end of determinacy, of tradition and of stability, and the birth of deconstruction, indeterminacy and a greater consciousness of the task at hand as a writer and the incertitude of the human condition. Zechariah, as a postprophetic text, is very similar to a postmodern text and is very much a prophecy of our own times, culturally speaking: it deconstructs the past and refuses to contemplate a determinate future. In it there is a breakdown of determinate meaning. Simultaneously, it self-consciously exposes the weaknesses of its predecessors.

In the postprophetic age, the nature of literary prophecy is laid bare. Prophecy is presented as art rather than as a guidebook. Guidebooks and determinate meanings belong to the past. Yet, Zechariah is not a pure parody of the prophets. Rather, Zechariah has moved prophecy into the realm of purely surreal art. In the postprophetic, the future is

---

4.   A good introduction to Holland's style of examining how readers read, which deals specifically with the difference between male and female readers in dialogue, is Holland and Sherman (1986); see also Holland (1980) for a brief introduction to his style of work.

indeterminate: it is the job of the reader to invent it. Zechariah as a postprophetic text is very similar to a 'postmodern' text. Determinate meanings lie in the past and belong to the world of the implied audience's ancestors. The future is indeterminate: it is the job of the reader to invent it. This is the nature of literary prophecy. This is the prophetic device that Zechariah has laid bare.

Concerning Zechariah, it is not so much that the author has produced an elusive text: he has produced more of a self-consciously evasive text. Confronted with the postprophetic, one must re-examine the prophetic to see how many postprophetic characteristics are shared by prophetic texts. Once again, Eco's comments are pertinent, 'In order to become a Sacred Wood, a wood must be tangled and twisted like the forests of the Druids, and not orderly like a French Garden' (1995: 128). Maybe 'tangledness' was essential to be included in the canon. The more I think about it the more I feel that perhaps the entire canon can or should be called 'The Evasive Text'.

On a personal level, I have discovered that closure is not the purpose of all games. The search for meaning can be an end in itself and is perhaps the intended purpose of the book of Zechariah. The threat of closure need not haunt the addict who can pursue the endless chains of meaning through infinity.

> They are looking for me, They must have picked up my trail... They know I am here now, They still want the Map. And when I tell Them that there is no Map, They will want it all the more.
>
> Eco 1992a: 641

Lest you despair, there is a 'positive' way to view this phenomenon.

> Both common people and intellectuals find your work conflictingly incoherent. That means you're a genius.
>
> Woody Allen (Bullets Over Broadway)

Perhaps Zechariah and the postprophetic, as well as the interpretation of them, are best seen as analogous to the birth of the novel.

> As God slowly departed from the seat whence he had directed the universe and its order of values, distinguished good from evil, and endowed each thing with meaning, Don Quixote set forth from his house into a world he could no longer recognize. In the absence of the supreme Judge, the world suddenly appeared in its fearsome ambiguity; the single divine Truth decomposed into myriad relative truths parceled out by men.
>
> Kundera 1988: 6

BIBLIOGRAPHY

Achtemeier, E.
1986   *Nahum–Malachi* (Interpretation: A Bible Commentary for Teaching and Preaching (Atlanta: John Knox Press).

Ackroyd, P.R.
1958   'Two Old Testament Historical Problems of the Early Persian Period', *JNES* 17: 13-27.
1962   'Haggai/Zechariah', in M. Black and H.H. Rowley (eds.), *The New Peake's Bible Commentary* (London: Thomas Nelson): 646-55.
1968   *Exile and Restoration* (London: SCM Press).

Amsler, S.
1972   'Zacharie et l'origine de l'apocalyptique', in Congress of the International Organization for the Study of the Old Testament, *Congress Volume: Uppsala, 1971* (VTSup, 22; Leiden: E.J. Brill): 227-31.
1981   'La parole visionnaire des prophètes', *VT* 31: 359-63.

Auld, A.G.
1983a   'Prophets through the Looking Glass: Between Writings and Moses', *JSOT* 27: 3-23.
1983b   'Prophets through the Looking Glass: A Response to Robert Carroll and Hugh Williamson', *JSOT* 27: 41-44.
1990   'Prophecy in Books: A Rejoinder', *JSOT* 48: 31-32.

Bach, A.
1993   'Reading Allowed: Feminist Biblical Criticism Approaching the Millennium', *CRBS* 1: 191-215.

Bakhtin, M.M.
1990   *The Dialogic Imagination* (ed. M. Holquist; trans. E. Caryl; Austin: University of Texas Press).

Baldwin, J.G.
1964   'Ṣemaḥ as a Technical Term in the Prophets', *VT* 14: 93-97.
1972   *Haggai, Zechariah, Malachi* (TOTC; London: Tyndale Press).

Bar-Efrat, S.
1989   *Narrative Art in the Bible* (JSOTSup, 70; Sheffield: JSOT Press).

Barker, M.
1977   'The Two Figures in Zechariah', *HeyJ* 18: 38-46.
1978   'The Evil in Zechariah', *HeyJ* 19: 12-27.

Barton, J.
1992   'Prophecy (Postexilic Hebrew)', in *ABD*: V, 489-95.

Bauer, L.
 1992 *Zeit des Zweiten Tempels: Zeit der Gerechtigkeit* (Beiträge zur Erforsch- ung des Alten Testaments und des antiken Judentums, 31; Bern: Peter Lang).

Bergdall, C.R.
 1986 'Zechariah's Program of Restoration: A Rhetorical Critical Study of Zechariah 1–8' (PhD dissertation, Fuller Theological Seminary).

Berlin, A.
 1987 *Poetics and Interpretation of Biblical Narrative* (Bible and Literature Series, 9; Sheffield: Almond Press).

Berquist, J.
 1989 'The Social Setting of Early Postexilic Prophecy' (PhD dissertation, Van- derbilt University).

Beuken, W.A.M.
 1967 *Haggai–Sacharja 1–8* (Assen: Van Gorcum).

Bič, M.
 1962 *Das Buch Sacharja* (Berlin: Evangelische Verlagsanstalt).

Bleich, D.
 1980 'Epistemological Assumptions in the Study of Response', in Tompkins 1980: 134-63.

Blenkinsopp, J.
 1984 *A History of Prophecy in Israel* (London: SPCK).

Blocher, H.
 1979 'Zacharie 3: Josué et le grand jour des expiations', *ETR* 54: 264-70.

Bloom, H.
 1989 *Ruin the Sacred Truths: Poetry and Belief from the Bible to the Present* (Cambridge, MA: Harvard University Press).

Boehmer, J.
 1938 'Was bedeutet der goldene Leuchter Sach. 4,2?', *BZ* 24: 360-64.

Booth, W.
 1983 'Rhetorical Critics Old and New: The Case of Gérard Genette', in L. Ler- ner (ed.), *Reconstructing Literature* (Oxford: Basil Blackwell): 123-42.

Borges, J.L.
 1971 'The Aleph', in *idem*, *The Aleph and Other Stories* (trans. N.T. di Gio- vanni; London: Jonathan Cape): 15-32.

Bowie, Malcolm
 1987 *Freud, Proust and Lacon: Theory as Fiction* (Cambridge: Cambridge University Press).

Brenner, A.
 1982 *Colour Terms in the Old Testament* (JSOTSup, 21; Sheffield: JSOT Press).

Brooks, P.
 1989 'Freud's Masterplot', in S. Felman (ed.), *Literature and Psychoanalysis* (Baltimore: The Johns Hopkins University Press): 280-300.

Brueggemann, W.
 1991 'At the Mercy of Babylon: A Subversive Rereading of the Empire', *JBL* 110: 3-22.

Burgess, A.
    1993   *The Independent* (27 November): 31.
Buss, M.
    1980   'The Social Psychology of Prophecy', in J.A. Emerton (ed.), *Prophecy: Essays Presented to Georg Fohrer on his Sixty-fifth Birthday, 6 September, 1980* (BZAW, 150; Berlin: W. de Gruyter): 1-11.
Butterworth, M.
    1992   *Structure and the Book of Zechariah* (JSOTSup, 130; Sheffield: JSOT Press).
Byatt, A.S.
    1994   'The Djinn in the Nightingale's Eye', in *idem, The Djinn in the Nightingale's Eye: Five Fairy Stories* (London: Chatto & Windus): 93-277.
Calvino, I.
    1993   *If on a Winter's Night a Traveler...* (trans. W. Weaver; London: David Campbell).
Carroll, R.P.
    1979   *When Prophecy Failed* (London: SCM Press).
    1983   'Poets Not Prophets: A Response to "Prophets through the Looking-Glass" ', *JSOT* 27: 25-31.
    1989   'Prophecy and Society', in R.E. Clements (ed.), *The World of Ancient Israel* (Cambridge: Cambridge University Press): 203-25.
    1990   'Whose Prophet? Whose History? Whose Social Reality? Troubling the Interpretative Community Again: Notes towards a Response to T.W. Overholt's Critique', *JSOT* 48: 33-49.
    1992   'The Myth of the Empty Land', *Semeia* 59: 79-92.
    1994   'So What Do We *Know* about the Temple? The Temple in the Prophets', in Eskenazi and Richards 1994: 34-51.
Carstensen, R.
    1972   'The Book of Zechariah', in C.M. Laymon (ed.), *The Interpreter's One-Volume Commentary on the Bible* (London: Collins): 504-10.
Cathcart, K.J., and R.P. Gordon
    1989   *The Aramaic Bible. XIV. The Targum of the Minor Prophets* (Edinburgh: T. & T. Clark).
Chary, T.
    1969   *Aggée–Zacharie, Malachie* (Paris: J. Gabalda).
Chatman, S.
    1983   *Story and Discourse* (Ithaca, NY: Cornell University Press).
Childs, B.S.
    1959   'The Enemy from the North and the Chaos Tradition', *JBL* 78: 187-98.
    1987   'The Canonical Shape of the Prophetic Literature', in J.L. Mays and P.J. Achtemeier (eds.), *Interpreting the Prophets* (Philadelphia: Fortress Press): 41-49.
Claassen, W. (ed.)
    1988   *Text and Context: Old Testament and Semitic Studies for F.C. Fensham* (JSOTSup, 48; Sheffield: JSOT Press).
Clark, D.
    1982   'The Case of the Vanishing Angel', *BT* 33: 213-18.
    1983   'The Perils of Pictures', *BT* 34.4: 440-41.

Clines, D.J.A.
    1990   'The Old Testament Histories: A Reader's Guide', in Clines 1990: 85-105.
    1993   'Metacommentating Amos', in McKay and Clines 1993: 142-60.
    1994   'Haggai's Temple, Constructed, Deconstructed and Reconstructed', in Eskenazi and Richards 1994: 60-87.
Clines, D.J.A. (ed.)
    1990   *What Does Eve Do to Help? and Other Readerly Questions to the Old Testament* (JSOTSup, 94; Sheffield: JSOT Press).
Coggins, R.J.
    1987   *Haggai Zechariah Malachi* (Sheffield: JSOT Press).
    1993   'Prophecy—True and False', in McKay and Clines 1993: 80-94.
Cohen, N.G.
    1985   'From *Nabi* to *Mal'ak* to "Ancient Figure"', *JJS* 26.2: 12-24.
    1987   ' "דבר...ב"': An Enthusiastic Prophetic Formula', *ZAW* 99: 219-32.
Cohn, D.
    1981   'The Encirclement of Narrative', *Poetics Today* 2.2: 157-82.
Collini, S. (ed.)
    1992   *Interpretation and Overinterpretation* (Cambridge: Cambridge University Press): 67-88.
Conrad, E.W.
    1992   'Heard but Not Seen: The Representation of "Books" in the Old Testament', *JSOT* 54: 45-59.
    1999   *Zechariah* (Readings; Sheffield: Sheffield Academic Press).
Coupland, D.
    1991   *Generation X* (New York: St Martin's Press).
Craig, K.M.
    1990   'The Corrections of the Scribes', *Perspectives in Religious Studies* 17: 155-65.
Craig, T.
    1991   'Rebuilding the Foundations: Metaphor and Social Drama in Early Post-exilic Texts' (PhD dissertation, Vanderbilt University).
  unpublished 'Critical Reading, Writing and (Re)Turn to the Body: Zechariah and the Transformation of Biblical Scholarship in a Post-Critical Age'.
Culler, J.
    1980   'Literary Competence', in Tompkins 1980: 101-17.
    1982   *On Déconstruction: Theory and Criticism after Structuralism* (Ithaca, NY: Cornell University Press).
    1988   *Framing the Sign: Criticism and its Institutions* (Oxford: Basil Blackwell).
Dalton, E.
    1979   *Unconscious Structure in The Idiot* (Princeton, NJ: Princeton University Press).
Davies, P.R.
    1992   *In Search of 'Ancient Israel'* (JSOTSup, 148; Sheffield: JSOT Press).
Davis, J.D.
    1920   'The Reclothing and Coronation of Joshua: Zechariah III and IV', *Princeton Theologiocal Review* 18 (1920): 256-68.

Day, P.L.
 1988 *An Adversary in Heaven: Śāṭān in the Hebrew Bible* (HSM, 43; Atlanta: Scholars Press).

De Vaux, R.
 1969 'Jerusalem and the Prophets', in *Interpreting the Prophetic Tradition* (The Goldenson Lectures, 1955–1966; Cincinnati: Hebrew Union College Press): 275-300.

Delcor, M.
 1975 'La vision de la femme dans l'épha de Zach., 5, 5-11 à la lumière de la littérature hittite', *RHR* 187: 137-45.

Demsky, A.
 1981 'The Temple Steward Josiah ben Zephaniah', *IEJ* 31: 100-102.

Derrida, J.
 1976 *Of Grammatology* (trans. G.C. Spivak; Baltimore: The Johns Hopkins University Press).

Donald, J.
 1989 'Introduction to Section Two', in Donald 1989: 136-45.

Donald, J. (ed.)
 1989 *Fantasy and the Cinema: A Reader* (London: British Film Institute).

Draisma, S. (ed.)
 1989 *Intertextuality in Biblical Writings: Essays in Honour of Bas van Iersel* (Kampen: Kok).

Driver, G.R.
 1930–31 'Studies in the Vocabulary of the Old Testament: II', *JTS* 32: 250-57.

Driver, S.R.
 1906 *The Minor Prophets II* (The Century Bible; Edinburgh: T.C. & E.C. Jack).

Eagleton, T.
 1985 *Literary Theory: An Introduction* (Oxford: Basil Blackwell).
 1989 'Bakhtin, Schopenhauer, Kundera', in K. Hirschkop and D. Shepherd (eds.), *Bakhtin and Cultural Theory* (Manchester: Manchester University Press): 178-88.

Eco, U.
 1992a *Foucault's Pendulum* (trans. William Weaver; London: Picador).
 1992b 'Between Author and Text', in Collini 1992: 67-88.
 1994 *Reflections on The Name of the Rose* (trans. William Weaver; London: Minerva).
 1995 *Six Walks in the Fictional Woods* (Cambridge, MA: Harvard University Press).

Eichrodt, W.
 1957 'Vom Symbol zum Typos', *TZ* 13: 509-22.

Eskenazi, T.C., and K.H. Richards (eds)
 1994 *Second Temple Studies. II. Temple Community in the Persian Period* (Sheffield: Sheffield Academic Press).

Eslinger, L.
 1989 *Into the Hands of the Living God* (JSOTSup, 84; Sheffield: Almond Press).

1992 'Inner-Biblical Exegesis and Inner-Biblical Allusion: The Question of Category', *VT* 42: 47-58.

Even-Shoshan, A.
1989 *A New Concordance of the Bible* (Jerusalem: Kiryath Sepher).

Eybers, I.H.
1971–72 'The Use of Proper Names as a Stylistic Device', *Semitics* 2: 82-92.
1975 'The Rebuilding of the Temple According to Haggai and Zechariah', *Die Ou-Testamentiese Werkgemeenskap in Suid-Afrika* 18: 15-26.

Feinberg, C.L.
1940a 'Exegetical Studies in Zechariah. I. An Exhortation to Repentance, 1:1-6', *BSac* 97.387: 318-24.
1940b 'Exegetical Studies in Zechariah. II. The Prophet's Night-Visions, 1:7–6:15', *BSac* 97.388: 435-47.

Felman, S.
1988 'On Reading Poetry: Reflections on the Limits and Possibilities of Psychoanalytical Approaches', in Muller and Richardson 1988: 133-56.

Fish, S.E.
1980a 'Interpreting the Variorum', in Tompkins 1980: 164-84.
1980b 'Literature in the Reader: Affective Stylistics', in Tompkins 1980: 70-100.

Fishbane, M.
1980 'Revelation and Tradition: Aspects of Inner-Biblical Exegesis', *JBL* 99: 343-61.

Fleming, D.M.
1989 'The Divine Council as Type Scene in the Hebrew Bible' (PhD dissertation, The Southern Baptist Theological Seminary).

Fohrer, G.
1968 *Introduction to the Old Testament* (Nashville: Abingdon Press).

Foucault, M.
1990 *The History of Sexuality*, I (trans. R. Hurley; Harmondsworth: Penguin Books).

Fowler, J.D.
1988 *Theophoric Personal Names in Ancient Hebrew: A Comparative Study* (JSOTSup, 49; Sheffield: JSOT Press).

Freer, K.O.
1975 'A Study of Vision Reports in Biblical Literature' (PhD dissertation, Yale University).

Freud, S,
1991 *The Interpretation of Dreams* (The Penguin Freud Library, 4; London: Penguin Books).

Frow, J.
1990 'Intertextuality and Ontology', in Still and Worton 1990: 45-55.

Frye, N.
1982 *The Great Code: The Bible and Literature* (New York: Harcourt Brace Jovanovich).
1985 'The Expanding World of Metaphor', *JAAR* 53: 585-98.

Galling, K.
   1964   'Die Exilswende in der Sicht des Propheten Sacharja', in *idem, Studien
             zur Geschichte Israels im persischen Zeitalter* (Tübingen: J.C.B. Mohr
             [Paul Siebeck]): 109-26.
Garbini, G.
   1994   'Hebrew Literature in the Persian Period', in Eskenazi and Richards 1994:
             180-88.
Gelston, A.
   1966   'The Foundations of the Second Temple', *VT* 16: 232-35.
Genette, G.
   1971   'Time and Narrative in *A la recherche du temps perdu*', in J. Hillis Miller
             (ed.), *Aspects of Narrative* (trans. P. de Man; London: Columbia Univer-
             sity Press): 93-118.
Gibson, W.
   1980   'Authors, Speakers, Readers, and Mock Readers', in Tompkins 1980: 1-6.
Glazier-McDonald, B.
   1992   'Zechariah', in C.A. Newsom and S.H. Ringe (eds.), *The Women's Bible
             Commentary* (London: SPCK): 230-31.
Good, R.M.
   1982   'Zechariah's Second Night Vision (Zech 2, 1-4)', *Bib* 63: 56-59.
Greenblatt, S.
   1988   *Shakespearean Negotiations* (Oxford: Clarendon Press).
   1989   'Towards a Poetics of Culture', in Veeser 1989: 1-14.
Greig, D.
   1989   'The Sexual Differentiation of the Hitchcock Text', in Donald 1989: 175-
             96.
Gunkel, H.
   1987   'The Prophets as Writers and Poets', in Petersen 1987: 22-73.
Gunn, D.M.
   1990   'Reading Right: Reliable and Omniscient Narrator, Omniscient God, and
             Foolproof Composition in the Hebrew Bible' in D.J.A. Clines, S. Fowl
             and S. Porter (eds.), *The Bible in Three Dimensions* (JSOTSup, 87; Shef-
             field: JSOT Press): 53-64.
Habel, N.
   1965   'The Form and Significance of the Call Narratives', *ZAW* 77: 297-323.
Halpern, B.
   1978   'The Ritual Background of Zechariah's Temple Song', *CBQ* 40: 167-90.
Hand, S.
   1990   'Missing You: Intertextuality, Transference and the Language of Love',
             in Still and Worton 1990: 79-91.
Hanson, P.D.
   1987   'In Defiance of Death: Zechariah's Symbolic Universe', in J.H. Marks
             and R.M. Good (eds.), *Love and Death in the Ancient Near East: Essays
             in Honor of Marvin Pope* (New Haven: Four Quarters): 173-79.
Harrelson, W.
   1982   'The Trial of the High Priest Joshua: Zechariah 3', *Eretz-Israel* 16: 116-
             24.

Haupt, P.
1918   'The Coronation of Zerubbabel', *JBL* 37: 209-18.
Hawkins, J.M., and R. Allen (eds.)
1991   *The Oxford Encyclopedic English Dictionary* (Oxford: Clarendon Press).
Henry, C.
1990   'The Image of a Word: Computer Generated Programs for the Trans-
            formation of Descriptive Language into Pictorial Representations for an
            Analysis of Axiomatic Thought Processes', in D.S. Miall (ed.), *Human-
            ities and the Computer: New Directions* (Oxford: Clarendon Press): 93-
            101.

Henshaw, T.
1958   *The Latter Prophets* (London: George Allen & Unwin).
Hertzberg, H.W.
1953   ' "Grüne" Pferde', *ZDPV* 69: 177-80.
Higginson, R.E.
1970   'Zechariah', in D. Guthrie and J.A. Motyer (eds.), *The New Bible Com-
            mentary Revised* (London: Inter-Varsity Press): 786-803.
Holladay, W.L.
1958   *The Root ŠÛBH in the Old Testament: With Particular Reference to its
            Usages in Covenantal Contexts* (Leiden: E.J. Brill).
1989   *Jeremiah 2: A Commentary on the Book of the Prophet Jeremiah Chap-
            ters 26–52* (Hermeneia; Minneapolis: Fortress Press).
Holland, N.
1980   'Unity Identity Text Self', in Tompkins 1980: 118-33.
Holland, N., and L. Sherman
1986   'Gothic Possibilities', in E. Flynn, and P. Schweickart (eds.), *Gender and
            Reading* (Baltimore: The Johns Hopkins University Press).
Horst, F.
1960   'Die Visionsschilderungen der alttestamentlichen Propheten', *EvT* 20:
            193-205.
House, P.R.
1990   *The Unity of the Twelve* (JSOTSup, 97; Sheffield: Almond Press).
Hubbeling, H.G.
1985   'Symbols as Representation and Presentation', *Neue Zeitschrift für sys-
            tematische Theologie and Religionsphilosophie* 27.2: 77-193.
Hyatt, J.P.
1937   'A Neo-Babylonian Parallel to BETHEL-SAR-EṢER, Zech 7$_2$', *JBL* 56:
            387-94.
Iser, W.
1980   'The Reading Process: A Phenomenological Approach', in Tompkins
            1980: 51-69.
James, F.
1934   'Thoughts on Haggai and Zechariah', *JBL* 53: 229-35.
Japhet, S.
1982   'Sheshbazzar and Zerubbabel', *ZAW* 94: 66-98.

Jeremias, C.
1977   *Die Nachtgesichte des Sacharja: Untersuchungen zu ihrer Stellung im Zusammenhang der Visionsberichte im Alten Testament und zu ihrem Bildmaterial* (FRLANT, 117; Göttingen: Vandenhoeck & Ruprecht).
Jobling, D.
1991   'Texts and the World: An Unbridgeable Gap?', in P.R. Davies (ed.), *Second Temple Studies*. I. *Persian Period* (JSOTSup, 117; Sheffield: JSOT Press): 175-82.
Jones, D.R.
1962   *Haggai, Zechariah and Malachi* (Torch Bible Commentaries, London: SCM Press).
Joubert, W.H.
1977-78   'The Determination of the Contents of Zechariah 1:7–2:17 through a Structural Analysis', *Die Ou-Testamentiese Werkgemeenskap in Suid-Africa*, 20–21: 66-82.
Joüon, P.
1991   *A Grammar of Biblical Hebrew* (with extensive commentary by T. Muraoka; 2 vols.; Subsidia biblica, 14.1, 2; Rome: Pontifical Biblical Institute Press, rev. edn).
Jung, C.G.
1977   *The Symbolic Life* (trans. R.F.C. Hull; London: Routledge & Kegan Paul).
Kafka, F.
1968   *The Trial* (trans. Willa and Edwin Muir; ed. E.M. Butler; London: Secker & Warburg, rev. edn).
Keil, C.F., and F. Delitzsch
1989   *Minor Prophets: Commentary on the Old Testament*, X (Peabody, MA: Hendrickson).
Kingsbury, E.C.
1964   'The Prophets and the Council of Yahweh', *JBL* 83: 279-86.
Kloos, C.J.L.
1975   'Zech. II 12: Really a Crux Interpretum?' *VT* 25, 4: 729-36.
Koch, K.
1978   *The Prophets*. I. *The Assyrian Period* (trans. M. Kohl; London: SCM Press).
1983   *The Prophets*. II. *The Babylonian and Persian Periods* (trans. M. Kohl; London: SCM Press).
Koehler, L., and W. Baumgartner
1953   *Lexicon in Veteris Testamenti Libros* (Leiden: E.J. Brill).
Kundera, M.
1988   *The Art of the Novel* (trans. Linda Asher; New York: Harper & Row).
Kurzweil, E.
1983   'Early Psychoanalytic Theory et al', in E. Kurzweil and W. Phillips (eds.), *Literature and Psychoanalysis* (New York: Columbia University Press): 19-23.
Lacan, J.
1988   'Seminar on "The Purloined Letter"', in Muller and Richardson 1988: 28-54.

Lambdin, T.O.
   1973   *Introduction to Biblical Hebrew* (London: Darton, Longman & Todd).
Landow, G.P.
   1992   *Hypertext: The Convergence of Contemporary Critical Theory and Tech-nology* (Baltimore: The Johns Hopkins University Press).
Landy, F.
   1993   'On Metaphor, Play and Nonsense', *Semeia* 61: 219-37.
Larkin, K.J.A.
   1994   *The Eschatology of Second Zechariah: A Study of the Formation of a Mantological Wisdom Anthology* (Contributions to Biblical Exegesis and Theology, 6; Kampen: Kok).

Le Bas, E.
   1950   'Zechariah's Enigmatical Contribution to the Corner-Stone', *PEQ* 82: 102-22.
   1951   'Zechariah's Climax to the Career of the Corner-Stone', *PEQ* 83: 139-55.
Leupold, H.C.
   1971   *Exposition of Zechariah* (Grand Rapids: Baker Book House).
Lipiński, E.
   1970   'Recherches sur le livre de Zacharie', *VT* 20: 25-55.
Lodge, D.
   1979   *Changing Places: A Tale of Two Campuses* (Harmondsworth: Penguin Books).
   1992   *The Art of Fiction* (London: Penguin Books).
Long, B.
   1976   'Reports of Visions among the Prophets', *JBL* 95: 353-65.
Lyon, E.
   1989   'The Cinema of Lol V. Stein', in Donald 1989: 147-74.
MacKay, C.
   1968   'Zechariah in Relation to Ezekiel 40-48', *EvQ* 40: 197-210.
Mare, W.H.
   1992   'Zion', in *ABD*: VI, 1096-97.
Marenof, S.
   1931–32   'Note concerning the Meaning of the Word "Ephah", Zechariah 5:5-11', *AJSL* 48: 264-67.
Marinkovic, P.
   1994   'What Does Zechariah 1–8 Tell Us about the Second Temple?', in Eske-nazi and Richards 1994: 88-103.
Marks, H.
   1987   'The Twelve Prophets', in R. Alter and F. Kermode (eds.), *The Literary Guide to the Bible* (London: Fontana Press): 207-33.
   1990   'On Prophetic Stammering', in R. Schwartz (ed.), *The Book and the Text* (Oxford: Basil Blackwell): 60-80.
Mason, R.A.
   1976   'The Relation of Zechariah 9–14 to Proto-Zechariah', *ZAW* 88: 226-39.
   1977a   *The Books of Haggai, Zechariah and Malachi* (The Cambridge Bible Commentary; London: Cambridge University Press).
   1977b   'The Purpose of the "Editorial Framework" of the Book of Haggai', *VT* 27: 413-21.

1982   'The Prophets of the Restoration', in R. Coggins, A. Phillips and M.
            Knibb (eds.), *Israel's Prophetic Tradition* (Cambridge: Cambridge Uni-
            versity Press): 137-54.

May, H.G.
1938   'A Key to the Interpretation of Zechariah's Visions', *JBL* 57: 173-84.

McCarthy, C.
1981   *The Tiqqune Sopherim and Other Theological Corrections in the Maso-
            retic Text of the Old Testament* (OBO, 36; Göttingen: Vandenhoeck &
            Ruprecht).

McHardy, W.D.
1968   'The Horses in Zechariah', in M. Black and G. Fohrer (eds.), *In
            Memoriam Paul Kahle* (BZAW, 103; Berlin: Alfred Töpelmann): 174-79.

McKay, H.A., and D.J.A. Clines (eds.)
1993   *Of Prophets' Visions and the Wisdom of Sages* (JSOTSup, 162; Sheffield:
            JSOT Press).

Meier, S.A.
1992   *Speaking of Speaking: Marking Direct Discourse in the Hebrew Bible*
            (VTSup, 46; Leiden: E.J. Brill).

Mettinger, T.N.D.
1993   'Intertextuality: Allusion and Vertical Context Systems in Some Job Pas-
            sages', in McKay and Clines 1993: 257-80.

Meyers, C.L., and E.M. Meyers
1987   *Haggai, Zechariah 1–8* (AB, 25B; Garden City, NY: Doubleday).
1992a   'Jerusalem and Zion after the Exile: The Evidence of First Zechariah', in
            M. Fishbane and E. Tov (eds.), *'Sha'arei Talmon': Studies in the Bible,
            Qumran, and the Ancient Near East Presented to Shemaryahu Talmon*
            (Winona Lake, IN: Eisenbrauns): 121-35.
1992b   'Zechariah, Book of (Zechariah 1–8)', in *ABD*: VI, 1061-65.

Michaels, W.B.
1980   'The Interpreter's Self: Peirce on the Cartesian "Subject" ', in Tompkins
            1980: 185-200.

Millard, A.R.
1991   'Variable Spelling in Hebrew and other Ancient Texts', *JTS* NS 42.1:
            106-15.

Miscall, P.D.
1991   'Isaiah: The Labyrinth of Images', *Semeia* 54: 103-21.
1992   'Biblical Narrative and Categories of the Fantastic', *Semeia* 60: 39-51.

Mitchell, H.G.
1980   *A Critical and Exegetical Commentary on Haggai, Zechariah, Malachi
            and Jonah* (ICC; Edinburgh: T. & T. Clark [1912]).

Moi, T.
1989   'Men against Patriarchy', in A. Jardine and P. Smith (eds.), *Men in
            Feminism* (repr.; London: Routledge).

Morgenstern, J.
1949   'Two Prophecies from 520–516 BC', *HUCA* 22: 365-427.

Morson, G.
1989   'Parody, History, and Metaparody', in G. Morson and C. Emerson (eds.), *Rethinking Bakhtin: Extensions and Challenges* (Evanston, IL: Northwestern University Press): 63-86.

Muilenburg, J.
1965   'The "Office" of the Prophet in Ancient Israel', in J.P. Hyatt (ed.), *The Bible in Modern Scholarship* (New York: Abingdon Press): 74-97.

Muller, J.P., and W.J. Richardson
1988   'Lacan's Seminar on "The Purloined Letter": Overview', in Muller and Richardson 1988: 28-54.

Muller, J.P., and W.J. Richardson (eds.)
1988   *The Purloined Poe* (Baltimore: The Johns Hopkins University Press).

Niditch, S.
1983   *The Symbolic Vision in Biblical Tradition* (HSM, 30; Chico, CA: Scholars Press).

Nogalski, J.
1993a   'The Redactional Shaping of Nahum 1 for the Book of the Twelve', in D.J.A. Clines and P.R. Davies (eds.), *Among the Prophets* (JSOTSup, 144; Sheffield: JSOT Press): 193-202.

1993b   *Literary Precursors to the Book of the Twelve* (BZAW, 217; Berlin: W. de Gruyter).

1993c   *Redactional Processes in the Book of the Twelve* (BZAW, 218; Berlin: W. de Gruyter).

North, R.
1972a   'Zechariah's Seven-Spout Lampstand', *Bib* 51: 183-206.

1972b   'Prophecy to Apocalyptic via Zechariah', in Congress of the International Organization for the Study of the Old Testament, *Congress Volume: Uppsala, 1971* (VTSup, 22; Leiden: E.J. Brill): 47-71.

Oppenheim, A.L.
1968   ' "The Eyes of the Lord" ', in W.W. Hallo (ed.), *Essays in Memory of E.A. Speiser* (AOS, 53; New Haven: American Oriental Society): 173-80.

Orr, A.
1956   'The Seventy Years of Babylon', *VT* 6: 304-306.

Overholt, T.W.
1990a   'Prophecy in History: The Social Reality of Intermediation', *JSOT* 48: 3-29.

1990b   ' "It is Difficult to Read" ', *JSOT* 48: 51-54.

Perowne, J.J.S.
1890   *Haggai and Zechariah* (The Cambridge Bible for Schools and Colleges; Cambridge: Cambridge University Press).

Person, R.F.
1993   *Second Zechariah and the Deuteronomic School* (JSOTSup, 167; Sheffield: JSOT Press).

Petersen, D.L.
1974   'Zerubbabel and Jerusalem Temple Reconstruction', *CBQ* 36: 366-72.

1981   *The Roles of Israel's Prophets* (Sheffield: JSOT Press).

1984a   *Haggai and Zechariah 1–8: A Commentary* (OTL; Philadelphia: Westminster Press).

1984b   'Zechariah's Visions: A Theological Perspective', *VT* 34: 195-206.

1987   'Introduction: Ways of Thinking about Israel's Prophets', in Petersen 1987: 1-21.

Petersen, D.L. (ed.)

1987   *Prophecy in Israel* (Issues in Religion and Theology, 10; London: SPCK): 1-21.

Petitjean, A.

1966   'La mission de Zorobabel et la reconstruction du temple', *ETL* 42: 40-71.

Pierce, R.W.

1984a   'Literary Connectors and a Haggai/Zechariah/Malachi Corpus', *JETS* 27: 277-89.

1984b   'A Thematic Development of the Haggai/Zechariah/Malachi Corpus', *JETS* 27: 401-11.

Pippin, T.

1992   'The Heroine and the Whore: Fantasy and the Female in the Apocalypse of John', *Semeia* 60: 67-82.

Polk, T.

1984   *The Prophetic Persona: Jeremiah and the Language of the Self* (JSOTSup, 32; Sheffield: JSOT Press).

Polzin, R.P.

1980   *Moses and the Deuteronomist* (New York: Seabury).

1981   'Reporting Speech in the Book of Deuteronomy: Toward a Compositional Analysis of the Deuteronomic History', in B. Halpern and J.D. Levensen (eds.), *Traditions in Transformation: Turning Points in Biblical Faith* (Winona Lake, IN: Eisenbrauns): 193-211.

Portnoy, S.L., and D.L. Petersen

1984   'Biblical Texts and Statistical Analysis: Zechariah and Beyond', *JBL* 103: 11-21.

Poulet, G.

1980   'Criticism and the Experience of Interiority', in Tompkins 1980:41-49.

Press, R.

1936   'Das erste Nachtgesicht des Propheten Sacharja', *ZAW* 54: 43-48.

Prince, G.

1980   'Introduction to the Study of the Narratee', in Tompkins 1980: 7-25.

1990   'On Narratology (Past, Present, Future)', in A.M. Hardee and F.G. Henry (eds.), *Narratology and Narrative* (French Literature Series, 17; Columbia: University of South Carolina): 1-14.

Prokurat, M.

1988   'Haggai and Zechariah 1–8: A Form-Critical Analysis' (PhD dissertation, Graduate Theological Union).

Pyper, H.S.

1993   'The Enticement to Re-read: Repetition as Parody in 2 Samuel', *BibInt* 1.2: 153-65.

Radday, Y.T., and D. Wickmann

1975   'The Unity of Zechariah Examined in the Light of Statistical Linguistics', *ZAW* 87: 30-55.

Radday, Y.T., and M.A. Pollatschek

1980   'Vocabulary Richness in Post-Exilic Books', *ZAW* 92: 333-46.

Redditt, P.L.
    1992   'Zerubbabel, Joshua, and the Night Visions of Zechariah', *CBQ* 54: 249-59.

Reider, J.
    1926   'Some Notes to the Text of the Scriptures', *HUCA* 3: 109-16.

Rendtorff, R.
    1986   *The Old Testament: An Introduction* (trans. J. Bowden; Philadelphia: Fortress Press).

Reventlow, H.G.
    1993   *Die Propheten Haggai, Sacharja und Maleachi* (ATD, 25.2; Göttingen: Vandenhoeck & Ruprecht).

Richter, H.
    1986   'Die Pferde in den Nachtgesichten des Sacharja', *ZAW* 98: 96-100.

Ricoeur, P.
    1974   'Metaphor and the Main Problem of Hermeneutics', *New Literary History* 6: 95-110.

Riffaterre, M.
    1980   'Describing Poetic Structures: Two Approaches to Baudelaire's "Les Chats" ', in Tompkins 1980: 26-40.
    1990   'Compulsory Reader Response: The Intertextual Drive', in Still and Worton 1990: 56-78.

Rignell, L.G.
    1950   *Die Nachtgesichte des Sacharja: Eine exegetische Studie* (Lund: C.W.K. Gleerup).

Robertson, E.
    1937   'The Apple of the Eye in the Masoretic Text', *JTS* 38: 56-59.

Robinson, D.F.
    1951   'A Suggested Analysis of Zechariah 1–8', *ATR* 33.2: 65-70.

Robinson, H.W.
    1945   'The Council of Yahweh', *JTS* 45: 151-57.

Ross, J.
    1987   'The Prophet as Yahweh's Messenger', in Petersen 1987: 112-21.

Rost, L.
    1952   'Bemerkungen zu Sacharja 4', *ZAW* 63: 216-21.

Rudolph, W.
    1976   *Haggai, Sacharja 1–8, Sacharja 9–14, Maleachi* (KAT, 13; Gütersloh: Gütersloher Verlagshaus).

Ruffin, M.L.
    1986   'Symbolism in Zechariah: A Study in Functional Unity' (PhD dissertation, The Southern Baptist Theological Seminary).

Samuels, A.
    1985   *Jung and the Post-Jungians* (London: Routledge & Kegan Paul).

Savran, G.
    1994   'Beastly Speech: Intertextuality, Balaam's Ass and the Garden of Eden', *JSOT* 64: 33-55.

Scott, R.B.Y.
    1949   'Secondary Meanings of אַחַר, *After, Behind* ', *JTS* 50: 178-79.

Scott, W.R.
1987   *A Simplified Guide to BHS* (Berkeley, CA: BIBAL Press).
Selden, R.
1989   *A Reader's Guide to Contemporary Literary Theory* (London: Harvester Wheatsheaf, 2nd edn).
Sellin, D.E.
1930   *Das Zwölfprophetenbuch* (Leipzig: Scholl).
Seybold, K.
1974a   *Bilder zum Tempelbau: Die Visionen des Propheten Sacharja* (BS, 70; Stuttgart: KBW).
1974b   'Die Bildmotive in den Visionen des Propheten Sacharja', in *Studies on Prophecy: A Collection of Twelve Papers* (VTSup, 26; Leiden, E.J. Brill): 92-110.
Sinclair, L.A.
1975   'Redaction of Zechariah 1–8', *BibRes* 20: 36-47.
Ska, J.L.
1990   *'Our Fathers Have Told Us': Introduction to the Analysis of Hebrew Narratives* (Subsidia biblica, 13; Rome: Pontifical Biblical Institute Press).
Smith, R.H.
1964   'The Household Lamps of Palestine in Old Testament Times', *BA* 27: 3-31.
Smith, R.L.
1984   *Micah–Malachi* (WBC, 32; Waco, TX: Word Books).
Sternberg, M.
1985   *The Poetics of Biblical Narrative: Ideological Literature and the Drama of Reading* (Bloomington: Indiana University Press).
Still, J., and M. Worton
1990   'Introduction', in Still and Worton 1990: 1-44.
Still, J., and M. Worton (eds.)
1990   *Intertextuality: Theories and Practices* (Manchester: Manchester University Press).
Stockton, E.D.
1978   'Zechariah: A New Approach', *Australasian Catholic Record* 47: 223-38.
Strand, K.A.
1982   'The Two Olive Trees of Zechariah 4 and Revelation 11', *AUSS* 20: 257-61.
Stuhlmueller, C.
1970   'Haggai–Zechariah–Malachi', in R.E. Brown, J.A. Fitzmyer and R.E. Murphy (eds.), *The Jerome Biblical Commentary* (London: Geoffrey Chapman): 387-401.
1988   *Rebuilding with Hope: A Commentary on the Books of Haggai and Zechariah* (ed. F.C. Holmgren and G.A.F. Knight; International Theological Commentary; Grand Rapids: Eerdmans).
Süring, M.
1980   *Horn-Motifs in the Hebrew Bible and Related Ancient Near Eastern Literature and Iconography* (Andrews University Seminary Doctoral Dissertation Series, 4; Berrien Springs, MI: Andrews University Press).

1985 'The Horn-Motifs of the Bible and the Ancient Near East', *AUSS* 22: 327-40.

Tatford, F.A.
1971 *The Prophet of the Myrtle Grove* (Worthing: Henry E. Walter; Eastbourne: Prophetic Witness Movement International).

Thomas, B.
1989 'The New Historicism and Other Old-fashioned Topics', in Veeser 1989: 182-203.

Thomas, D.W.
1931–32 'A Note on מחלצות in Zechariah iii₄', *JTS* 33: 279-80.

Thompson, T.L.
1992 *Early History of the Israelite People: From the Written and Archaeological Sources* (Studies in the History of the Ancient Near East, 4; Leiden: E.J. Brill).

Tidwell, N.L.A.
1975 'WĀ'ŌMAR (Zech. 3.5) and the Genre of Zechariah's Fourth Vision', *JBL* 94: 343-55.

Tollington, J.
1993 *Tradition and Innovation in Haggai and Zechariah 1–8* (JSOTSup, 150; Sheffield: JSOT Press).

Tompkins, J.P.
1980a 'An Introduction to Reader-Response Criticism', in Tompkins 1980: ix-xxvi.
1980b 'The Reader in History: The Changing Shape of Literary Response', in Tompkins 1980: 201-31.

Tompkins, J.P. (ed.)
1980 *Reader-Response Criticism: From Formalism to Post-Structuralism* (Baltimore: The Johns Hopkins University Press).

Torrey, C.C.
1936 'The Foundry of the Second Temple at Jerusalem', *JBL* 58: 247-60.

Torrington, J.
1993 *Swing Hammer Swing* (London: Minerva).

Tucker, G.
1987 'Prophetic Speech', in J.L. Mays and P.J. Achtemeier (eds.), *Interpreting the Prophets* (Philadelphia: Fortress Press): 27-40.

Unger, M.F.
1963 *Unger's Bible Commentary: Zechariah* (Grand Rapids: Zondervan).

VanderKam, J.C.
1991 'Joshua the High Priest and the Interpretation of Zechariah 3', *CBQ* 53: 553-70.

Veeser, H.A. (ed.)
1989 *The New Historicism* (London: Routledge, Chapman & Hall).

Verhoef, P.A.
1988 'Notes on the Dates in the Book of Haggai', in Claassen 1988: 259-67.

Vorster, W.S.
1989 'Intertextuality and Redaktionsgeschichte', in Draisma 1989: 15-26.

Vriezen, T.C.
1948 'Two Old Cruces', *OTS* 5: 80-91.

Wallis, G.
1978 'Die Nachtgesichte des Propheten Sacharja', in VTSup, 29 (Leiden: E.J. Brill): 377-91.

Waltke, B.K., and M. O'Connor
1990 *An Introduction to Biblical Hebrew Syntax* (Winona Lake, IN: Eisenbrauns).

Waterman, L.
1954 'The Camouflaged Purge of Three Messianic Conspirators', *JNES* 13: 73-78.

White, H.
1989 'New Historicism: A Comment', in Veeser 1989: 293-302.

Whitley, C.F.
1954 'The Term Seventy Years Captivity', *VT* 4: 60-72.

Williamson, H.G.M.
1983 'A Response to A.G. Auld', *JSOT* 27: 33-39.

Wilson, R.
1980 *Prophecy and Society in Ancient Israel* (Philadelphia: Fortress Press).

Winterson, J.
1990 *Sexing the Cherry* (London: Vintage).

Wolde, E. van
1989 'Trendy Intertextuality?', in Draisma 1989: 43-49.

Wolfe, R.E.
1935 'The Editing of the Book of the Twelve', *ZAW* 53: 90-129.

Wolff, H.W.
1977 *Joel and Amos* (trans. W. Janzen, S. Dean McBride, Jr and C.A. Muenchow; Hermeneia; Philadelphia: Fortress Press).

Woude, A.S. van der
1974 'Die beiden Söhne des Öls (Sach. 4:14): messianische Gestalten?', in M.H. van Voss, Ph. H.J. Houwink ten Cate and N.A. van Uchelen (eds.), *Travels in the World of the Old Testament* (Assen: Van Gorcum): 262-68.
1988 'Zion as Primeval Stone in Zechariah 3 and 4', in Claassen 1988: 237-48.

Wright, E.
1982 'Modern Psychoanalytic Criticism', in A. Jefferson and D. Robey (eds.), *Modern Literary Theory: A Comparative Introduction* (London: Batsford): 145-65.

Yeivin, I.
1980 *Introduction to the Tiberian Masorah* (ed. and trans. E.J. Revell; Masoretic Studies, 5; Missoula, MT: Scholars Press).

Zanghi, R.J.
1986 'God's Program for Israel in Zechariah's Night Visions' (ThD dissertation, Dallas Theological Seminary).

Zijl, P.J. van
1971 'A Possible Interpretation of Zech. 9:1 and the Function of "The Eye" ('Ayin) in Zechariah', *JNSL* 1: 59-67.

INDEXES

INDEX OF REFERENCES

OLD TESTAMENT

NEW TESTAMENT

INDEX OF AUTHORS

JOURNAL FOR THE STUDY OF THE OLD TESTAMENT
SUPPLEMENT SERIES